BA 0571 23␣

Leabharlanna Fhine
BLANCHARDSTOW
Inv/06 : 06/BA187 P␣␣␣ ␣␣␣␣␣
Title: Abour Hare the playwr
Class:

REF 822·914

ABOUT HA

ABOUT HARE

Author and Series Editor: Richard Boon is Professor of Performance Studies at the University of Leeds. He is the author of a number of studies of modern British political theatre, including *Brenton the Playwright* (Methuen, 1991), and is also co-editor of *Theatre Matters: Performance and Culture on the World Stage* (CUP, 1998). He is also the author of *About Hare: The Playwright and the Work*.

Series Editor: Emeritus Professor Philip Roberts was Professor of Drama and Theatre Studies, and Director of the Workshop Theatre, at the University of Leeds from 1998–2004. Educated at Oxford and Edinburgh, he held posts in the Universities of Newcastle and Sheffield before arriving in Leeds. His publications include: *Absalom and Achitophel and Other Poems* (Collins, 1973), *The Diary of Sir David Hamilton, 1709–1714* (Clarendon Press, 1975), *Edward Bond: A Companion to the Plays* (Theatre Quarterly Pubs., 1978), *Edward Bond: Theatre Poems and Songs* (Methuen, 1978), *Bond on File* (Methuen, 1985), *The Royal Court Theatre, 1965–1972* (Routledge, 1986), *Plays without Wires* (Sheffield Academic Press, 1989), *The Royal Court Theatre and the Modern Stage* (CUP, 1999).

ABOUT HARE
The Playwright and the Work

Richard Boon

faber and faber

First published in 2003
by Faber and Faber Limited
3 Queen Square London WC1N 3AU
This edition published in 2006

Typeset by Faber and Faber Limited
Printed in England by Bookmarque Ltd, Croydon

All rights reserved
© Richard Boon, 2003

The right of Richard Boon to be identified as author of this work
has been asserted in accordance with Section 77 of the Copyright,
Designs and Patents Act 1988

*This book is sold subject to the condition that it shall not, by way of trade
or otherwise, be lent, resold, hired out or otherwise circulated without the
publisher's prior consent in any form of binding or cover other than that in
which it is published and without a similar condition including this
condition being imposed on the subsequent purchaser*

A CIP record for this book
is available from the British Library

ISBN 978-0-571-23012-9
ISBN 0-571-23012-1

2 4 6 8 10 9 7 5 3 1

For my mother and father

Contents

Editors' Note

There are few theatre books which allow direct access to the playwright or to those whose business it is to translate the script into performance. These volumes aim to deal directly with the writer and with other theatre workers (directors, actors, designers and similar figures) who realize in performance the words on the page.

The subjects of the series are some of the most important and influential writers from post-war British and Irish theatre. Each volume contains an introduction which sets the work of the writer in the relevant historical, social and political context, followed by a digest of interviews and other material which allows the writer, in his own words, to trace his evolution as a dramatist. Some of this material is new, as is, in large part, the material especially gathered from the writers' collaborators and fellow theatre workers. The volumes conclude with annotated bibliographies. In all, we hope the books will provide a wealth of information in accessible form, and real insight into some of the major dramatists of our day.

A Chronology of Plays, Teleplays and Screenplays

By date of first professional production, broadcast or release; it has not been possible to establish precise dates for some of the work. All are original works of single authorship unless otherwise specified.

1968   *Inside Out* (with Tony Bicât; adaptation of Kafka's diaries), September, Arts Lab, London.

1969   *How Brophy Made Good*, Brighton Combination.

1970   *What Happened to Blake?* 28 September, Royal Court Theatre Upstairs, London.

  –   *Slag*, 6 April, Hampstead Theatre Club, London.

1971   *The Rules of the Game* (adaptation of Pirandello), June, National Theatre (at the New Theatre), London.

  –   *Lay By* (with Howard Brenton, Brian Clark, Trevor Griffiths, Stephen Poliakoff, Hugh Stoddart and Snoo Wilson), 24 August, Traverse Theatre Club, Edinburgh.

  –   *Deathsheads* (one-act play), December, Traverse Theatre Club, Edinburgh .

1972   *The Great Exhibition*, 28 February, Hampstead Theatre Club, London.

  –   *England's Ireland* (with Tony Bicât, Howard Brenton, Brian Clark, David Edgar, Francis Fuchs and Snoo Wilson), September, Mickery Theatre, Amsterdam.

1973   *Man Above Men* (TV play), 19 March, BBC Television ('Play for Today').

  –   *Brassneck* (with Howard Brenton), 19 September, Nottingham Playhouse; subsequently broadcast 22 May 1975, BBC Television ('Play for Today').

1974   *Knuckle*, 4 March, Comedy Theatre, London (adapted for BBC radio, Walter Hall, 1981; also televised 7 May 1989, BBC Television 'Theatre Night'.)

1975   *Fanshen* (based on the book by William Hinton), 22 April, ICA Terrace Theatre, London; televised 18 October 1975, BBC Television.

–   *Teeth 'n' Smiles*, 2 September, Royal Court Theatre, London.

1978   *Plenty*, 7 April, National Theatre (Lyttelton), London.

–   *Deeds* (with Howard Brenton, Trevor Griffiths and Ken Campbell), 8 March, Nottingham Playhouse.

–   *Licking Hitler. A Film for Television*, 10 January, BBC Television.

1980   *Dreams of Leaving. A Film for Television*, January, BBC Television.

1982   *A Map of the World*, March, Opera Theatre, Adelaide, Opera House, Sydney; 20 January 1983, National Theatre (Lyttelton), London.

1983   *Saigon: Year of the Cat* (television film), November, Thames Television.

–   *The Madman Theory of Deterrence* (sketch, in *The Big One*), London.

1985   *Pravda, A Fleet Street Comedy* (with Howard Brenton), 2 May, National Theatre (Olivier), London; adapted for radio by the authors, 28 September 1990, BBC Radio.

–   *Wetherby* (film), 8 March, Greenpoint/Film Four/ Zenith (Simon Relph).

–   *Plenty* (adapted for film by the author), TCF/RKO (Edward R. Pressman).

1986   *The Bay at Nice* and *Wrecked Eggs*, 4 September, National Theatre (Cottesloe), London.

1987   *The Knife* (libretto; lyrics by Tim Rose-Price, music by Nick Bicât), New York.

1988   *Paris by Night* (film), Virgin/British Screen/Film Four International/Zenith.

- *The Secret Rapture*, 4 October, Royal National Theatre (Lyttelton), London; adapted for radio by Chris Venning, BBC World Service, 1991.
- *Strapless* (film) Virgin/Granda/Film Four International (Rick McCallum).

1990 *Racing Demon*, 1 February, Royal National Theatre (Cottesloe), London.

1991 *Heading Home* (teleplay), 13 January, BBC Television ('Screen Two').

- *Murmuring Judges*, 10 October, Royal National Theatre (Olivier), London.

1992 *Damage* (film, adapted from the novel by Josephine Hart), Entertainment/Skreba/NEF/Canal (Louis Malle).

- *The Rules of the Game* (adaptation of Pirandello), 12 May, Almeida Theatre, London.

1993 *The Secret Rapture* (adapted for film by the author), Oasis/Greenpoint/Channel 4 (Simon Relph, David Hare).

- *The Absence of War*, 2 October, Royal National Theatre (Olivier), London; (performed as third part of a trilogy; the first two parts, *Racing Demon* and *Mumuring Judges*, were performed on the same day; also adapted for TV, BBC, 1995).

1994 *The Life of Galileo* (adaptation of Brecht), 11 March, Almeida Theatre, London.

1995 *Mother Courage and her Children* (adaptation of Brecht), 14 November, Royal National Theatre, London.

- *Skylight*, 4 May, Royal National Theatre (Cottesloe), London.

1997 *Amy's View*, 13 June, Royal National Theatre (Lyttelton), London.
 Ivanov (adaptation of Chekhov), 2 June, Almeida Theatre, London.

1998 *The Judas Kiss*, 19 March, Almeida Theatre Company at the Playhouse Theatre, London.

- *Via Dolorosa*, 8 September, Royal Court Theatre, London; also adapted for TV (BBC) by the author, 2000.
- *The Blue Room* (adaptation of Schnitzler, *La Ronde*), 10 September, Donmar Warehouse, London.

2000 *My Zinc Bed*, 14 September, Royal Court Theatre, London.

2001 *Platonov* (adaptation of Chekhov), 11 September, Almeida Theatre, London.

2002 *The Hours* (film, adapted from the novel by Michael Cunningham), February, Paramount (Robert Fox, Scott Rudin).

- *Lee Miller* (film, in progress).
- *The Corrections* (film, adapted from the novel by Jonathan Franzen, in progress).
- *The Breath of Life* (stage play, in progress).

A Chronology of British History, 1945–2001

1945 Second World War ends; Attlee's Labour government replaces Churchill's wartime coalition; family allowance system introduced; BBC introduces Light Programme (radio); Orwell's *Animal Farm*. Truman replaces Roosevelt as US President.

1946 New Towns Act; nationalization of Bank of England, Civil Aviation, coal industry; opening of London Airport. Churchill's 'Iron Curtain' speech in US; Bulgaria becomes communist; UN replaces League of Nations.

1947 First nuclear reactor, Harwell; nationalization of electricity and transport; free passage to Australia for British servicemen; India granted independence. Communist government established in Poland; US Marshall Plan brings aid to war-torn Europe; flying saucers first reported in US.

1948 First successful heart surgery, London; first post-war Olympics, London; Laurence Olivier's *Hamlet* wins Oscar.

1949 Clothing rationing ends. People's Republic of China and Republic of Ireland created.

1950 British general election turnout 84 per cent; 49 per cent of British people have bathrooms.

1951 Morale-boosting Festival of Britain, London; J. Sainsbury opens first self-service supermarket, London; Britain's first National Park (Peak District). USA tests first H-bomb, Marshall Islands.

1952 Death of George VI; first James Bond novel (*Casino Royale*). Nobel Peace Prize awarded to Albert Schweitzer.

1953 Coronation of Elizabeth II (shown on TV); Hillary and Tensing climb Everest; Britain tests first atom bomb, Monte Bello Islands. Soviet leader Stalin dies.

1954 Bannister runs first 4-minute mile. Disneyland built, California. France expelled from Vietnam, which splits into communist North and anti-communist South.

1955 Britain submits dispute with Argentina over Falklands to UN; Ruth Ellis the last British woman to be legally executed; commercial television (ITV) introduced. End of post-war occupation regime in West Germany.

1956 Transatlantic telephone service introduced; anti-nuclear CND Aldermaston march. First wave of rock 'n' roll (Bill Haley, Elvis Presley); Yul Brynner wins Best Actor Oscar for *The King and I*.

1957 Entertainment duty on live theatre abolished. Treaty of Rome establishes Common Market (EEC). USSR launches first orbital satellites (Sputniks I and II).

1958 First parking meters in London. USA launches first satellites; US Supreme Court orders Little Rock High School, Arkansas, to admit blacks. First stereo gramophone records.

1959 First hovercraft crossing of English Channel; first section of M1 motorway opened; Mini launched (cost: £500). First meeting, European Court of Human Rights. Communist Fidel Castro becomes leader of Cuba.

1960 Last year of National Service; heart pacemaker developed, Birmingham; Sylvia Pankhurst, suffragette, dies. Kennedy becomes US President; US Senate passes Civil Rights Bill; US spy plane shot down by USSR.

1961 Crick and Watson crack DNA code, Cambridge; contraceptive pill available on NHS; 'spy trials' in London; 1300+ arrested in Trafalgar Square CND demonstration. US severs relations with Cuba. Berlin Wall built. Russian

Yuri Gagarin is first man in space. *West Side Story* wins Best Picture Oscar.

1962 Thalidomide scandal. Cuban Missile Crisis heats up Cold War. Telstar – first TV satellite – launched.

1963 Great Train Robbery; Beatles make 'Mersey sound' international. US: President Kennedy assassinated; Johnson sworn in; black rights demonstrations. Nuclear Test Ban Treaty. Rachel Carson's book *Silent Spring* launches ecology movement.

1964 Typhoid epidemic in Aberdeen; BBC2 opens; Beatles, *A Hard Day's Night*. Mandela jailed for life, South Africa. Harlem race riots, New York; Martin Luther King wins Nobel Peace Prize. China explodes atom bomb. Tokyo Olympics.

1965 Churchill dies; death penalty abolished; GPO Tower opens. Rhodesia makes Unilateral Declaration of Independence from Great Britain. US: air raids, Vietnam; Malcolm X, black Muslim leader, assassinated; race riots, Los Angeles.

1966 116 schoolchildren killed by collapsing coal-slag heap, Aberfan, Wales; England wins football World Cup; measles vaccination starts. Vietnam War spills into Cambodia.

1967 Abortion Bill becomes law. Race riots in US; Israel defeats Arabs in Six-Day War; first heart transplant, South Africa.

1968 Anti-war riots, Grosvenor Square, London; Enoch Powell's anti-immigration 'rivers of blood' speech; Beatles, *Sergeant Pepper*. US: Martin Luther King, Robert Kennedy assassinated; riots, Democratic Convention, Chicago; Nixon becomes President. Tet Offensive in Vietnam. USSR invades Czechoslovakia.

1969 Test-tube fertilization pioneered; North Sea oil discovered; 100,000 strike against trades union reform; British troops into Northern Ireland. US: 25,000 in anti-war demonstration, Washington; Stonewall Riots, New York, launch gay rights movement; 500,000 attend Woodstock Festival, New York. Neil Armstrong walks on moon.

1970 Edward Heath becomes Conservative PM; 18-year-olds get vote; successful mass campaign against South African cricket tour. US: American troops invade Cambodia; 6 student demonstrators killed by National Guard.

1971 Decimal currency launched; 66 football fans die in Ibrox disaster; 'Angry Brigade' bombs home of employment minister; internment without trial begins in Northern Ireland. Barnard performs first heart-and-lung transplant.

1972 Miners' strike leads to blackouts; 'Bloody Sunday' massacre in Northern Ireland, direct rule by London imposed. US: break-in at Democratic HQ, Watergate. Munich Olympics: 11 Israeli athletes killed by pro-Palestinian guerrillas.

1973 IRA bombs Old Bailey; 2 million strike on May Day; State of Emergency and three-day week imposed over second miners' strike; VAT introduced. US: Watergate hearings begin.

1974 Free family planning for all on NHS; nurses get 58 per cent pay rise; Wilson wins general election. US President Nixon resigns over Watergate cover-up.

1975 Thatcher defeats Heath to become Conservative leader; Britain votes 'yes' in EEC referendum; half NHS beds are closed; average wage-earner paying 25 per cent direct tax (3.3 per cent in 1955). Vietnam War ends with Communist victory. Baader-Meinhof terrorist trials begin, Germany.

1976 IRA bomb campaign in England; Callaghan replaces Wilson as Labour Party leader and PM; riots at Notting Hill Carnival. South Africa: Soweto killings. China: Chairman Mao dies.

1977 'Lib-Lab' political pact between Liberals and Labour; 'Grunwick' industrial dispute; fire-brigade workers strike; Sex Pistols' *God Save the Queen* launches punk movement. South Africa: anti-apartheid activist Steve Biko dies in detention. Czechoslovakia: dissidents publish 'Charter 77'. US: Elvis Presley dies; first space-shuttle flight.

1978 'Lib-Lab' pact collapses; Labour Party Conference rejects all forms of wage restraint; Anti-Nazi carnival in London; Louise Brown, first 'test-tube baby', born in Oldham. Italian ex-PM Aldo Moro killed by Red Brigade terrorists. Vietnamese troops invade Kampuchea.

1979 'Winter of Discontent' as public-service workers strike; Lord Mountbatten and Airey Neave, Shadow Northern Ireland Secretary, assassinated by IRA; Blair Peach killed in anti-Nazi demonstration, London; Margaret Thatcher elected first woman PM; government decides to deploy nuclear Cruise missiles in Britain. Muslim revolution in Iran. US: near nuclear disaster at Three-Mile Island; *Kramer versus Kramer* wins 5 Oscars. USSR invades Afghanistan.

1980 SAS storms Iranian Embassy in London; unemployment tops 2 million; Labour Party Conference supports unilateral nuclear disarmament; Foot replaces Callaghan as Labour Party leader; independence for Zimbabwe; John Lennon shot in New York. US boycotts Moscow Olympics over USSR invasion of Afghanistan. Independent Trade Union Solidarity formed, Poland.

1981 'People's March for Jobs'; unemployment reaches 3 million; riots in London, Liverpool and Manchester; Social Democratic Party (SDP) formed by four right-wing ex-Labour MPs; Prince Charles marries Lady Diana Spencer. Ronald Reagan becomes US President. Free elections in communist Poland followed by imposition of martial law.

1982 Falklands War between Britain and Argentina; CND

revivifies as US nuclear missiles deployed; Labour Party expels hard-left Militant Tendency faction. Massacres in refugee camps as Israel invades Lebanon.

1983 Thatcher wins surprise re-election; Kinnock replaces Foot as Labour leader; £500 million cut in government spending, including £140 million on health. Anti-nuclear demonstrations in Britain and across Europe. Iran–Iraq war. Drought in Ethiopia. US troops invade Grenada.

1984 Year-long miners' strikes begin; biggest ever trade deficit; pound at record low against dollar; IRA bombs Grand Hotel, Brighton, during Conservative Party Conference; British Telecom privatized; new Arts Council funding policy reallocates £6 million from London to regions. Reagan re-elected US President. AIDS virus discovered.

1985 Miners' strikes end; financial markets in turmoil; riots in Birmingham and London; NHS prescription charges up from 40p to £2; England banned from European football after Heysel Stadium (Belgium) riots kill 38; Ulster Unionist MPs resign *en masse* against Anglo-Irish agreement. 'Band Aid' concerts in London and Philadelphia raise £50 million for Ethiopian famine relief. Mugabe wins election victory in Zimbabwe.

1986 Unemployment, 3.2 million; Stock Exchange has record one-day fall; start of year-long industrial dispute as Murdoch moves Fleet Street offices to Wapping. US planes attack Libya; Reagan renounces Strategic Arms Limitation Treaty with USSR. Chernobyl nuclear disaster in USSR. Lebanon in tenth year of civil war. State of Emergency in South Africa.

1987 Thatcher wins third general election; British Gas privatized; Wapping dispute ends; 'Black Thursday', London, as £50 million wiped off shares in worldwide financial crisis; IRA bomb kills 11, Enniskillen. State of Emergency extended in South Africa. Chinese students demonstrate in Tiananmen

Square, Beijing. Israel intervenes in Palestinian dispute in Gaza Strip.

1988 Thatcher becomes longest-serving British PM; plans announced for privatization of British Steel and Coal; radical review of NHS; Liberals merge with SDP; IRA terror campaign grows; 275 killed as Libyan terrorists bomb Pan Am flight over Lockerbie. George Bush Snr becomes US President; *Rain Man* wins Best Picture Oscar. Gorbachev begins restructuring of USSR. End of Iran–Iraq War.

1989 'Poll Tax' demonstrations, Scotland; privatization of nuclear industry announced; Britain refuses to join European Exchange Rate (ERM); 95 killed at Hillsborough football stadium. US invades Panama. First contested elections in USSR for 70 years. Berlin Wall torn down; democratic movements gain pace in communist East Germany, Hungary, Poland, Czechoslovakia, Romania. Pro-democracy demonstrations in China. De Clerk becomes South African President.

1990 Anti-'Poll Tax' riots in Trafalgar Square; Britain in recession; Margaret Thatcher forced to resign as PM by own party and replaced by John Major. USSR: Gorbachev elected President, unrest continues. West and East Gemany reunified. Warsaw Pact dissolved. Ethnic unrest grows in Yugoslavia. Nelson Mandela freed in South Africa. Iraqi troops invade Kuwait; Allied forces prepare for armed response.

1991 'Poll Tax' abolished; IRA bombs 10 Downing Street; unemployment 2.4 million. Gulf War. Apartheid abolished in South Africa. Boris Yeltsin becomes President of USSR; Soviet Union disbanded; Gorbachev resigns. Yugoslavia begins slide to civil war.

1992 Major leads Conservatives to unexpected fourth general election victory, announces 'Back to Basics' campaign; Kinnock replaced by John Smith as Labour Party leader; 'Black Wednesday' as pound plummets and interest rates soar;

General Synod votes for ordination of women. US: Clinton replaces Bush Snr as President; race riots in Los Angeles. Continuing unrest in old Soviet republics. Civil war in Yugoslavia: 500,000 dead by end of year.

1993 Privatization plans for British Rail and London Underground announced; unemployment, 3 million; hospital waiting lists at record high; 'Downing Street Declaration' paves way for peace in Northern Ireland. US invasion of Somalia ends in farce. Savage fighting between Serbia and Bosnia. Israel and Palestinians sign historic peace agreement.

1994 Labour leader John Smith dies, replaced by Tony Blair; 'sleaze' scandals rock Conservatives; ceasefires in Northern Ireland. Mandela elected President of South Africa. Bloody war in Rwanda and Burundi.

1995 Blair's Party Conference speech establishes principles of 'New Labour'; rebellion grows in Conservative Party, especially over Britain's part in the EC; water restrictions imposed after drought. US: Oklahoma bombing. Israeli leader Rabin assassinated by Jewish extremist. 'Dayton Accord' creates fragile peace in Bosnia.

1996 Docklands bomb ends IRA ceasefire; outbreak of 'mad cow' disease (BSE); gunman kills 16 children in Dunblane. Russians pull out of Chechnya. New Constitution in South Africa. Israeli–Palestine relations deteriorate.

1997 New Labour wins general election under Tony Blair ending 18 years of Conservative rule; William Hague replaces Major as Conservative leader; IRA disrupts Grand National; Blair meets Sinn Fein leader Gerry Adams; Diana, Princess of Wales killed in Paris car crash; Hong Kong reverts to Chinese rule. Middle East peace negotiations.

1998 Omagh bombing is worst single atrocity in Northern Ireland 'Troubles'; 'Good Friday' peace agreement reached; devolution for Scotland and Wales. EC agrees common currency, the 'euro'. US: Lewinsky scandal breaks, President Clinton impeached; al-Qaeda bombs US embassies in Africa. Russia on point of financial collapse.

1999 Britain spearheads Nato operations in Kosovo; Irish peace talks hit trouble; Britain argues with France over beef imports. Russia: President Yeltsin survives impeachment, takes military action against Chechnya. Nelson Mandela retires.

2000 Large-scale protests against fuel taxes; floods kill 12. US: Bush edges presidential election over Gore amidst accusations of impropriety; US Navy ship damaged by al-Qaeda bomb. Yugoslav President Milosevic overthrown.

2001 'Foot and mouth' outbreak costs millions to agriculture and tourism; Blair wins second election victory, commits to referendum on Britain joining 'euro'; Ian Duncan-Smith replaces Hague as Conservative leader; IRA begins decommissioning arms. US: 'September 11' – al-Qaeda hijackers pilot two planes into World Trade Center; US and Britain bomb Afghanistan. Israel: Sharon wins election amidst worst Israel–Palestine violence for years. Yugoslavia: Milosevic charged with war crimes. 'Kyoto Protocol' signals world (minus US) agreement on climate control.

Post-war British Prime Ministers
Clement Attlee (Lab.), 1945–51; Sir Winston Churchill (Con.), 1951–5; Sir Anthony Eden (Con.), 1955–7; Harold Macmillan (Con.), 1957–63; Sir Alec Douglas-Home (Con.), 1963–4; Harold Wilson (Lab.), 1964–70; Edward Heath (Con.), 1970–74; Harold Wilson (Lab.), 1974–6; James Callaghan (Lab.), 1976–9; Margaret Thatcher (Con.), 1979–90; John Major (Con.), 1990–97; Tony Blair (Lab.), 1997–.

Foreword by Dame Judi Dench

Whenever I have been asked to appear in a David Hare play, I have always said 'Yes', before even reading the script. (Not that failing to read the script is out of the ordinary for me!) However, having played in *Wetherby, Saigon: Year of the Cat* and *Amy's View*, I know that anything written by David Hare is going to be something challenging for the audience and for me. I believe that theatre should stimulate its audience, and David Hare has never failed to do that. He is a unique and remarkable writer.

He also has the audacity to perform his own work – *Via Dolorosa*!

August 2002

Preface

The purpose of this book is to trace the evolution of the work of one of our leading dramatists. Its intention is, so far as possible, to allow David Hare and a number of his collaborators to speak for themselves about how his work has developed, what is particular about it, how it works on stage, and how it has contributed to the theatrical, social and political life of modern Britain.

The book is divided into three parts: an Introduction sets Hare's life and career in historical context. To readers of Hare's own generation, much of this material may already be familiar, but the same can be said less and less of later generations. Knowledge of the history of the post-war years in Great Britain and beyond is essential to an understanding of the work of a playwright to whom the recent past – and, on a more personal level, memory – is of paramount importance. The early part of this introduction, then, offers an account of the huge political and social changes that occurred in Britain during Hare's formative years – changes that in many ways are *the* subject of his career. The latter part of the introduction continues to give what seems to me essential context, but shifts the emphasis to analysis of his plays and screenplays. This is inevitably a highly selective and limited process: more exhaustive critiques of the plays are to be found variously in the monographs and articles indicated in the annotated bibliography at the end of the book.

The second part of the book consists of a digest of interviews given by Hare from the early days of his career to the present. It also includes other material of various kinds – letters, journalism, polemic and so on – committed by him, as it were, directly to paper, without the intercession of the interviewer. Here, I have been primarily concerned with allowing Hare's voice to be heard as directly as possible. Hare has written not only about his own work, but about theatre, society, politics and culture generally; more so, indeed, than any other playwright of his generation. Much of this material is readily available, sometimes in more than one published form (see Bibliography), so I have tended to avoid merely reproducing it in favour of concentrating on less immediately accessible sources. *Writing Left-handed*, *Asking Around*, *Acting Up* and the Introductions to the various collections of plays are, of course, strongly recommended to the reader. The section concludes with a new interview with Hare, done especially for this book.

The third and final section consists of a series of new interviews with practitioners who have been particularly involved in Hare's work. These interviews tend to concentrate on the playwright's later work, which is less well covered by existing secondary material; they also attempt, in part at least, to give some idea of the *practice* of acting, lighting, designing and directing his plays. The section concludes with an interview with Sir Richard Eyre, whose long personal and professional association with Hare gives him a unique perspective on the playwright's career.

Richard Boon

May 2002

Introduction

Since he began writing in the late 1960s, David Hare has produced, as writer, co-writer or adapter, some fifty performed
plays, television plays and screenplays, and the libretto for one
opera. It is a body of work as remarkable for its variety – of
medium, subject, form and style – as for its size. It has won its
author multiple awards, and has found a home on some of the
biggest stages in Great Britain (including the National Theatre,
with which he has had a particularly close association) and in
the USA (where, in the late 1990s, he had three shows running
concurrently on Broadway), as well as on our television and
cinema screens. Hare has also worked as a stage and screen
director, not only of his own work, but also of the work of
other contemporary dramatists, and of Vanburgh, Shaw and
Shakespeare. In addition to the plays and screenplays, he has
published three books and numerous articles related to his own
work and to the theatre, politics, society and culture generally.

When, in 1998, Hare received a knighthood in recognition
of his services to the theatre, it seemed to confirm his position
as a leading figure of the establishment (other recipients in the
same honours list included the footballer Geoff Hurst, the
chairman of the British Medical Association, the Director-
General of the BBC, various 'captains of industry' and lawyer
and fellow playwright John Mortimer). The honour seemed to
sit well with the former public-school boy and graduate of
Jesus College, Cambridge. Yet throughout his career Hare has
been a passionate and unrelenting critic of the establishment,
and of what we may call 'the official culture'. Plays such as
Pravda (1985), *Racing Demon* (1990), *Murmuring Judges* (1991)
and *The Absence of War* (1993) attack the very pillars of

Leabharlanna Fhine Gall

contemporary society – the press, the Church, the law and politics respectively – with savage relish and not a little despair. Indeed, his whole career may be seen as one long assault on some of our most deeply held assumptions about what it is to be British in the latter part of the twentieth century – assumptions about our society, politics, history and sense of morality. One commentator has suggested that Hare is 'like Le Carré's Honourable Schoolboy, forever trying to undermine England from within and enjoying every minute of it'.* There may be a certain truth in that, although it hardly does justice to Hare's seriousness and sense of purpose as a dramatist.

Hare is a 'political playwright'. It is in some ways a disingenuous and slippery term: disingenuous, because, in common usage, it refers only to playwrights whose work comes from a broadly leftist, socialist position (the politics of right-wing writers tend to sit invisibly within the accepted conditions of the status quo, the 'this-isn't-politics-this-is-just-how-things-are' argument that always gives the right a political advantage over the left); slippery, because it covers a wide range of different kinds of theatre practice that are extremely varied – sometimes to the point of mutual contradiction – in what should be said, why, how, and to whom. Move only a little way beyond the shared basic belief that society needs changing radically – to be made more just, more equal, and more free – and that the theatre can and should play its part in that, and you may find 'political playwrights' as much at odds with each other as with those on the right. (The cynic may observe that infighting seems traditionally a necessary feature of left-wing politics generally, never mind of political theatre.)

Hare himself gives us some help in beginning to define what particular kind of political playwright he is. In 1978, he gave a lecture at King's College, Cambridge, the views of which he continued to endorse as late as the 1990s. It began

* Reported by Michael Coveney in 'Worlds Apart', *Time Out*, 21–7 January 1983, p. 12. John Le Carré's novel *The Honourable Schoolboy* was published by Hodder and Stoughton in 1977.

with the obvious: the playwright writes plays. He chooses plays as his way of speaking. If he could speak more clearly in a lecture, he would lecture; if polemic suited him, he'd be a journalist. But he chooses the theatre as the most subtle and complex way of addressing an audience he can find. Because of that, I used to turn down all invitations to speak in public, because I didn't want an audience to hear the tone of my voice. I don't like the idea that they can get a hand-down version of my plays sitting in a lecture hall sizing me up. In the theatre I am saying complex and difficult things. I do not want them reduced either by my views on the world, or, more important, the audience's idea of my views. I want no preconceptions. I don't want, 'Oh, of course, Hare is a well-known anti-vivisectionist, that's why there's that scene where the dog is disembowelled.' I want the dog cut up and the audience deciding for themselves if they like the sight or not. The first lesson the playwright learns is that he is not going to be able to control the audience's reactions anyway; if he writes an eloquent play about the sufferings of the Jews in the Warsaw Ghetto there is always going to be someone in the audience who comes out completely satisfied with the evening, saying at last someone's had the guts to say it, those Nazis knew what they were about. As you can't control people's reactions to your plays, your duty is also not to reduce people's reactions, not to give them easy handles with which they can pigeon-hole you, and come to comfortable terms with what you are saying . . .*

'Complex', 'subtle', 'difficult' plays, then, which put squarely on the audience's shoulders the responsibility for engaging with the ideas they contain; and plays which, unlike some kinds of

---

* The lecture was first published by the RSC in 1978, then appeared as an appendix to Faber's 1978 publication of Hare's *Licking Hitler*. It is reprinted, with some cuts, as 'The Play is in the Air: On Political Theatre', in *Writing Left-Handed*. See Bibliography.

political theatre work, are not driven by single issues. Indeed, hardly any of Hare's plays (the early, co-authored *England's Ireland* [1972] and *Deeds* [1978] are rare exceptions; see below) are 'issue-driven' in that sense, and none is a quick response to topical events. This goes some way to explaining why, for example, in the early 1980s – a time of great political turmoil – Hare was *not* writing plays about the Falklands War, the Brighton bombing or the year-long miners' strikes. In fact, he claims at one point (see p. 97*) that his average gestation period for a play is about seven years; but that offers only a partial answer. Hare does not put his plays at the service of a particular cause, or make responses to particular events, because that is not what he believes political theatre – or at least, his brand of political theatre – is *for*. For similar reasons, it is also the case that, apart from *The Great Exhibition* (1972) and *The Absence of War* (1993), his plays seldom deal centrally with characters directly and publicly engaged in political life.

These are issues over which Hare's critics have chewed throughout his career, and generally to his great irritation (he is famously 'a critic of the critics' in both Great Britain and the USA). For some on the left, this lack of engagement with politics in its most obvious sense is a sign of a dramatist who had 'sold out' long before getting his knighthood. Conversely, the critical establishment has sought to claim him as 'one of its own' almost from the earliest days of his career – seeking to place him in a particular tradition of English bourgeois theatre, best represented by a playwright such as Terence Rattigan – and has generally struggled to accommodate within its view not only some of the more difficult things he has had to say, but also some of the theatrical and stylistic ways in which he has chosen to say them. Too often Hare has, as it were, taken his roses to the critical flower show, only to be told that, while

---

* Unless otherwise indicated, all quotations are taken from the digest of interviews that follows this introduction. Sources are indicated there and, more fully, in the Bibliography.

they are nice enough flowers, they make poor carnations: a glance at critical responses to *A Map of the World* (1983; see p. 102 ff.) confirms that, but it is also true of his career generally. The stylistic experimentation of the unique *Fanshen* (1975), or the passionate polemic of *Via Dolorosa* (1998), might have led critics to suspect that an apparently straightforward love story such as *Skylight* (1995) may not be quite what it first appears to be. Hare has always had, and perhaps treasured, the ability to wrong-foot his critics, and has preferred instead to trust to the intelligence of his audiences.

Indeed, Hare's views, as represented at least in part by the digest of interviews and other materials that follows this introduction, may sometimes seem contradictory and paradoxical: see, for example, how his mind changes, and changes back, about documentary theatre, or the value of making adaptations, or working in television. Similarly, he is often ambivalent about subjects where one might expect certainty, such as the important roles played in his career by the Royal Court and National Theatres. This apparent contrariness to some extent begs the question as to how possible it is to 'trace his evolution as a dramatist', which is the declared intention of this book. 'Evolution' may imply a kind of purposeful, linear progression, a clear and coherent sense of development. It may even suggest that later work must by definition be 'better' than earlier work. There is, of course, some truth in this: playwrights, like any other committed professional workers, have a sense of the direction of their own careers, and learn their craft, gain experience, and become more confident as they grow older; but there is a neatness to the idea that is misleading. A glance at the Catalogue of Hare's personal papers, held at the Ransom Center of the University of Texas at Austin,* reveals a career littered with abandoned projects, unproduced plays and screenplays (such as the undated 'The Bloody Workers'), draft versions of work (sometimes under working titles very different from what

---

*Available on-line: see Bibliography.

eventually appeared in the public arena: 1991's *Heading Home* began life as 'Safe as Houses'), rehearsal scripts, rejected scenes and discarded pages. What this tells us is that the public – and, to a degree, the academic and the critical – view of a playwright's career is (reasonably enough) only partial, and that the business of writing plays, and of understanding how plays are written, is less than straightforward. What appears on a stage or in a cinema is in many ways only the tip of an iceberg. An individual piece of work may gestate over years; a scene discarded from one project may appear, in adapted form, in another; scripts change in the rehearsal room (see Lia Williams on *Skylight* below). A play may be as much a response to events in its writer's private life as to events in public life. Nor should the importance of simple *opportunity* be underestimated – opportunity to work on a particular stage, or with a particular director or actor, or on a particular subject can be an important factor in determining the kind of work produced. In all, any one play may be seen as a kind of condensation of many different ideas, experiences, factors and influences that play with and bounce off each other in the writer's imagination. It is part of the academic's job, and the critic's job, to find pattern and discern order, but it is not necessarily a pattern or an order intended or even felt by the playwright.

This is probably true of any playwright, but it is certainly true of Hare. His career spans a period of enormous political, social and cultural change. At its start, the willingness of people – audiences – to engage with political issues, both inside and outside the parliamentary system, was, arguably, much greater than it is now. As a dramatist he has, pèrhaps more than any other of his generation, succeeded in capturing the *zeitgeist* – the spirit of the age – through the many changes the period has seen. He has been able to do that because – to paraphrase his friend and collaborator Howard Brenton – he has, with his plays and screenplays, constantly set up, dismantled and set up again the 'scaffolding' of his work. If the digest of his interviews suggests something of the complexity and variability of that process, then it also, I hope, makes it apparent that both his socialist conviction and his belief in the ability of drama to play a meaningful part in political debate have not wavered. To begin to answer the question of what *kind* of political dramatist Hare is, I return to his 1978 lecture at King's:

> When I look back on 1978 it will not be [Labour Prime Minister] Callaghan's face that I shall want to remember; the bleak logistics of his world will evoke very little to me, I am sure. Instead, I shall perhaps remember a tramp stretched across three seats in the warm, on the Victoria line, fast asleep, his right hand gently cradling his cock, while the rest of us in the carriage stared impassively ahead. What historical forces drew him there? What armies fought? What families fell apart? What compensating impulse guides his hand?*

Early life

Hare was born in 1947 at St Leonard's, in Sussex, to Clifford (a merchant seaman) and Agnes Gilmour Hare. In 1952, the family moved the few miles to Bexhill-on-Sea, where Hare attended the local preparatory school. In 1960 he became a boarder at the Anglo-Catholic Lancing College, where he first met his lifelong friend and fellow playwright Christopher Hampton. After leaving Lancing he spent some time in California, before going up to Jesus College, Cambridge, to read English. He graduated in 1968 and went on to work briefly for Pathé News before beginning a career in theatre.

It is tempting to try to mine a playwright's formative years for experiences that inform his later life and work. Certainly, Richard Eyre sees Hare's early life as having an abiding influ-

---

* The quoted passage was cut from the version that appears in *Writing Left-Handed*, but appears towards the end of the version appended to *Licking Hitler*.

ence on his work (see below, pp. 219–20), and, as the playwright's interview with Jeremy Isaacs below shows, there are a number of recurrent interests and themes in the plays that may be traced back to youthful experience: the love of film, the ambivalent interest in religion, the morbid curiosity about the workings of closed, private institutions similar to those in which he was educated. It might even be suggested that a teenage visit to America not only began a lifelong fascination with that country, but also gave him, at a crucial point in his life, an outsider's view of his home country, and with it an almost anthropological interest in the particularity of its society and culture. That interest, it might be argued, drives the forensic dissections of British institutions in many of the plays and screenplays. Yet Hare himself is not only generally uncomfortable about the danger of his plays being 'reduced' by too high an authorial profile, but also (see p. 87) specifically warns us of the dangers of trying to account for his work in autobiographical terms. (One thing, for example, that the student of Hare's early life will *not* find is evidence of any great desire to write plays. As a child, he regularly accompanied his mother to the local theatre; he also acted a little at school, and directed one or two plays at university. As shall be seen, however, he did not begin to think of himself as a playwright first and foremost until several years into his career.) Moreover, many theorists and critics argue that it is a dangerously misleading, even irrelevant, way of approaching the work of any artist, particularly that of one whose chosen medium is the public forum of live theatre. What *is* important, however, is to understand the historical, political and social context in which Hare grew up, not least because that context has provided him with the subjects of many of his best-known plays. More than that, there is a very real sense in which the post-war history of Britain – or at least Hare's perception of it – remains the dominant subject of his career overall.

The political and historical context

The years immediately following the Second World War – the years of Hare's early childhood – were characterized by a radical transformation of British society, a transformation that in many ways created the Britain we know today. The reforming zeal that lay behind this fundamental recreation of the country was motivated by the economic disasters of the pre-war years, which had produced poverty on a scale scarcely imaginable in a Western country today, and also, of course, by the hardships of the war itself. It is significant that the landslide that brought Clement Attlee's Labour administration to power at the end of the war in the general election of 1945 (a landslide that, for the first time, truly established Labour as the second party of government) was built in substantial part on the votes of returning soldiers, who, to put it at its simplest, wanted to know why the war had been fought if not for the creation of a better Britain. The wartime Prime Minister, the Conservative Winston Churchill, famously felt betrayed by what he saw as his rejection by the British people, and not entirely without cause: the government he led for much of the war was a coalition of all the main parties, and that government had, even in the worst days of the conflict, begun the process of reform. In 1942 the Beveridge Report identified 'five evil giants' that threatened the national well-being: idleness, squalor, need, want and ignorance. In 1944, the Education Act tackled the last of these, introducing a 'free' state education service to the age of fifteen; but it was the Attlee government that created what came to be known as the Welfare State. A series of Acts between 1946 and 1948 enshrined the principle that 'a wide range of publicly provided benefits and "universal" services should be available to all on demonstration of need and, in the case of the services, "free" at the point of receipt'.* The

* Bill Coxall and Lynton Robins, *Contemporary British Politics* (third edition, London: 1998), p. 20. Specifically, the legislation in question was the Family Allowances Act (1945), two National Insurance Acts (1946), the National Health Service Act (1946), and the National Assistance Act (1948).

co-operative spirit of the wartime coalition also lived on in two vital ways: first, that the country's economy should be 'mixed' (an idea based on the theories of liberal economist John Maynard Keynes), combining private enterprise with public sector intervention, and, second, that whatever their other differences – and they were many – the two main parties of government, Labour and Conservative, would operate on the basis of a broad agreement on fundamental aspects of home and foreign policy. It was in many ways a remarkable accommodation between the opposing forces of left and right, between socialist and capitalist philosophies. Later this accommodation became known as 'Butskellism', after Conservative and Labour politicians R. A. Butler and Hugh Gaitskell, but it is better known as the 'post-war consensus', and it provided the fundamental basis on which Britain was to be governed until the election of Margaret Thatcher's first Conservative administration in 1979.

If the post-war consensus was to last for over thirty years, the euphoria and optimism that marked the years immediately after the war proved rather more short-lived. Although the programme for social reconstruction enjoyed widespread support within the establishment, and was carried on the back of a general ideological shift to the left in the general public, conditions on the ground were slow to improve. The effects of the severe winter of 1947, for example, were exacerbated by a fuel crisis (coal production having failed to regain pre-war output levels) and by a massive balance-of-payments crisis. Rationing of basic foodstuffs and materials, brought in as a necessary means of managing the country's wartime survival, continued well after the war and in some cases was not lifted until the early 1950s. Against this background of continuing austerity, the national economy struggled to improve, and the impact was felt by the newly founded Welfare State. In 1949, the cost of the NHS (2/6d, or 12.5p, per head per week) exceeded its budget, with the result that government gave the 'free' service the power to charge for prescriptions, leading to the ministerial resignations of the radical Aneurin Bevan (the architect of the NHS) and future Prime Minister Harold Wilson; a ceiling on NHS spending was imposed the following year. Attlee continued in government until 1951, but the sense of compromise and betrayal that was to afflict so many subsequent Labour governments had set in some time before that.

The loss of national confidence that beset Britain in the late 1940s and early 1950s was made worse by the dawning realization that it was no longer the world power it had been. The British Empire, despite the ravages of the First World War and the economic crises of the twenties and thirties, was still at its peak as late as 1933, when it covered a quarter of the world's land surface and administered, in one form or another, a similar percentage of the world's population. Even in 1945, Britain was still perceived as the third (after the USA and the USSR) 'great power', in part at least because of Churchill's international prestige and personal magnetism, both of which he cleverly exploited. The wartime leader's 'Iron Curtain' speech at Fulton, Virginia, in 1946 effectively signalled the start of the Cold War between West and East that was to dominate world politics until Gorbachev's *perestroika* ('restructuring') reforms and the collapse of Eastern European communism in the late 1980s. By 1947 Britain had nuclear capability and was firmly aligned behind the USA, turning its back on the moves towards European integration that were already beginning. Yet its status as a genuine world power was already recognized by some as largely illusory. For all the genuine heroism of the country's effort between 1939 and 1945, the war had been won largely by the sheer might of the USA and the USSR. The Empire was no longer sustainable, and in 1947–8 Britain granted independence to – or made strategic withdrawals from – its colonies in the Far East (including India, the 'jewel in the crown'). That began an often difficult process of decolonization that peaked between 1960 and 1964, when no fewer than seventeen colonial territories became independent.

The sense of crisis in national identity came to a head, however, in 1956. In that year, Britain and France, together with

Israel (founded as a nation-state in 1948, in part as a result of post-imperial British policy), attempted to mount a military expedition to repossess the Suez Canal, recently nationalized by the Egyptian President, Gamal Abdel Nasser. The initiative collapsed, all too obviously through lack of American support, 'thereby dealing a shattering and long-lasting blow to (Britain's) self-image as a great power'.* The blow was felt most keenly by the Conservative government of the day under Harold Macmillan (Attlee's election defeat in 1951 led to thirteen years of Tory rule); but if the right had little to celebrate, then neither had the left: the same year saw the USSR invade Hungary to overthrow what it saw as a too liberal communist regime. For many on the pre-war left, Soviet Russia had stood as an example of the achievability of a socialist utopia on earth; their faith, which had withstood the evidence to the contrary which emerged in the post-war years – evidence of the murderous repressiveness of Stalin's regime – could not survive the invasion of Hungary.

From the mid-1950s onwards, consensual politics came increasingly under strain, prefiguring the rifts that were to open on right and left in the 1970s. Generally speaking, the major parties still managed to accommodate each other in policy terms – the Conservatives denationalized the road haulage and steel industries in the fifties; the Labour government renationalized steel in 1967 – but Britain's decline as an economic and world power continued. Despite government efforts, economic growth fell behind that of its major competitors. In particular, European economies were strengthening, in large part as a result of the creation of the European Economic Community (EEC) in 1957, which Britain had tried to block; by the mid-sixties it had become apparent that the Commonwealth, which Britain had created both to disguise its retreat from Empire and to set up an alternative economic *bloc*, was not a real world force. A rapid policy shift led to two attempts to join the EEC

* Coxall and Robins, p. 24.

(in 1960 and 1967), both of which were humiliatingly rebuffed by the French President, Charles De Gaulle; Britain was finally admitted in 1973 under Edward Heath's Conservative government, and then on rather disadvantageous terms. At the same time, Britain sought to cling to its status as a world power at the cost of a debilitatingly huge defence budget, though it was still forced to abandon its ambitions to independent nuclear deterrence when it cancelled the Blue Streak missile in 1960, leading to a reliance on American nuclear military hardware that continues today. The issue of defence spending was particularly acute, as the Welfare State was consuming an ever larger percentage of the country's income, through the National Health Service, social services and education. Education in particular saw a large expansion in university and polytechnic provision, as well as a rapid move towards comprehensive schools, which was begun by Labour in the sixties and was continued, somewhat against the ideological grain, by the Conservatives after 1970.

However, despite deep-seated problems and an ongoing, underlying trend of national decline, Britain in the sixties saw an explosion of social and cultural energy that stood in marked and, for many, welcome contrast to the dour fifties. The wave of optimism occasioned by John F. Kennedy's election as US President in 1960 was reflected, albeit palely, in Harold Wilson's new Labour government of 1964, which promised a Britain rebuilt in 'the white heat of technology' and the possibility of finally implementing in full the broad socialist vision of the 1945 Attlee government. Wilson's government may have succumbed all too rapidly to compromise, but it rode for a while on a tide of low unemployment and relative prosperity. The period, crucially, also saw the coming of age of those born in the post-war 'baby boom': in 1965 there were one million more fifteen-to twenty-four-year-olds than a decade earlier. Many of those were reaping the benefits of the 1944 Education Act and the subsequent expansion of the higher education sector, and the majority of those not in full-time education were in work and had money in their pockets. Moreover, this was a generation that had, or took, freedoms unknown to its parents.

In popular memory – or, at least, in contemporary media representations of popular culture – the 'permissive sixties' have too often been reduced to no more than a series of superficial tropes: this was the era of 'sex 'n' drugs 'n' rock 'n' roll', of hippies, flower power and free love. The key (though by no means the only) means of expression of the new freedom was music – specifically, rock and roll, which came to dominate the popular culture of the West. One commentator remarked at the time: 'The closest Western civilization came to unity since the Congress of Vienna in 1815 was the week when [the Beatles'] *Sergeant Pepper* was released – in every city in Europe and America, the stereo system and radio played.'* Greater sexual freedom was enabled by the development of the contraceptive pill and the liberalization of the abortion laws. Drug culture developed. An American writer, returning to California in 1968 after a long absence, noted that

> people even looked different. Peace symbols and crystal pendants had replaced crucifixes and Stars of David as emblems of religious conviction. Clothes were tie-dyed and bucolic, colours psychedelic, and hair long . . . women were going bra-less . . . a band, booming through amplified speakers . . . produced an effect something like entering a new dimension . . . I felt: a new world is possible.†

It was certainly a decade that provided a useful Aunt Sally for Margaret Thatcher's efforts, in the 1980s, to reclaim Britain's 'glorious past': the sixties were characterized as the time when Britain lost its way, when national self-indulgence betrayed the legacy of former greatness. But 'the sixties' were much more than that: they were a time when the young, disenchanted with

---

* Quoted by Andreas Whittam Smith in '1968', *Independent on Sunday*, 8 February 1998, p. 7.
† David Horowitz, quoted by Whittam Smith.

the tired compromises of their political masters, for a while discovered their own political power. Influenced by Marx, Freud, Marcuse and Sartre, young radicals rethought traditional socialism to envision new forms of social governance and organization, and whilst some of their philosophies might have passed through idealism into impracticality, their power was real and, in many instances, their influence long-lasting. That power reached its peak in 1968, when there were student, or student/worker, demonstrations in every month of the year and all around the world. Their causes were various, ranging from civil rights to gay and women's liberation, but they centred on the Vietnam War, where the USA and its allies (including Britain) had become increasingly involved in defending the South of that country from the threat posed by the communist North. Crucially, this was the first – and, in terms of uncontrolled access, the last – war to be comprehensively covered by television, making its justification and its conduct subject to public scrutiny and debate in a way that had never happened before.

> the Vietnam war was the perfect *cause célèbre*. Had not the USA got into Vietnam without consulting its people? Was not the war kept going by the defence establishment, which was indifferent to public opinion? Did not the success of the North Vietnamese Tet Offensive, when the walls of the US embassy in Saigon were breached, show the hopelessness of American policy? And did not the remarks attributed to an American officer that it was sometimes 'necessary to destroy a town in order to save it' demonstrate the utter futility of the whole enterprise?*

The most significant protests were in France, with *les événements* ('the events') of May 1968. John Bull explains:

> What happened there that spring is historically without precedent – the creation of a potentially revolutionary

---

* Whittam Smith, *ibid*.

situation within the context of a stable and securely affluent society. It was a situation that was fermented and stage-managed not by the traditional organs of political conflict – the unions and political organisations of the working-class – but by a young, radical and alienated intelligentsia. A movement that started in a university in the suburbs of Paris was briefly to bring France to a standstill, and to threaten even the Gaullist regime, as serious attempts were made to construct a revolutionary counter-society that would bypass the machinery of the modern state . . . They sought nothing less than a redefinition of political struggle as it affected the individual in his everyday life. Factional dispute was, as always, rife, but the dominant analysis, and that which found its way most forcibly back across the Channel, was that of the Situationists . . .*

Put simply, the situationist analysis insisted on the need radically to change society, but rejected not only conventional parliamentary means but also the classic Marxist revolutionary view of how that might be done: these were seen only as tactical manoeuvres within a system that would remain fundamentally unchanged, a system defined as 'the society of the spectacle', in which

. . . the main agent of capitalist oppression had ceased to be located at the point of production – the factory floor – and had transferred to a point of consumption: the consumption of bourgeois ideology as transmitted through culture generally and the mass media in particular. The relationship between the individual and society was thus analogous to that between the spectator and the events on a screen: both were passive consumers of a two-dimensional charade. It was by shattering the hegemony of received images that individuals had of society that the ground-work of revolutionary change could be established; smashing the

* John Bull, *New British Political Dramatists* (London: 1984), pp. 10–12.

screen of *public* life would expose the realities of *private* and *daily* life beneath.*

It is worth outlining the tenets of situationism simply because their influence – and the influence of 'May '68' generally – on the politically engaged young in Britain was so important. As the sixties drew to a close, the domestic political situation was deteriorating: the Wilson government's moral bankruptcy was evident to all (the Conservatives under Edward Heath were to return to power in 1970, prefiguring a decade in which the post-war consensus would be driven to collapse by accelerated economic decline, industrial militancy and new policies from the Conservative New Right and the Labour left) and armed conflict in Northern Ireland was escalating towards the disaster of the 'Bloody Sunday' killings in early 1972. For a while, the radical, even utopianist vision of the situationists and the visible success of protests not only in France but around the world seemed to offer a model for how things might be handled differently. In fact, there is an ironic sense in which the most important influence of *les événements* lay in their inevitable failure: the loose leftist alliance from which they drew their energy fractured, and the backlash from the French government appalled many by its severity. Just as the USSR – again in 1968 – was unafraid to use physical force to quash the liberal communist regime that had developed in Czechoslovakia under Alexander Dubcek, so the Gaullist government had no qualms in sending the riot police on to the streets of Paris – nor did the British government hesitate in dealing severely with an anti-war demonstration in Grosvenor Square in London. In the words of Howard Brenton,

> May 1968 was crucial . . . [it] disinherited my generation in two ways. First it destroyed any remaining affection for official culture. The situationists showed how all of them,

* Richard Boon, *Brenton the Playwright* (London: 1991), p. 55. See also Guy Debord, *The Society of the Spectacle* (Detroit: 1970).

the dead greats, are corpses on our backs – Goethe, Beethoven – how gigantic the fraud is. But it also, secondly, destroyed the notions of personal freedom, anarchist political action. And it failed. It was defeated. A generation dreaming of a beautiful utopia was kicked – kicked awake and not dead. I've got to believe not kicked dead. May '68 gave me a desperation I still have.*

This was the context in which Hare began his career in the theatre.

Hare's career in context

Fringe origins
One of the effects of the political upheavals of the late 1960s was to produce in Great Britain a whole generation of radical theatre practitioners of various kinds committed to social, political and cultural change. If much of what we now take for granted in terms of the range and variety of theatre available to us, from theatre-in-education to community work to performance art, did not actually begin in the sixties, then it certainly benefited hugely from the burst of creative and dissident cultural energy that characterized the period, and from the increased public subsidy to the arts ushered in by the Wilson government. These were practitioners who worked on the 'fringe' of mainstream culture, who took their work outside the established theatre into new venues: community halls, working-men's clubs, the new 'arts labs' and the studio spaces that belonged to the new universities and colleges. What concerns us most here was the emergence, as one aspect of this explosion of theatrical energy, of a group of figures whose commitment was to the writing of politically engaged plays, and who were to exert a considerable influence over the British theatre scene for the next thirty years. Prime

* In Catherine Itzin and Simon Trussler (interviewers), 'Petrol Bombs Through the Proscenium Arch', *Theatre Quarterly*, December 1975–February 76, p. 20.

amongst them were David Edgar, the late John McGrath, Trevor Griffiths, Howard Brenton and, of course, David Hare.

Grouping these playwrights together in this way implies a commonality of interest. They certainly shared basic principles, notably regarding the need for a new theatre to engage in public life in a way in which – it seemed to them – the old theatre had signally failed to do. Indeed, many of them were to work together, in various combinations, in the years to come. However, it is difficult to argue that they ever amounted to a 'movement'; their work shows as much difference as similarity of content, argument, form and style, and this was true even at the earliest stage of their careers. Identifying the differences between them, however, at least helps us define the particular origins and nature of Hare's engagement of politics with theatre. Edgar, McGrath and Griffiths were, broadly, committed to placing their work within a conventional socialist analysis of how society needed changing and how theatre might play a part in that (McGrath, indeed, saw himself very much as belonging to a tradition of such work that extended back through Joan Littlewood and Theatre Workshop to the Workers' Theatre Movement of the 1920s and 1930s): whatever the particular content or form of the work, it was at the service of the class struggle. Brenton, on the other hand, was influenced more by the new situationist philosophies, which, as I suggest above, saw conventional socialist thought and the dominant capitalist ideology as two sides of the same unacceptable coin. It was Brenton who, in 1969, introduced situationism to the founders of Portable Theatre, Tony Bicât and David Hare.

I have already said that Hare's route to writing for the theatre was by no means an obvious one. It was largely through the influence of Bicât, whom Hare met at Cambridge (most of these writers, including Brenton, were exactly of the first generation to benefit from the post-war expansion of education; Hare himself went to Lancing as a 'scholarship boy'), that his interest began to develop. Even then, he seems largely to have been motivated by a sense of disgust at the established theatre of the day which, like Bicât, he saw as 'rhetorical, overproduced, lavish, saying nothing, conventional' (see p. 62). His views are most readily associated with the commercially driven, formulaic product of the West End, and perhaps with the tiredness and lack of ambition of many of the provincial repertory theatres; whether or not they should also be taken to include the work of that earlier generation of new British playwrights – Osborne, Arden, Wesker, Bond, Jellicoe and so on – whose work at the Royal Court Theatre in London from 1956 onwards had already done so much to revivify British theatre, is less clear. It is true that the work of many, though by no means all, of those writers tended to operate within more or less conventional theatrical forms ('well-made plays'); equally, Hare today speaks of that work, and of its authors, with affection and respect (see 'Conversation', pp. 164–5). Be that as it may, it is telling that his initial engagement with theatre came about as much out of disillusionment with it as an established cultural form as out of any desire to find a vehicle through which to advance a specific political agenda; at this stage, he wanted to direct, not write. It is clear that he shared with others of his generation a disgust at the obscenities of the Cold War, particularly as represented by the American action in Vietnam, and that, domestically, he had an acute sense of the economic decline and social decay of Britain in the sixties (feeling particular anger at the betrayal of the Wilson governments), but he saw little on the established left to give him grounds for optimism. His tutor at Cambridge, the Marxist critic Raymond Williams, argued for the inevitability of socialist revolution, an inevitability that Hare himself simply could not see; the two remained at loggerheads for years (Hare's memoir of Williams, 'Cycles of Hope', appears in his 1991 collection of essays, *Writing Left-Handed*: see Bibliography). Perhaps more significant was Hare's attitude to his English course at Cambridge: its concentration on the canonical, on established 'great books', to the exclusion of supposed lesser work, infuriated and alienated him. Insofar as what is emerging here is a figure entertaining revulsion and anger about official politics and official culture, theatrical and literary, it seems that Hare was very ready to hear Brenton's account of the new French thinking.

The pre-Brenton work at Portable began with literary adaptations from Kafka and Genet, which is in itself perhaps further evidence of interest in the dark underbelly of official culture. Hare is dismissive today of his own first original plays (*How Brophy Made Good* [1969] and *What Happened to Blake?* [1970]), claiming they were written simply out of the necessity of giving the fledgling company something to stage. He identifies Brenton's *Christie in Love* (1968)* – in which audience sympathy is uncomfortably directed towards the eponymous sexual mass-murderer, with the representatives of social propriety, in the shape of two inept and voyeuristic policemen, being ruthlessly lampooned – as the play with which Portable found its voice. Hare directed, and Bicât built the set. The play, with its confrontational style, savage jokes and provocative claim that Christie acted out of a kind of love for his victims, gave situationist-inspired structure and purpose to Portable, and stands as a paradigm of its work to come: self-consciously avant garde, experimental, and taking theatre to places – literal and metaphorical – where it did not normally go. The aim was nothing less than an assault on the audience's sensibilities, on its *cultural* values: the play took what it saw as its spectators' own hypocrisy – that combination of righteous condemnation and prurient, salacious interest typical of tabloid coverage of such events – and threw it back in their faces. Later Portable projects that Hare had a hand in writing included the multi-authored *Lay By* (1971) and *England's Ireland* (1972); Griffiths contributed to the former and Edgar to the latter, but neither play can be seen as falling within conventional political debate in its narrow sense. The attack is broader and, in some senses, deeper than that. The company's targets in the audience were as likely to be members of the counterculture as of the

---

* Howard Brenton, *Christie in Love*, in *Plays: One* (London: 1986).

official one, and its targets in terms of subject – sex murder, pornography, Northern Ireland – were targets that could not under normal circumstances easily be put onstage at all. *England's Ireland* was banned by over fifty theatres, though the Portable cause generally was aided by the Theatres Act of 1968, which abolished censorship of the stage in Britain (a victory won largely by the Royal Court and the '1956' generation of playwrights). A piece such as *Lay By* took full advantage: it not only tackled its subject – pornography – through openly staging it, but also had its cast members handing out hard-core photographs to the audience. This refusal to accept, and indeed actively to undermine and dislocate, the conventional proprieties of stage–audience relationships went further. When Hare directed Brenton's *Fruit* in 1970, he did so in such a way as to forbid 'any aesthetic at all . . . It was impossible to make aesthetic patterns, and it was impossible to apportion moral praise or blame' (pp. 64–5). This kind of 'pared down' stagecraft owed something to the work of innovative American performance groups such as Café La Mama (indeed, the American influence on fringe theatre practice generally was considerable, though Hare claims to have been largely unaware of it at the time; he does, however, acknowledge the debt owed by *Blake* to the La Mama group).

In all, Hare wrote two, co-wrote three and directed five Portable shows before the group collapsed in bankruptcy in the early seventies. The impact of its work – violent, nihilistic, disturbing and determinedly offensive – was as significant as that of any of the groups working on the fringe at the time. It is as difficult to imagine much of the work being stageable today as it is to see in the Hare who was one of the group's three or four key members the same figure who was to produce *Amy's View* or *My Zinc Bed*. Yet Portable provided a crucial apprenticeship. Not only did it introduce him to the craft of writing and directing plays, but its situationist-inspired formulation of the particular relationship between public and private life, and its insistence on addressing questions of what values lie behind the easy assumptions and lies of official culture, set, or at least confirmed, a theme that is central to his whole career. When he describes the Portable work as addressing 'closely-knit social situations in a process of extreme decay' (p. 69), he could be offering a manifesto for much of his subsequent work.

The first half of the 1970s saw Hare produce a series of original plays in which his distinctive personal voice began to emerge. Each of these plays is located within one of those 'closely knit social situations': *Slag* (1970) and *The Great Exhibition* (1972), pieces written during his time with Portable but not for the company, were set in an exclusive girls' school and in the Hampstead home of a morally bankrupt Labour MP respectively; *Knuckle* (1974) in the Surrey stockbroker belt, and *Teeth 'n' Smiles* (1975) at the 1969 May Ball at Jesus College, Cambridge (Hare's alma mater). All these settings have in common their location within the confines of the ruling class, and the degree to which the small groups of characters who inhabit them are isolated from the larger world outside. What is reflected here is partly Hare's lifelong fascination with the internal workings of closed communities and institutions, partly his determination to write 'truthfully' (in other words, to write about what he knows about), and partly a desire to carry his arguments into 'the enemy camp'; to this extent, these plays establish a pattern that obtains almost exclusively throughout his career. This stands in marked contrast to much of the post-Portable work of his contemporaries: Brenton's 1973 play *Magnificence*,* for example, has a scene set in the Cambridge home of a Tory cabinet minister, but that is located in and played against a larger social context peopled by characters of very different social outlook and class; and, indeed, it is the clash between these separate worlds that forms the political substance of the play. Few outsiders intrude into the world of Hare's early plays: his analysis is made almost entirely from within upper-class institutions, and only in *The Great Exhibition*

* Howard Brenton, *Magnificence*, in *Plays: One*.

is that analysis in any *overt* sense political. Where Brenton glories in adopting a range of stylistic voices to express the fragmentation of social experience and political attitude, Hare speaks in variations of one quickly recognizable voice – a voice that is laced with wit, loves jokes and is often heavy with irony.

In what sense, then, may these plays be seen as 'political theatre'? *Slag* – the play in which Hare feels he discovered his gift as a writer – satirizes the impractical idealism and ultimately anarchic self-indulgence of the post '68 countercultural movements, as does the later *Teeth 'n' Smiles*. *The Great Exhibition* similarly offers an indictment of the wasted years of the Wilson governments of the sixties. Yet even in the more obviously 'political' *Great Exhibition* the analysis is made without any great sense of historical specificity or detail, and *Slag* makes no direct reference at all to outside events. The kind of ideological conflict that is made overt in Brenton's work is in Hare's subsumed into the private lives of individuals. Bull makes the point well:

> Where [Brenton] is concerned primarily with characterization as a product of social reality, Hare works from the inside. He is intensely interested in the particular individuality of the individual, and most of his central characters are misfits, living out their disillusionment through the dismal unrolling of post-1939 British history. His characters do not embody the confusion of social reality but struggle against it, and it is in this clash that Hare seeks to define the area of political debate.*

These pieces play out narratives of the struggle of idealism against disillusionment and despair, and to a very great extent the battle is seen as already lost. The attempts of the three women teachers in *Slag* to create their own alternative society within the exclusive Brackenhurst School founder laughably, whilst Hammett, the corrupted Labour MP of *The Great*

---

* Bull, pp. 61–2.

Exhibition, drifts towards resignation as his personal and professional life collapses around him. *Teeth 'n' Smiles* offers a little more optimism, but only to a minimal and highly qualified extent. Brackenhurst, the intended 'battleground of the future', continues on its quietly declining way, its practices and rituals drained of meaning but crucially still intact; as such, it stands for all the institutions in these plays, which either carry on undented (*The Great Exhibition*) or flex slightly to accommodate dissidence and opposition (*Teeth 'n' Smiles*). The system wins. Hare's interest, and his means of engaging his audiences in understanding the social relevance of his work, lie in showing the price paid by his characters for clinging to any kind of hope. These are figures characterized by their desperation, their madness or their cynicism, figures whose behaviour through its very oddness demands understanding and explanation. Characters' frustrations turn in on themselves, creating inward-looking worlds of fantasy, power games and role play. Indeed, performance is a strong leitmotif throughout, whether it be the imaginary games played in *Slag*, Hammett's self-conscious acting out of his personal and professional life in *The Great Exhibition*, or the similarly self-conscious adoption of 'rock-star behaviour' of the band in *Teeth 'n' Smiles*. Performing, rather than being, the self is the only way of dealing with reality. There is a hint here of Genet, and perhaps of Pirandello, whose *Rules of the Game* Hare adapted for a 1971 National Theatre production with Paul Scofield: the self-reflexive theatricality of the writing (which also includes references to Shakespeare) serves to force audiences to question the reliabilty of what is before them. Hare has, in fact, described these early plays as 'puzzles' (p. 73) for audiences to solve, and that idea is made most literal in *Knuckle*. Here, the form is that of the kind of 1940s *'noir*-ish' detective thriller best exemplified by the work of Raymond Chandler and Dashiell Hammett [*sic*], but the convention is invoked only to be exploded: not only does the setting – Guildford – stand in ironic disjuncture to downtown LA, but our detective hero, Curly, too readily accepts defeat in his quest to rescue his idealistic missing sister from the web of corruption, blackmail and murder in which she has become lost. Hare's adoption of the detective thriller becomes, as he explains himself, an investigation into the possibility of morality within contemporary capitalism, and whilst he goes on to describe Sarah, the missing sister, as 'the most admirable person I've ever drawn', the fact that she is never found, and never appears on stage, means that she sits in the play as a kind of vacuum, defined more by what she *isn't* – or, more accurately, by what she refuses to be – than by what she *is*.

Going mainstream

If, by the mid-1970s, Hare was already identifying his political battlefield as essentially a *moral* arena, then that was a position arrived at, as he explains himself (p. 74), through the 'ruthlessly truthful' process of his writing. However, questions remained about his wider social and theatrical role as one of the generation of new British political dramatists, and indeed about the role of that generation generally. It is tempting to suggest that the attitudes to institutions expressed by the plays to some extent reflect his own position with regard to the contemporary theatrical establishment. From 1968 to 1971 he worked as Literary Manager and subsequently Resident Dramatist for the Royal Court Theatre, which may suggest a symbolic moment of the coming together of the two great 'movements' – Court and Fringe – of post-war political theatre. In fact, it was not entirely a happy personal experience for Hare. However, his ambivalence towards the institution that was the Court – and in some ways it prefigured his relationship with the National Theatre later in his career – must also be placed in the wider context of developments in contemporary theatre generally. By the early 1970s many of Hare's generation were beginning to doubt the continuing viability of the Fringe as a means of creating their new theatre and reaching the wider audiences they desired. Brenton came to view the Fringe as a kind of cultural 'cul-de-sac', its radicalism spent and its audiences – very largely middle-class and already converted to the political cause – as exclusive in their way as those of the West End. As the decade progressed, the ''68 generation' (with the exception of McGrath, who founded his two '7:84' companies in 1971 and 1973 to take theatre to working-class audiences in Scotland and Northern England respectively) moved increasingly into the publicly sub-sidized theatres of the mainstream culture: Brenton produced work for the National (where Hare directed his *Weapons of Happiness* in 1976), Edgar's *Destiny* saw him leave his agitprop work and the smaller venues for a big play for the RSC, and Griffiths concentrated on television work.* The Court too hosted work by a number of the new writers – including, of course, Hare's *Teeth 'n' Smiles* – and as early as 1970 hosted a 'Come Together' Festival (though even here the relationship between the old and new guard was often tense). For some on the hard left of the Fringe, this was 'selling out'; for the writers con-cerned, it was an opportunity to reach bigger audiences and to produce work larger in scope and ambition, whilst at the same time (and not unproblematically – Brenton described Hare's production of *Weapons* as being like 'an armoured charabanc' encamped within the National) bringing into the mainstream the political and formal concerns of the Fringe.

Hare's own position – one is tempted to say, not untypically – was a little different. By 1974 he had already had two plays produced on the commercial stage: *Slag* and *Knuckle*, the latter being his first West End show. Using the commercial stage to attack commerce unsurprisingly proved a little difficult for the West End audience, but it clearly signals Hare's political inten-tions at the time. Furthermore, Hare's view was that if he could use the commercial theatre for his work, he should, if only to free up the subsidized spaces for other writers. Beyond that, and notwithstanding the feelings of theatrical 'homelessness' he confessed to at the time, he found two further outlets for his work in this period, and produced through them two plays –

* Howard Brenton, *Weapons of Happiness* in *Plays: One.*

27

Brassneck and *Fanshen* – that were in their different ways quite unlike anything that had gone before or, in the case of *Fanshen* at least, would come after.

Brassneck (1973) was co-written with Howard Brenton for the Nottingham Playhouse, then under the artistic directorship of Richard Eyre. Eyre had already directed the première of *The Great Exhibition* at the Hampstead Theatre Club, and his close association with Hare was to reach full fruition during his later stewardship of the National (see the interview below, p. 218). His regime at Nottingham was dedicated to producing the work of the new writers, and produced some of the seminal plays of the post-war period: Brenton's *The Churchill Play* (1974), Griffiths's *Comedians* (1975) and, of course, *Brassneck*. The play charts the rise, fall, and rise again of the Bagley business dynasty, and through it offers a panoramic view of British history from 1945 to the 1960s. Its story of corruption and betrayal, as generations of the Bagley family move from bent property to heroin dealing, offers a satirical view of the voracious nature of capitalism and of inexorable post-war decline; typically for the kind of work the new writers brought to the big stages – *Brassneck* is one of the first of those plays, and in many ways paradigmatic – it is as damning of the left as of the right.

The question of the play's authorship is in a sense a vexed one, for both Brenton and Hare acknowledge that the piece is quite unlike anything that they have produced individually: they are happy with the view of one critic that the play was in fact written by 'Howard Hare'. It is oversimplistic, but nonetheless accurate, however, to suggest that the form of the play marries Hare's 'private' focus with Brenton's more 'public' overview. The structure is episodic, the narrative discontinuous. Key private and domestic moments are placed in often ironic historical context by the use of projected slides showing public events. Little attention is paid to the psychological development of character or to the naturalistic fleshing-out of scenic location: audiences are invited to 'fill in the gaps' themselves. These characteristics are the central components of what Brenton and Hare were beginning to develop as a 'British epic theatre': theatre on a large scale, ambitious in historical sweep, and dealing with the great issues of public life as reflected by and mediated through the private and domestic lives of its characters.

The use of the word 'epic' inevitably invokes the name of Brecht, though in fact many of the new writers were suspicious of his influence (Brenton referred to his plays as 'museum pieces', though later went on to adapt *The Life of Galileo* for the National, just as Hare produced a version for the Almeida, as well as one of *Mother Courage* for the National in the 1990s) and sought to distance themselves from him. In *Fanshen* (1975), however, Hare produced what is, with Caryl Churchill's *Light Shining in Buckinghamshire*, the most Brechtian of modern British plays. The play was written for the young Joint Stock Theatre Group. Hare had played a part in founding the group, with Max Stafford-Clark, formerly artistic director of the Traverse Theatre in Edinburgh, and David Aukin, who had founded the Freehold and Foco Novo companies; as with Hare, the origins of both men lay on the Fringe. When William Gaskill joined the group from the Royal Court, two traditions merged in a practical, creative context (Stafford-Clark, indeed, himself went on to run the Court). It was the process of creating *Fanshen* that was largely to determine the work process of the group – the 'Joint Stock method' – throughout its life. The play was adapted from a book by William Hinton* that tells the story of the Chinese Revolution through the experiences of one village. Hare was drawn to the project because he was 'sick to death with writing about England' (p. 82) and relished documenting a situation in which the possibility of *change* was a battle to be won, and not one apparently already lost. The means by which the villagers affect *fanshen* ('turning over') is through a constant and demanding process of 'Self-Report,

---

* William Hinton, *Fanshen: A Documentary of Revolution in a Chinese Village* (New York: 1966).

Public Appraisal' through which are collectively judged the many difficult decisions they have to make to bring equality and justice to their impoverished lives. A parallel process was put to use by the Joint Stock group during the five weeks of practical workshops, research and discussion that provided Hare with the raw material out of which, over a period of four months, he wrote the text. That text (typically for most of the playwrights who produced work with the group) is quite different from any of the rest of the writer's plays. Individual psychology is rejected in favour of the individual's socio-economic role within the collective; language is pared down to an essential simplicity devoid of irony, wit or double meaning. The process of making the play is shown in it, partly as a reflection of the process the villagers themselves went through and partly to induce within the audience an appropriately critical response: it too must test arguments, judge the rightness of decisions made. Not surprisingly, and somewhat to Hinton's displeasure, Hare's initial version made a slight shift of focus away from the book, stressing the moral, rather than the more specifically political, aspects of its arguments; a later version redressed the balance.

By the mid-1970s, then, Hare had seen work – of various different kinds – on commercial and subsidized mainstream stages and on tour round Fringe venues. His next play, *Plenty* (1978), took him to the heart of the theatrical establishment, and confirmed his position as one of our leading young dramatists. He describes *Plenty* as the piece he had 'been trying to write for a long time' (p. 93): it certainly represents a kind of summative statement of the concerns of his earlier writing, and was formally his most ambitious play to date. Its subject is again the price paid by 'the moral dissenter', but, influenced in part by *Brassneck*, it places its central characters in a fuller and more detailed historical context: the play sweeps from 1943 to 1962, from the war through the Festival of Britain to the Suez Crisis and the last years of Conservative government before Harold Wilson's first election victory. The central story is that of Susan

Traherne. When we first meet her, she is an idealistic young woman, a Special Operations Executive agent working behind enemy lines in occupied France, and living her dangerous life with the kind of brilliant intensity to which Maggie in *Teeth 'n' Smiles* self-destructively aspires. Nothing in the post-war years of decline can provide her with the same, almost magical existence. One of the many ironies of the play (its title is another: the fifties were the years when, according to Macmillan, 'we never had it so good') is that Susan, who as a spy is essentially a professional liar, cannot deal with a society seen to be increasingly built on lies. The world she moves in is that of an enclosed diplomatic establishment that looks not outward to the new Britain of the Welfare State, but inward to the old values of Empire; significantly, her descent into madness mirrors those public events (notably the Suez Crisis) that signal the actuality of the redundancy of those values. Susan's refusal to lie, her insistence on clinging to her idealism, is destructive of herself and of others around her, including her husband Brock. Between them, Susan and Brock represent the desperate logic of the play: not to consent to society drives you mad; to consent makes you complicit in its cynical dishonesty and moral turpitude.

Hare came to feel his own direction of the play underplayed the importance of other characters, especially Brock. By favouring Susan too much he unbalanced the argument, and ran the risk of allowing her particular psychological individuality (her personal tragedy) rather than the greater analysis (the historical tragedy of many wasted lives) to dominate the play, representing a potential clouding of its political intent. This was a mistake he had earlier recognized with Hammett in *The Great Exhibition*, and which he was to correct in his 1980 television film *Dreams of Leaving*, where the authority of the key protagonist and narrator, William, is constantly undercut by, amongst other things, the unreliability of his character. In most other regards, however, *Plenty* offers a brilliant exposition of the principles of 'British epic', sustaining a richly meaningful interplay between public and private life through an episodic structure that dramatizes, rather than merely asserts, crucial arguments and actions. This is the epic theatre that was in Hare's mind when he asked of the sleeping tramp on the London Underground (in the King's lecture given in the same year as *Plenty* premièred), 'What historical forces drew him there? What armies fought? What families fell apart?' (see above, p. 7). The debt to Brecht is clear, though Hare also acknowledges the importance of what he learned from Shakespeare, and indeed from his own earlier work. (In *Teeth 'n' Smiles*, for instance, too much of the historical context of the play is clumsily loaded into one rather hefty speech by the band's business manager, Saraffian.) Equally, there is a real sense in which, in *Plenty*, he truly found his subject: history.

According to Jonathan Kent, Hare has said 'that the seminal event in his life happened before he was born: the war. The war was the defining moment in the lives of a whole generation' (p. 216). All of Hare's work up to and including *Plenty* must be seen to a greater or lesser extent in this context, as must most of it afterwards. *Plenty* itself was heavily influenced by his reading of Angus Calder's *The People's War*,* a book that gave an account of the effects of the war on civilian life and that in doing so debunked some of the popular mythology and received opinion of official history. (Calder had also influenced Brenton's *The Churchill Play*.) Hare continued his historical revisionism in the 1978 television film *Licking Hitler*. Here, the conventions of the British war movies of the forties and fifties are used to investigate the lives of workers in the wartime 'black propaganda' agencies: more 'professional liars' who are seen to go on to key positions in post-war public life, and who are presumably well equipped to do so. The overwhelming sense in all this work is of a better Britain that has been lost – or rather betrayed and thrown away – and of brilliant lives wastefully diminished through the sad decline of the post-war years. There

---

* Angus Calder, *The People's War: Britain 1939–45* (London: 1969).

is undoubtedly a sense of tragedy, and maybe romanticism (the writer himself may perhaps be seen as the kind of embattled idealist who appears in so many of his plays) in Hare's revisionist analysis, though set alongside that are rare moments, achieved briefly by a few characters, of a kind of utopian grace. Susan's last lines in *Plenty* – 'There will be days and days and days like this' – delivered as 'flashback' on a blissfully sunny hillside in wartime France are not *only* bitterly ironic: they are also suggestive of the rich possibility of human experience, its capacity for intense vitality. Nor do such moments lessen in importance in the later parts of Hare's career; indeed, they are in some senses crucial, for Hare's view of history is to set how things *are* in the context not only of how things *were*, but also in the context of how things *might have been*.

In opposition

If 1968 was a watershed year in the development of modern British theatre, then 1979 was hardly less so – though discussions about the future of the theatre understandably did not loom large in the national consciousness following the election of Margaret Thatcher's first administration in that year. As I have already suggested, that event effectively marked the end of the post-war consensual politics that had governed Britain for over thirty years. Thatcher's 'New Right' policies were designed to halt the national decline that had accelerated throughout the 1970s, culminating in the 'Winter of Discontent' in 1979, when a wave of public-service strikes half-paralysed the country. Legislation to curtail the freedom of trades unions was therefore a priority. More profoundly, the market, rather than government intervention, was to determine the national economy: taxes were cut, key industries privatized, market forces introduced into welfare services (the universal availability of which was threatened) and the level of public spending ruthlessly forced down. In terms of foreign policy, the emphasis was more than ever on alliance with the United States, with Europe coming a poor second.

It was the cuts in public funding to the arts that impacted most directly on the theatre, and in particular on many of the ''68 generation', who had spent much of the seventies developing large-scale, big-cast 'state of the nation' plays that now became, crudely, too expensive to perform. Brenton's controversial *The Romans in Britain* (1980) and Edgar's no less ambitious *Maydays* (1983) were effectively the last plays of their kind to be produced; the two writers' output in the eighties was of necessity reduced in scale as they searched for new, or in some cases old, forms capable of carrying oppositional debate forward (Edgar's *That Summer* addressed the miners' strike of 1985 through the medium of romantic comedy). Generally speaking, the effect of increasing financial pressure on the subsidized mainsteam theatre was to force it into a box-office dependency that threatened an end to risk-taking and experiment, and a return to the narrowly formulaic, commercially driven product of pre-public subsidy days; the effects on theatre outside the mainstream were no less severe, with financial hardship and constant changes in Arts Council funding policy producing confusion and fragmentation.

The right also – and more profoundly – stole the theatrical left's ground on an ideological level. It is easy, at least in terms of the simple number of plays performed, to overestimate the dominance of left-wing political theatre pre-Thatcher, but it is generally true that the work done did much to set the theatrical agenda and stimulate discussion. The radical swing to the right – not without irony, given that they had put so much energy into attacking the left – seemed to leave many of the new writers relatively speechless, especially as the overall political context saw the left, from the Parliamentary Labour Party to street activists, disintegrate into separate and often bitterly opposed interest groups offering no single, clear oppositional voice. Brenton, in a voice not so far removed from Hare's, has the poet Byron articulate the dilemma in his 1984 play, *Bloody Poetry*: 'A war. If only there were a war in England, not that endless – slow, sullen defeat. Why don't the bastards take up arms against such a government? Then we poets would be of some use, we'd do the songs, the banners, the shouts, but no. Sullen silence.'*

In fact it was the reaction to Brenton's *The Romans in Britain* that signalled the new government's attitude to the theatrical left. The play is a critique of imperialism in general and the British presence in Ireland in particular, but its political points were obscured by the furore that developed over its depiction of an attempted homosexual rape. Media coverage was intense, and a prosecution on the grounds of obscenity was launched by the right-wing National Viewers' and Listeners' Association (neatly finding a loophole in the 1968 Theatres Act, which had abolished stage censorship). The prosecution was ultimately withdrawn, but the damage had been done. The fact that the play was performed in the (publicly owned) *National* Theatre, that it assaulted deeply held notions of national identity, that it refused the easy answers of bourgeois humanism and, moreover, that it was written by a child of the cursed 'permissive sixties', made it a useful *cause célèbre* for political opponents inside and outside government. This was especially true given that it was Thatcher's declared intention to restore pride in national identity, to put the 'Great' back into Britain, and to reject the revisionism of much contemporary historical thinking in favour of a celebration of the traditional glories of our imperial past.†

How, then, did Hare fare in the eighties? Given that he was a political dramatist whose main subject to date had been history, he might justifiably have felt personally victimized by the new government. His opposition to Thatcherism remained unrelenting and angry throughout the decade, and was often expressed through his journalism, as was his consistent and robust defence of the beleaguered theatre. At first glance, however, his own work for the stage seems to have been adversely

---

* Howard Brenton, *Bloody Poetry*, in *Plays: Two* (London: 1989).
† For a fuller account of *The Romans in Britain* and its place in the history of modern British theatre, see Boon, *Brenton the Playwright*, chapter 6.

affected: he produced only three full-length pieces – *A Map of the World* (1983), *Pravda* (1985, the second play by 'Howard Hare') and *The Secret Rapture* (1988) – and two shorter exercises, *The Bay at Nice* and *Wrecked Eggs* (both 1986). So (relatively) limited an output might well say something about the difficulties of producing new work for the theatre at the time; what it does not take into account, however, is Hare's work in film for both television and the cinema, which not only constituted the greater part of the decade's work but which also, when added to the theatre work, indicates a level of overall productivity almost identical to that of the seventies.

This is not to say that he did not feel to some degree disenchanted by the theatre, and by the theatrical establishment, after the reception of *Plenty*, claiming he felt 'worn down by the criticism' (p. 93). It was not at all unreasonable of one interviewer to ask, in 1982, whether he had 'left the theatre for good'.* Hare's answer was in the negative, but he also acknowledges that the work on film was liberating. *Dreams of Leaving* (1980), *Saigon* (1983), *Wetherby* (1985), the screenplay for *Plenty* (1985), *Paris by Night* (1988) and *Strapless* (1988) may be seen as a manifestation of a lifelong love of film, but, at least as important, four of the pieces (the exceptions are *Saigon* and *Plenty*) were also directed by the writer, giving him a degree of control, and the opportunity fully to realize personal vision, that the more collaborative theatre does not permit. Not that television was without its censorship problems (it never has been): Hare bemoaned the difficulties of writing about the 'harder' subjects, such as sex and Northern Ireland (see, for example, Caryl Churchill's difficulties with her 1975 television play, *The Legion Hall Bombing*), but he also relished the chance of mass audiences that screen work affords, and it may also be the case that the lack of *overt* or *obvious* political content in his work helped him avoid the kinds of problem that Trevor Griffiths, for example, increasingly faced.

* Alison Summers: see p. 94 and Bibliography.

Saigon: Year of the Cat is set in that other war that so influenced Hare: Vietnam. Specifically, it is concerned with events surrounding the chaotic American withdrawal from Saigon in 1974, a story told through what was to become an increasingly important narrative device in his work: a love story. The protagonists are Barbara Dean, an English bank official, and Bob Chesneau, an American CIA agent attached to the US embassy. Their tentative, exploratory discovery of each other as lovers mirrors and investigates how they deal both individually and as a pair with the crisis that is growing outside their institutions: on both the private and the public levels, they have to try to accommodate within their world views events that are alien to them and not within their control. Unlike the characters in Hare's earliest work, they are forced outside their closed communities literally and psychologically, and they manage with very limited success. Indeed, it is the failure of the US ambassador to see outside his own, private reality – to conceive that things really are as bad as they seem, and that US forces are being defeated by the advancing communists – that leads directly to the panic of the last-minute evacuation and the chaos that causes Chesneau to forget his responsibilities to the safety of pro-American Vietnamese workers, leaving them to an inevitable fate. Part of Hare's intention is to correct the dominant view in the West, that Vietnam was an American tragedy: it was more of a tragedy for the Vietnamese, who are strongly represented in the film. By questioning how, on both personal and more widely political and cultural levels, people can break out of closed mind-sets and establish a common, shared reality, *Saigon* parallels the interests of Hare's next stage play.

A Map of the World represents something of an experiment in Hare's theatre work. If he felt that the stage version of *Plenty* had taken the epic as far as it could go, then the new play looks to a different form (albeit one that borrows some of the characteristics of epic). The play is set in a Bombay hotel, at a UNESCO conference on world poverty. The setting is itself significant: the conference gathers delegates from around the world – each to his or her own room – then has them meet in the common area of the lounge. The only representatives of the country outside the hotel are its Indian waiters, a reality that from the beginning undermines the theatrical authority of the delegates, for all their articulate discussion and witty discourse. At the centre of the play is a debate between a distinguished novelist, Victor Mehta, and a journalist, Stephen Andrews, about how best to address the problems of the developing world. What adds layers of complexity to the play is that it transpires that what the audience is watching is in fact the shooting of a film, based on a book by the real Mehta about a similar – real – conference: the ultimate 'puzzle', perhaps (and indeed the world of the play is not so very far removed from the bizarre, isolated worlds of the early plays). The play, then, not only offers a critique of the glib, often self-serving assumptions the West habitually makes about the developing world, but does so in a way that constantly questions the reliability of what is being said, why and by whom, and therefore questions the ways in which we judge what *is* real and right. By Hare's own admission, *A Map of the World* is not a complete success as a play: its complex political purpose comes to some extent at the cost of its theatrical drive; but its insistence on the need to acknowledge the difficulties, ambivalences and paradoxes of the debate with which it engages says something about the left-ist theatre of the early eighties: those qualities had most often been associated with the kind of traditional bourgeois theatre of which many on the left were deeply suspicious; but asking some very basic and not-easily-answered questions about how political theatre can and should engage its audiences with its ideas – and how far it could be *trusted* – had become inevitable in the new climate.

Good and evil

These were questions that Hare took with him when he became Associate Director of the National Theatre in 1984. Typically, he took the position (under the theatre's then director, Sir Peter Hall) with a certain degree of ambivalence, but with a clear personal agenda: to continue to bring into the heart of mainstream culture the kind of big public play he and others had pioneered in the seventies. The theatre, he argued, was 'the unique forum in which a society can discuss itself' (p. 111). It is perhaps unsurprising, then, that he began his project by turning to his old collaborator, Howard Brenton. *Pravda* began life as a straightforward satirical comedy on the institution of the press: '*Pravda* means "the truth". English newspapers aren't propaganda sheets. The question is, why do so many of them choose to *behave* as if they are?', asked Brenton.* The eventual play retained all the delights of rumbustious – and very funny – satirical comedy, playing to packed houses over an extended run; but answering Brenton's question had led him and Hare to a wider, and in some ways darker, challenge to the nature of society in 'Thatcher's Britain'. In the play's central figure, the South African newspaper proprietor Lambert Le Roux (brilliantly and monstrously incarnated by Anthony Hopkins; see the interview with Bill Nighy below, pp. 181–2), the two writers not only offered a scathing attack on a figure not entirely dissimilar to the media tycoon Rupert Murdoch and his aggressive acquistion of large parts of the British press, but also explored what happens to society when only power matters. Le Roux is a nihilistic 'force of nature': those who oppose him fail to understand that, for him, power is not a means to an end, but the end itself. Ultimately they realize that they must fight him with his own weapons, but, lacking his absolute certainty, they are doomed to failure. Le Roux may be shown to be quite insane, but he emerges triumphant, systematically destroying or co-opting his enemies to his cause. In a depressing reflection of the state of the contemporary left, his opponents emerge as confused, traduceable and effete liberals who realize far too late the nature of the forces they are up against. The play had

---

* Quoted in the Programme for *Pravda*, National Theatre, 1985.

become, in the eyes of its writers, an examination of evil, and searching for the force that could counteract that evil became an overriding concern for both of them in their subsequent work.

Pravda, like Caryl Churchill's *Serious Money* (1987), offered a genuine and widely celebrated theatrical critique of the new Britain. Yet it could not and did not stand as a viable model for later work, either for Brenton and Hare or for other writers. As Hare makes clear, the collaborations with Brenton were of their own kind, arising out of particular circumstances; more generally, economic conditions continued to militate against larger-scale work. In the same year that *Pravda* was such a success, Peter Hall closed one of the National's stages, cut jobs and announced his own departure. Moreover, there was no 'third generation' of political dramatists beating at the doors of the theatres in the way that the '56 or '68 cohorts had. As Trevor Griffiths was to observe, it became hard for people to make politics out of theatre when people were not making politics out of politics: such were the chaos on the left and the dominance of the right.

In one sense Hare perhaps held an advantage over his contemporaries when it came to surviving in the new climate. The lack of overt political content in his writing may have eased his path at a time when political debate in mainstream culture was becoming rather unfashionable; similarly, his concentration on questions of morality – often personal morality – married well with a widely felt need on the left to re-examine its beliefs and policies on a deep-seated philosophical level. One of the discoveries made by *Pravda* was that opposition to Thatcherism was compromised not just by disorganization and woolly thinking, but by a more profound moral uncertainty: what, in the end, did the left *believe*, in its heart? These were questions that Hare had already begun to explore, and, moreover, often on a smaller – and hence more viable – scale than the big 'state of the nation' plays of some of his contemporaries. Furthermore, as he acknowledges himself, working with Brenton had given him 'an energy' that was to carry him through to *The Secret Rapture* and the trilogy (p. 109).

The way in which Hare positioned himself in the new moral climate of the eighties is best illustrated by a brief comparison of his first two feature films, *Wetherby* (1985) and *Strapless* (1988). In *Wetherby*, the comfortable, rather anaesthetized life of Jean, a Yorkshire schoolteacher, and her circle of friends is disrupted by the mysterious arrival at their dinner party of a volatile stranger, John Morgan. Here, the outsider penetrates the closed community, with shattering results. It is worth quoting the following interchange:

MORGAN Well, I don't know. I only know goodness and anger and revenge and evil and desire . . . these seem to me far better words than neurosis and psychology and paranoia. These old words . . . these good old words have a sort of conviction which all this modern apparatus of language now lacks.
(*People have stopped eating and are looking at him. There is a silence.*)
MARCIA Ah, well, yes . . .
MORGAN We bury these words, these simple feelings, we bury them deep. And all the building over that constitutes this century will not wish these feelings away.
[. . .]
. . . They don't need defining. If you can't feel them you might as well be dead.

Morgan is unbalanced by his desperate need to *feel* in a society that seems no longer to feel, or to care about feeling (it is interesting here to note Hare's comments on Osborne and the "'56 generation' in the 'Conversation' below). Like Maggie and Susan Traherne in *Teeth 'n' Smiles* and *Plenty*, he 'mainlines' experience and sensation, and cannot handle the personal consequences: on a second visit to Jean, he blows his brains out. Yet his action, however tragic, has a kind of integrity compared to the easy bourgeois existence of Jean's circle and the desolate morality of the wider world, and he awakens a similar potential in Jean herself. Indeed, there is the brief potential of theirs becoming a love story. This is a complex film in which games are played with the viewer: episodes are replayed in subtly different flashbacks, where things are as they are differently remembered by the one remembering, raising questions about the reliability of memory (further explored in the 1991 television film *Heading Home*) and of the medium through which the story is being told (as in *A Map of the World*). It is also a tragedy of, at times, terrifying bleakness; but Morgan's insistence on the 'good old words' and the values they represent is also Hare's insistence, and his means of grounding the moral debate that to him seemed essential. *Strapless* is a lighter piece, but exercises similar themes. It is a love story, but its implications reach beyond the domestic to the wider social canvas. Raymond's destructive hunger for sensation is mediated through a passion for romance that leads him into bigamy, with the inevitably damaging results for his doctor wife, Lillian. The debate, however, moves on from *Wetherby* and Hare's earlier work: Lillian is able to recognize that she cannot ignore what Raymond has awoken in her, that 'the bill must be picked up' for personal feelings and instincts, that the 'good old words' and what they represent cannot be ignored. As in private life, so in public life: truth to one's conscience, to one's emotions, and resistance to faithlessness and amorality are crucial not only personally, but also, by extension, politically: Lillian not only survives Raymond, but becomes active in her hospital in defence of the NHS.

Paradoxically, it is both logical and ironic that Hare should gain confidence in his own idealism and that of his characters at the moment when society at large seemed to have lost its own. It is by no means an unqualified idealism, as *Heading Home* shows. The complexity of the moral debate is articulated most fully, however, in *The Secret Rapture* (1988), a play that is about 'the intractability of goodness' (p. 122), and what happens when Thatcherite Britain forces its way into the living room. Essentially, it tells the story of two sisters during the aftermath of their father's death. Isobel is 'lumbered with being good' (p. 121): caring, honest, selfless and with a deep-seated faith in humanity. Marion, a junior minister in the Conservative government, is quite the opposite: like Hare's Euro MP Clara in the 1988 film *Paris by Night*, she is conscienceless, selfish and self-regarding, and callous in the ruthless pragmatism with which she deals with the 'softness' of others. Like Clara, she is responsible (though less directly so) for a murder: Isobel's. Stated like this, the moral and political parameters of the play seem obvious, even crude, and indeed Isobel is manipulated and exploited by Marion throughout the play. Yet, as with Janetta in *Heading Home*, there is, as Marion recognizes, an innocence about Isobel that is dangerous, an innocence that is damaging to others. There is a sense in which Isobel is another in the line (Maggie, Susan Traherne, John Morgan, Raymond) of what one critic calls Hare's 'spiritual extremists',* figures whose moral absolutism throws into chaos the lives of those around them. Nor is Marion a two-dimensional caricature of the Thatcherite politician: there is an attractiveness in her practicality and dynamism. Her ability simply to get on with her life stands in welcome and, Hare suggests, genuinely significant contrast to Isobel's oddly detached selflessness. More importantly, she learns from Isobel's death, at least to the extent that it grants her an awareness of and insight into herself, the lack of which, she realizes, had made her what she was. It has always been characteristic of Hare's writing that even those characters to whom he might be deeply opposed on political and moral grounds are not simply dismissed, but given ideas, attitudes and arguments as fully deserving of attention and respect as those of the characters with whom an audience might expect his natural sympathies to lie (see Bill Nighy, below). 'Rightness' does not reside within any one figure, but is something that has to be beaten out in complex arguments

---

* Duncan Wu, *Six Contemporary Dramatists* (London: 1995), p. 97.

between characters and hence, crucially, between stage and audience. The play is fierce in its condemnation of the Thatcherite world that Marion inhabits, but it not only seeks to understand it, it also draws something from it. For all that, *The Secret Rapture* remains, ultimately, a kind of tragedy.

Finding a new politics

All these themes are further explored and developed in what remains Hare's most ambitious project to date: the trilogy. *Racing Demon* (1990), *Murmuring Judges* (1991) and *The Absence of War* (1993) were six years in the writing, and taken as a whole – they were also performed as a whole in 1993 after their individual premières, all directed by Richard Eyre at the National – they constitute a uniquely epic view of contemporary British society. In a real sense they are, in ambition, subject, and – not least – the location of their production, the ultimate 'state of the nation' play. The subject is the social and moral cost of Thatcherism, and it is painted on a broad English canvas through the investigation of three great British institutions: the Church, the Law and the Labour Party (Hare also briefly flirted with the possibility of plays on education and the health service). The view they offer is consistent but, crucially, *found* rather than given: whatever Hare brought to them from his earlier work, they were heavily informed by the extensive research he conducted in their preparation – research that is documented in his *Asking Around: Background to the David Hare Trilogy*.* The plays ask a number of key questions: what is the state of these institutions at a time when society is facing huge problems of a gross division between rich and poor, with the latter effectively disenfranchized and disbarred from power? How do those on the cutting edge of their work survive and continue to operate? And, to repeat Hare's own question in the introduction to *Asking Around*, 'if not through institutions, how do we express the common good?'

* See Bibliography.

Nothing indicates better what kind of political dramatist Hare had become than that these questions should be uppermost in his mind at a time when domestic and international politics were in turmoil. Nationally, unemployment rose to record levels as the economy locked into a cycle of 'boom and bust', with industrial disputes and protests against government policies an inevitable result. Parliamentary opposition remained divided and stuggling to realign itself, with Neil Kinnock still battling to reform the Labour Party and the Liberals merging with the SDP, itself an offshoot of old Labour. IRA activity was high. Abroad, the collapse of apartheid in South Africa, ongoing strife in the Middle East and political unrest in China made for high levels of international tension. Most significantly, the dramatic unravelling of communism in the USSR and the Eastern bloc reshaped the world, signalling – or so it seemed – the final triumph of capitalism over socialism. It was a series of events that effectively 'stole the subject' of many of Hare's contemporaries (like him, committed socialists all); but, as I have already suggested, Hare was, perhaps through accident of subject and style as much as anything, better placed to respond to the volatile and rapidly changing political situation (though Richard Eyre, in the interview below, points out that the writer has always had the instinct of the sure-footed producer, knowing how best to locate his work in changing circumstances).

The focus of the trilogy falls squarely on the real lives of (mainly) ordinary people: 'the people who do the dirty work' (p. 126). There is an element of celebration here: as one of the characters in *Murmuring Judges* puts it, 'Let's hear it for the guys who keep turning up.' 'Keeping turning up' may seem slender grounds for political optimism, but, as the plays show, the forces arraigned against those who hold to and work for 'the common good' are considerable. The characters at the heart of *Racing Demon* and *Murmuring Judges* are figures – vicars, policemen, a conscience-stricken lawyer – who are left isolated to deal with daily reality because the institutions of which they are part are seen to have abdicated their responsibities. Those institutions are peopled by an intellectual elite, inward-facing and concerned above all with the preservation of its own status and power. Part of Hare's argument is to demonstrate the preposterousness of expecting such institutions to function within a society organized along lines dictated by market forces, though any student of his work will immediately recognize an older enemy: this is the 'moral gumrot' of *Knuckle*'s Surrey, but on a much larger and more influential scale. These are social institutions devoid of social responsibility. In *Racing Demon*, the Church of England's mission to propagate the gospel has become little more than an evangelistic advertising strategy; in *Murmuring Judges*, the Law, with all its ritual and paraphernalia, is seen as a gentlemen's club, concerned above all with guarding its own privileges and, in the process, 'chewing up' citizens' lives through miscarriages of justice. In both cases – though the Church's real power is less than the Law's, Hare saw it as a 'sort of metaphor for other institutions' (p. 129) – the essential political function is anaesthetic and repressive, leaving those 'at the coal-face' who actually connect with real people stranded and confused.

Racing Demon, like *The Secret Rapture*, deals with the nature of goodness. A small group of vicars finds itself *de facto* in the position of social workers, 'bandaging society's wounds', and seeking ways of negotiating the conflicts between what they believe to be their calling and the daily reality of their lives. For the caring and doubting Lionel, that means steering an essentially pragmatic course, simply doing what he can; for Tony, it means the evangelical route. Whatever he may feel about the Church's institutional dedication to evangelism, Hare is careful to show Tony's growing commitment as motivated at least in part by the genuine desire to 'get people emotionally involved'; here, the 'spiritual extremist' is given a theological framework. But it is also an unacceptable political framework: unacceptable, because power is flowing down from the top and Tony's 'emotional involvement' amounts to a form of repression. Lionel, on the other hand, can ultimately only patch and mend, not cure. Most significant is the stance of the Reverend 'Streaky' Bacon, who has no theology but who sees God in people's happiness, the taste of a drink, the love of friends: 'The whole thing's so simple. Infinitely loving. Why do people find it so hard?'

In many ways, this simple, even romantic sentiment represents a key moment in Hare's evolution as a political dramatist. If, as he claims, he 'found his politics' in *Racing Demon*, then that discovery lay at least in part in the fact that there is 'something which isn't just what we're conditioned by . . . If a writer doesn't have a sense of the other, by which I mean spirit or soul, I don't want to know.'* It is a large step for a socialist dramatist used to conceiving character primarily as a function of economic and cultural materialism (and who still, to a large extent, does), but it is prefigured in earlier work, in *Wetherby* and *The Secret Rapture*. The value Streaky finds in simple, everyday, often physical pleasures, experienced in *moments*, does not necessarily subscribe to a conventional religious theology, but *is* the basis of a moral value system that can extend *beyond* the moment. If *Pravda* detected the possibility of evil, *Racing Demon* detects the possibility of goodness. *Murmuring Judges* ends with a young policewoman and a young lawyer committing to reform of the law; *Racing Demon*, with a moment of sublimity similar to the one that ends *Plenty*.

The Absence of War, on the other hand, is a darker play, but one that is accommodated within Hare's revised world view. Its subject is the shock election defeat suffered by Labour under Neil Kinnock in 1992, when, for those on the left, the real possibility of an end to thirteen years of Conservative rule was snatched away. Inevitably, the play was seen as being 'about' Kinnock in a way that Hare had not intended, though he admits to having taken insufficient care to prevent the identification. It is best seen, however, in the light of the trilogy as a

---

* Quoted in Malcolm Page, *File on Hare* (London: 1990), p. 83.

whole. George Jones, Hare's Labour leader, leads his party to defeat because, as Duncan Wu argues,* he surrenders to the psychology of repression precisely in the way in which key characters in the preceding plays do not. Jones is both idealist – he has something of Isobel's selflessness – and pragmatist, who understands that the Party, with all its difficulties, offers the only practical way of bringing about essential social change. In putting the needs of the Party and the country above his own needs – he suppresses his natural instincts as a leader in favour of the more cautious and presentation-obsessed policies of the party machine – he alienates himself *from* himself and from the electorate. By the time he realizes he must 'connect', he cannot, and, faced with an opportunity of speaking from the heart about what he believes, flounders to silence. Jones's story is the tragedy of an honourable man who pays the price for not trusting in the power of 'the old words'.

Towards a poetry of the stage

The decade since the trilogy has been marked, in historical and political terms, by confusion and uncertainty. On the one hand, the 1997 general election victory of 'New Labour' under Tony Blair brought to an end eighteen years of Conservative rule, the last of which were characterized by continuing national economic problems and, within Conservative ranks, 'sleaze' scandals, backbiting and, above all, division over Britain's role in the EC. Blair's victory was, in terms of seats gained, a landslide, though that disguised the fact that it rested on only 44 per cent of the national vote. Nonetheless, the new government's immediate actions promised to deliver profound change, with devolution for Scotland and Wales quickly brought on to the statute books and the Bank of England freed from political control. New Labour promised a new consensus: by adopting large parts of the Thatcherite agenda – particularly regarding the control of public spending, the involvement of private finance

* Wu, p. 111ff.

48

in the public sector, and low taxation – and allying it to a general approach that was more compassionate, it sought to have the best of both worlds. Although the government delivered welcome economic stability, and retained power in the 2001 election, its genuine radicalism – as had so often been the case with Labour administrations – had come quickly into question. Major institutional reform such as that of the House of Lords dragged on unresolved, public services still faced huge problems, and the new pro-European stance did not translate into hard action: Britain continued to face across the Atlantic as resolutely as ever. Despite the growth of worldwide anti-globalization movements finding vociferous and occasionally violent support in the country, general political apathy in Britain, particularly among the young, seemed as high by the end of the decade as it had at its beginning. Whereas the post-war consensus had, at least for a while, rested on a contract of trust between governors and governed, the new consensus struggled to reach any such agreement.

In terms of the theatre, a sense of stasis also continued to dominate. New Labour's early 'cool Britannia' initiative, which sought to raise the national and international profile of the British arts generally, came to seem more concerned with the purely presentational 're-branding' of Britain on the one hand and with simply making money on the other: there was no return to the kind of large-scale public subsidy that had done so much to enable new work in the sixties and seventies. Many of what had become the older guard – Hare himself, Howard Barker, Caryl Churchill and Timberlake Wertenbaker – still produced important new work, but the damage that had been done in the eighties had a lasting legacy. Newer, younger writers, such as the late Sarah Kane, Joe Penhall, Mark Ravenhill, Jez Butterworth, Clare McIntyre and Conor McPherson, have offered grounds for hope, producing often innovative and exciting work (and belying the argument of some cultural critics that the theatre is dead). Yet many have struggled to escape the smaller theatres or to create (notwithstanding the energy of

'In Yer Face' theatre) 'that kind of rallying point which every theatregoing generation needs to provide a focus for its own wishes and dreams' (p. 141).

Hare's own work in the last ten years has been characterized by two general trends. First, he has made no fewer than seven adaptations, five in the theatre and two from novels to film. I shall say little of these, as they are (as more recent work) covered extensively in the digest and the interviews with collaborators that follow. That is not, however, to diminish their value as works in their own right. The versions of Brecht – *The Life of Galileo* (1994), and *Mother Courage and her Children* (1995) – and of Chekhov – *Ivanov* (1997), and *Platonov* (2001) – gave Hare the chance to 'enter into dialogue' with some of the world's greatest writers (p. 161). Jonathan Kent, joint Artistic Director of the Almeida Theatre in London where most of this work was performed, suggests that Hare has that critical quality of all good adapters, the ability to be 'true to the spirit of the original, while retaining [their] own particular voice'; the adaptations 'are seen through the prism of [Hare's] own sensibilities, his own political beliefs' (p. 213). It is that notion of a 'dialogue' that is important: these adaptations do not represent Hare making the work of others his own, but rather give himself the opportunity to test and develop some of his own themes as an original playwright against comparable explorations. All these plays, albeit in very different ways, focus on the actions of particular individuals who live in societies undergoing huge, even cataclysmic, change. Hence what attracted Hare to the Brecht plays was their examination of 'people struggling with the devastating effects of bad faith in a fast changing society' (p. 139). The location of the Chekhov pieces (and Kent suggests Hare has a particular affinity with Chekhov) in a pre-Revolutionary Russia, where an ancient feudalism disintegrated under the new capitalism, likewise held considerable appeal to a writer working in his own *fin de siècle*, especially as *Platonov* in particular embodies these wider social and historical forces in its concentration on the private life of its eponymous hero, who tries to 'discover in love a purpose and meaning that eludes him elsewhere' (p. 149). *The Blue Room* (1998), 'freely adapted' from Schnitzler's *La Ronde*, similarly pits individual desire against social role and socialized behaviours – behaviours in which are embedded wider issues of public and private power.

The second trend in Hare's output from 1995 to the present resides within the series of original works that he has produced: *Skylight* (1995), *Amy's View* (1997), *The Judas Kiss* (1998), *Via Dolorosa* (1998) and *My Zinc Bed* (2000) show a steady progress towards increasingly 'private' plays. Their themes – the roles and responsibilities of the individual (including the creative artist) within an uncaring, amoral and dehumanizing modern society – both parallel many of the concerns of the adaptations and, of course, are deeply rooted in earlier work. *Skylight*, one of Hare's most popularly successful plays, is another love story. The protagonists are Tom Sergeant, a rich restaurateur who, on the face of it, has everything, and his former mistress, Kyra Hollis, a schoolteacher. Their relationship ended under the pressure of the terminal illness of Tom's wife and Kyra's decision to leave her comfortable job in private education for a position in a 'difficult', run-down London school. Prompted by his recent widowhood, Tom visits Kyra in her cold north London flat. The debate that follows takes place within the context of their continuing passion and desire for each other pitted against their growing realization that, although they are incomplete without each other, neither can they be together. Typically for Hare, an apparently simple political framework – post-Thatcherite businessman with a private Caribbean beach, set against committed public-sector teacher – contains a richly complex and ambivalent debate. Tom has everything, and is comfortable with his wealth, but is confused by his need for Kyra and by his inability to understand her resolute commitment to a life that is, by his standards, impoverished. Kyra stands in a line of Hare's characters that extends back to Lillian in *Strapless* and through to 'the guys who keep turning up' in the trilogy. She 'has' nothing, bar her determination to help the disenfranchized, disempowered pupils at her school; yet there is within her a streak of self-righteousness and self-destructiveness. She is not entirely the idealistic saint the audience might wish her to be. It is left to the audience to weigh the moral values represented in this intimate, domestic situation, and to extrapolate them to the wider world. What is central to an understanding of the play's political intent is the broader social context: what is outside the window of Kyra's flat is human, social and physical desolation. As Bill Nighy says, the play invokes and taps into what an audience 'thinks about several times a day in one form or another . . . every time you check your wallet, every time you look across the street and see someone who is disenfranchised or lonely or ill, and every time you pick up a newspaper and read that children have been abandoned, by the government or by individuals . . . it's everything' (pp. 182–3). The utterly opposed values represented by the two characters effectively deny the possibility of their private relationship, yet if they cannot ultimately reconcile their differences, they have by the end of the play at least come to a fuller understanding of them, as has the audience. The concluding image of a sumptuous meal shared by Kyra and Tom's son, Edward, again offers an image of simple human potential rooted in a moment of physical pleasure.

The necessity of beginning to resolve large, social issues of morality on an intimate, personal level is in many ways Hare's central theme of the nineties. The form he finds, as represented by *Skylight*, is a kind of 'submerged epic', and it is further developed in *Amy's View*. Here, a pastiche of precisely the kind of Rattiganesque fifties play that Hare's critics have often seemed to want him to write is invoked only to be exploded. It is essentially 'a family play' in which the opportunity of reconciliation between a mother (Esme) and daughter (Amy) whose relationship has broken down is tragically missed; reconciliation, repeatedly deferred, is rendered impossible by the unexpected – and, in terms of the formal conventions invoked, genuinely shocking – death of Amy. Her mother's values are shown to have been rooted in the past, as represented by her dead artist husband (as in *The Secret Rapture*, the drama is haunted by the ghost of a character who has died before the play begins). That the action of the piece, which begins in 1979, should span sixteen years – years that see the decline of the theatre (and, by metaphorical implication, of society generally) in which Esme makes her living – gives wider historical context to the failure of mother and daughter to connect with the realities of their relationship. *The Judas Kiss*, though afforded an unsympathetic critical reception on its British première, develops the tragic theme and also begins to experiment with a form – that of 'stage poetry' (p. 153) – which is capable of expressing Hare's arguments not just on an intimate domestic level, but within the psychology of an individual, by attempting to capture the mysterious, essential spirit of a character. The play attempts to demythologize the figure of Oscar Wilde, rejecting the effete, cynical wit in favour of a more robust, hugely generous man with a 'genius for love'. Wilde's almost literally suicidal decisions both not to leave England when threatened with prosecution over his homosexual affair with Lord Alfred Douglas, and then, after the end of his subsequent prison sentence, to go back to his lover, are thus accounted for by his fundamental belief that 'you only really see a person through love'. Wilde may be destroyed by his passion, but Hare sees it as essential.

In my interview with him below, Hare speaks of his growing sense of affinity with the 'romantic individualists' who constituted the "56 generation' of playwrights, particularly John Osborne. What he sees in a figure like Osborne is anger at the absence of 'good brave causes', and a determination to shock audiences into passion: 'Everybody's telling us not to feel, well, damn you all, *I* feel' (p. 165). Leaving aside his contribution to the Portable work, Hare himself has never been a 'shocking' figure in the way that he attributes the term to Osborne, but his belief in the ability of theatre, in times of political apathy (and it is political apathy that links the late fifties with the late nineties), to play a part in stirring audiences up, in forcing them to *feel*, is a characteristic he does share with his predecessor. To this extent, his next stage play, *Via Dolorosa*, should come as no surprise; yet, at the same time, it remains a unique departure in his career.

The play, which is an account of Hare's experiences of a visit to Israel and Palestine, is a dramatic monologue, performed by the writer himself. It was the first time he had acted since school, and, he maintains, it will remain the last. (The full story of its creation and performance is told, often hilariously, in *Acting Up*.)* There is a particular sense in which the very form of the play is in itself a political statement: it is arguable that by the late nineties politics and culture had become so fragmented that the kind of passionate, personal statement that *Via Dolorosa* represents could be seen as the only effective form of political play ('damn you all, *I* feel . . .'). The notion that the play is 'personal', however, needs to be treated with some caution. For one thing, the writer makes it clear that it was performed not by David Hare, but by 'David Hare': a dramatized, semi-fictional and selective version of himself. For another, the play 'has no opinions' (p. 157), but seeks instead, through the collision of radically opposed, often contradictory voices (thirty-three of them) both on each side of the conflict and within each side, to ask questions. The relationship between David Hare and 'David Hare' and the lack of 'editorial comment' both engage with a debate within the play about the value of any kind of art in dealing with the horrors of the Holocaust, which led to the desperate ongoing situation in the Middle East. (This meditation on the usefulness and reliability of art and the media, including the theatre, to deal with so profound and difficult a subject, develops a theme that was articulated in *A Map of the World* and *Wetherby*, but that is also present, in nascent form, in the 'puzzles' of the early work.) Hare's

* See Bibliography.

positioning of himself as a faithless figure in a context where faith means all, from governmental to street level, pits one society – Britain – where there are 'no' politics, against another – Israel/Palestine – where there are far too many. In one way, for all the mind-numbing and often paradoxical complexity of the issues it describes, the play simply reports back from the front line, giving much-needed basic information; in another, it throws down an implicit challege to its audiences to ask themselves how they would react in such circumstances. As such, it demonstrates Hare's conviction that passionate belief, whether it be religious or secular, lies only just beneath the surface of apathy, and awaits political awakening and testing by the kind of sudden, unexpected and dramatic change of which history provides myriad examples.

It seems characteristic of Hare's recent responses to events – or lack of them – in politics and history that the greater the issues involved, the narrower and more precise the focus of his writing becomes. This is perhaps what he means when he talks about one function of his work being to 'clean the gutters' (p. 166), to dismantle and discard what *isn't*, in order to establish what *is*; in a sense, the absence of Sarah as the moral centre of *Knuckle* asks a question that his work ever since has been trying to answer. The increasing emphasis on the spirit or 'soul' of characters (their 'is-ness'), as explored in *The Judas Kiss*, demonstrates his continuing search for the solid human ground on which might be built the public morality necessary to enable a just and liberating politics. His chosen form – 'stage poetry' – is developed further in his most recent performed stage piece, *My Zinc Bed*. The play focuses with great intensity on the relationship of three people, who 'materialize out of the air' (see the interviews with Rick Fisher and Vicki Mortimer below, pp. 193ff, 202ff) into a glittering and immensely seductive world of power, money and luxury. The piece rehearses many of Hare's recurrent themes, but specifically asks whether those moments of intense physical pleasure that so often in earlier plays offer a kind of redemption for the characters that experience them, might, in the form of addiction – to alcohol, to power, to love – themselves prove entrapping and delimiting of the soul. Is there, finally, such a thing as genuinely free will? Again, it is left to the audience to make its own judgement; but what Hare insists on is that, despite all the pressures of contemporary reality, where the mediations of consumer culture reduce people to little more than a shallow, entirely knowable uniformity, people are complex, profound and mysterious, and deserving of the kind of intense scrutiny that he believes only the theatre can provide.

As I write, Hare is continuing to explore the possibilities of 'stage poetry' in his latest, as yet unperformed and unpublished play, *The Breath of Life*. He also awaits the British release of the film *The Hours*, the screenplay of which he adapted from the novel by Michael Cunningham, and is working on a second film adaptation, of Jonathan Franzen's novel, *The Corrections*. In my interview with him, he quotes a favourite metaphor of his friend and fellow playwright, the American Wallace Shawn, 'about a man sitting down to enjoy a cup of coffee, but the dog's barking outside, and if only that fucking dog would stop barking he could enjoy his coffee' (p. 167). Until the dog falls silent, Hare will continue to write.

2

Hare on Hare: A Digest of Interviews, Articles etc.

There are several substantial interviews with Hare from which I draw repeatedly. To avoid the clumsy repetition of full references, and to preserve, I hope, a clear narrative flow, these are identified (after a fuller initial reference) only by the name(s) of the interviewers. The following list is offered as an *aide-mémoire*:

Ansorge: *Plays and Players, 1972*
Dugdale: *The Listener, 1988*
Ford: *Plays and Players, 1971*
Gaston: *Theatre Journal, 1993*
Itzin and Trussler: *Theatre Quarterly, 1975–6*
Summers: *Centennial Review, 1992*
Tynan: *Interview, 1989*
Wyver: *City Limits, 1985*
Zeifman: *David Hare: A Casebook, 1994*

Interviews and other materials used only once or twice are given a fuller reference. In all cases the reader is referred to the Bibliography for full details of sources used.

Origins

The following is taken from 'The Director's Cut', a 1989 BBC Television interview Hare gave to Jeremy Isaacs.

HARE: My father was a sailor with the P&O and he was on those big boats that still in the forties and fifties sailed to take those who ran the Empire out to run the Empire; that's to India and Australia. And my mother was Scottish. She was born in Paisley and there's a Scottish element in my work that's quite strong.

ISAACS: *Were you closer to your mother than to your father?*
HARE: Well, inevitably. I mean my father was just a glamorous figure who came into my life for a month every year and unloaded goods into it, which he'd bought in every port in the world. Then he went away again. He had a roll of notes; like many sailors he didn't approve of bank accounts or cheques, and so he had an enormous roll of pound notes and a rubber band. And so we went from times of austerity to a brief month of plenty and then back to austerity . . .

In my childhood films made a fantastic impression on me, in a way the theatre didn't, and because of my particular age group, the films that I first saw were *Doctor in the House* and *Genevieve*. The world that Dirk Bogarde inhabited with Muriel Pavlow was a world I wanted to live in . . . I wanted to be a doctor and I wanted to kiss nurses. It wasn't that I coveted things in film, but I just loved the world, and good films when I was young were under a sort of glaze that made them fantastically attractive. I try in my films to create whole worlds that have that appeal. You should want to use the objects, sit in the furniture, eat the meals, make love to the men and women. It should be your dream. I love trying to create that dream . . .

Where did you go to school?
I went to school in the local prep school, which was still quite barbaric; I mean these were the post-war years and so the school teaching in those days was very eccentric. It was mostly people who'd been in the army, and were looking for ways to spend their declining years. The level of violence in schools still, in the forties and fifties, I remember as being very shocking. I remember boys coming back having been beaten by the headmaster of my prep school; blood across their bottoms, blood on their chests, shirts ragged and it really was . . . I think all that died away in the sixties and I feel that those are the last days where all that still went on.

After the prep school?
Then I went to Lancing College, which was not like that at all.

That's an Anglo-Catholic College in Sussex; very religious.

Was that religion important to you then?
Very, very. I was a very devout, pious boy. I'd say pious rather than devout. It appealed to me and I liked having it as a protection against the world, I think.

What appealed to you about it?
Well, I'd say at the worst it gave me a sense of superiority. I don't think it was a very attractive thing.

Did you fit in easily at that school?
No, I found it quite difficult to begin with; I did eventually. I went with what I've called an 'off' accent. I went with some accent that wasn't quite the accepted accent of the middle class and I remember terrible things being said about it in my first term, so I then adopted the accent I now speak with. I also had a break with religious feeling, which I think was brought on by my being asked to . . . I was a Server at Communion in private chapel at quiet times, and it was assumed that I'd become a Sacristan and move on to serve the Chaplain in front of four hundred boys. I found the idea of parading your religion so disgusting that it was that, more than anything, that made me give it up and I had a terrible row at the school about it and they said, 'But you're being groomed to be the Sacristan'. And I said, 'The idea of marching down an aisle and showing my religion is quite revolting to me'. And I think that instinct was a saving instinct in me as a rather unhappy boy, perhaps . . .
. . . it was a benign place; it was a liberal school. There were a lot of extremely friendly and interesting masters teaching there, so it had a good influence on me . . .

Cambridge, how about that?
Not so good.

Why not?
I think because I'd seen California. I went to California before I went to Cambridge and I'd been very impressed with how exotic

West Coast culture then was, and how different from English culture. The two over the years have grown much more similar; maybe through television or travel everyone knows what Los Angeles looks like, but I went not really knowing what it was going to look like. I found the palm trees and the surf boards and the cut-off jeans (to a boy who had come from austere fifties, sixties Britain) heaven ... and the girls were heaven, and it was completely different from anything I'd known, and I had therefore very little wish to go to Cambridge.

What did you get then from reading English at Cambridge?
Well, I got into terrible arguments with myself. I wasn't born to be a critic and I went thinking that I wanted to study with a particularly famous Marxist literary critic, Raymond Williams, with whom I had an extremely disputatious and unhappy relationship for three years. I'm happy to say we made up before he died a few years ago. And I realized that the business of criticism was profoundly inamicable to me. The drawing up of an approved list, the Cambridge method of saying certain writers were good because they were morally sound or serious and that certain other writers were despicable, this seemed to me just a complete waste of time as an activity, partly because I didn't understand what the criteria were and I didn't think the criteria were just. I was aware that bad writers in many ways interested me more than the good writers; the so-called 'bad', the so-called 'good', but I didn't want to spend my life judging.

What were you disputing with Raymond Williams about?
The hopelessness of his politics. It was a time in the mid-sixties in which he was much attached to the drawing up of manifestos for the coming revolution and I tried to convince him that it was very unlikely; first of all that there would be a revolution in England, but secondly that were there to be a revolution the first thing they would do before storming the Post Office would be consult his programme, his document about what form the Revolution should take.

*So you were sceptical about a sort of sixties feeling that was
going on around you?*
Yes, I was sceptical about the socialist programme because it
seemed to me that academics were so irrelevant to the political
process and so unable to grasp the elements of what was happening, that they seemed to me completely irrelevant. I was
angry about him not seeing this.

How much theatre were you involved in at Cambridge?
Not a great deal. I did some and I think I was aware that it
wasn't satisfying me because I didn't know that I was a writer. I
only discovered I was a writer when I left Cambridge . . . and . . .

What did you do as soon as you left Cambridge?
I went to work for Pathé, for A.B. Pathé, Pathé News and then
very soon after that I founded Portable Theatre and that was
to take sharply political plays around the country, I would say;
in fact, in retrospect, anarchist plays round the country, in
order to shock people by putting plays on where they weren't
expected . . .

Portable Theatre

*Hare co-founded Portable Theatre with Tony Bicât in 1968.
Over the course of its short and turbulent history, Hare wrote
two of its plays, collaborated in the writing of three others, and
directed five. Outside Portable, he wrote* Slag *and* The Great
Exhibition.

*Unless they are otherwise attributed, his comments here are
taken from an interview with Catherine Itzin and Simon
Trussler, which appeared in* Theatre Quarterly *in 1975–6. This
was the first substantial interview with Hare to be published,
and it remains a valuable source of information on his career
up to the mid-seventies.*

As I remember, it was mostly [Tony Bicât's] idea – it was certainly his idea calling it Portable Theatre. It came out of a long

series of conversations about the theatre, in which he was very interested, and in which I became interested . . . He was a lot more cogent about what he wanted to do. What happened was, we were both directors and we didn't have any writers. It's very difficult, because in retrospect people say it was a writers' theatre. That's how it fell out, but we began with Kafka and Genet. Once we were even going to do Lawrence Durrell. Neither of us were writers, and the Kafka show was a literary thing, really – not very different from Emlyn Williams reading Dickens, as four square as that.

The idea was to take theatre to places where it normally didn't go. We weren't to see that a variety of arts centres and groups would spring up to accommodate that. But when we started we played more army camps and bare floors than we were playing at the end . . . We both thought the theatre of the day was rhetorical, overproduced, lavish, saying nothing, conventional – all those things.

. . . the Kafka show, *Inside Out*, worked because the neurosis is so pure in it. Somehow if you dramatize Kafka's life it's oddly more accessible than Kafka's books, because in the books you are conscious of the art – but put his diaries on stage and everyone recognises their own worst fears. Tony and I did the dramatization from the diaries – not changing the words much. There were a few improvized passages – an extreme avant-garde technique to be dabbling with! We did the basic script, then changed it with the actors. We were both extremely ignorant, and the actors did well to keep their patience with us.

[Portable developed] through Howard Brenton, really. One night Howard came and was literally the only person in the audience, so we said, would you like to go to the pub? And that's how we met, and when we wanted to do new writers, Brenton's *Christie in Love* was certainly the best play that came our way . . .

What we had in common was that we thought we were living through a period of extreme decadence, both socially and theatrically. We just couldn't believe that the official culture was incapable of seeing the extreme state of crisis that we thought the country was in.

Hare expanded on his views about the politics and culture of the sixties – and about his early doubts regarding the importance of plays – in a 1981 interview with Alison Summers (published in the Centennial Review *in 1992):*

Culture here in the mid-1960s was extremely psychologically oriented. Plays were about how much you loved your mother or how your mother didn't love your father, and so on. Plays were family-based psychological dramas, or comedies of menace, or plays set in rooms. If you thought that the country was suppurating, it didn't seem important to write plays.

In the late 1960s, capitalism appeared to be undergoing a deep trauma out of which would come deep change. We've lived with years and years of economic deterioration now, but in the mid-1960s when the pound was falling, it was very dramatic, because we had lived through years of comparative prosperity. It was similarly dramatic when the students allied with the workers in France, because it seemed as if a new political alliance was possible between the intellectuals and the working class; this was something we had seen little of in England. Never had there been so dramatic a contrast – between what a government was elected to do and what it did – as the treachery that Wilson's wretched Labour government provided. Now, you may say that it was because I was twenty-one and knew nothing, but these seemed like vivid events.

'Culture' seemed irrelevant to what we then thought was the grave crisis of capitalism. Culture, as I had experienced it, was mainly literary culture. I'm still completely outside it. I feel no connection with the culture you read about in Sunday newspapers; I have nothing to do with the culture of the day.

Indeed, Hare told Itzin and Trussler that his first two original stage plays were written for Portable only out of necessity:

[*How Brophy Made Good* was written] because we were waiting for a play from Snoo Wilson . . . which he'd rashly
promised to do, but failed to deliver. So *Brophy* was written to
fill that hole, very fast. I can say almost nothing about it now. I
didn't like it very much when I saw it, and I don't think it's a
particularly interesting piece of work. I haven't read it for a
very long time.

[*What Happened to Blake?* was written] because Portable
needed a play. And, though it's hard to believe it now, we were
interested in literary biographies, in trying to represent the lives
of writers. That was through Tony's influence: he was interested in artists. Blake was a man I had wanted to write about, and
it also meant I could develop a line of work that Portable was
doing, a kind of stripping down of stagecraft. Though I think
Blake came out like an imitation of a La Mama play, like a Paul
Foster play. [*Playwright Paul Foster is a past president of the
influential Café La Mama group.*] I admired Blake, and loved
his poems. But I found his madness useless. I don't think artists
going bananas are very interesting, it's their job to stay sane.
That contradiction in my attitude to him blew the play apart. I
couldn't handle it. The most successful passages in the play are
about Mrs Blake, for whom I have a great deal of time.

*Something of what Hare means about Portable's development
of a particular kind of stagecraft can be gleaned from his comments on directing Brenton's* Fruit, *the play* Blake *opened with
in a double bill at the Royal Court's Theatre Upstairs in
September 1970.* Fruit *is a savage and nihilistic piece described
by its author as 'a play of slander, lies, torture, perversion in
high places, vile plans in low places, a rotting bag of half-truths
for an audience to throw where they will'.*

. . . we worked on a deliberately and apparently shambolic
style of presentation, where people simply lurched on to the
stage and lurched off again, and it was impossible to make
patterns. That is to say, we worked on a theatrical principle of
forbidding any aesthetic at all . . . It was impossible to make

aesthetic patterns, and it was impossible to apportion moral praise or blame.

Between Brophy *and* Blake, *Hare wrote his first play for a non-Portable, 'commercial' audience,* Slag. *Its production at the Hampstead Theatre Club won him an* Evening Standard Award:

I was amazed. I thought I must have a gift I didn't realize I had. The innocence was incredible – compared with the amount of time I now take to write a play, I thought then that I could just dash one off . . . The subject matter came from a zealotry about women, I suppose. It was written at a time when I was deeply impressed, delighted with women. I always protest when people claim it's a misogynist play . . . I think it is schematic, that is its vice. But that is a vice of plays which have three characters and happen in an enclosed space. You inevitably polarize in a way that in a large scale play you don't. And the point is that it's really a play about institutions, not about women at all. Only that I thought it was delightful to see three women on the stage. It's about every institution that I'd known – school, Cambridge, Pathé, and so on. They are all the same. That is how institutions perpetuate themselves. With rituals that go on inside them – ever more baroque discussions about ever dwindling subjects. But it happens to be peopled with women, partly because it was the sort of play that I thought I would enjoy going to see – women on the stage, represented as I thought more roundly and comprehensively than was then usual . . .

. . . I don't really think of the audience when I write. Certainly not in the case of *Slag* – though this again was partly through ignorance, because I had no idea of what 'writing for [*the commercial producer*] Michael Codron' entailed. I know what it entails now – one set and three characters! But I have been very happy with Codron, enjoyed writing for him . . . I think that if you can possibly survive in the commercial theatre you should, because otherwise you're just blocking up the subsidized theatres for new writers . . .

Talking to Peter Ansorge in Plays and Players *in 1972, Hare had this to say about the relationship between* Slag *and the Portable work:*

I regarded *Slag* as an exercise for the proscenium arch – using what I had learned from Portable. It was meant to conjure up everything out of the air – the empty space –which is almost always the starting point for a Portable show. I wanted to assault a particular citadel of the conventional theatre . . . that whole discussion about genetics (the superiority of the female to the male chromosomes) was painstakingly researched. It was meant to be like elastic – to see how far people can stretch themselves and an argument. Portable plays are concerned with the language of technology and biochemistry . . .

Slag, *like the Portable work, certainly had the power to offend the offendable: in 1972 the headmaster of a boys' school in Surrey 'discovered' a copy in the school library, and wrote to the publisher, Faber, to complain. The play was 'at least a bad influence and likely to corrupt in the School situation . . . I propose to burn [it].'*

The play, however, which perhaps best exemplifies the Portable aesthetic was the controversial Lay By, *which was created collaboratively by seven writers, including Hare and Brenton, and Snoo Wilson, who also directed.*

Lay By came out of a writers' conference where, having discussed all day what was wrong with the situation of writers, I suggested that anyone who wanted should try writing a play collectively, given the guarantee that it would be presented at the Royal Court on a Sunday night. In fact, the Court let us down on that guarantee. But we went off and wrote, seven of us together, based on a clipping that appeared in the paper that day and which Trevor Griffiths happened to have – an extremely prurient description of an alleged rape on a motorway, and the trial. We started work the following Wednesday with wallpaper and crayons. An experiment in public writing.

John Ford's 1971 interview with Hare, Brenton and Wilson in Plays and Players *gave some idea of the working atmosphere and method out of which the play came:*

WILSON: Brenton turned up on the first morning with three rolls of wallpaper and a set of crayons – which was very useful because it altered the scale of one's thinking. We rolled the wallpaper out on the floor and started crawling over it writing, and that was a good way of breaking the ice. And everyone jumped round, and David got asthma, and I bought a rotten pineapple that day.

HARE: That way of working on the first day meant there was no possibility of anyone huddling in a corner and writing their own stuff.

WILSON: You cannot write small with a wax crayon. In fact, the wax crayons were abandoned after a bit but people were still writing very big, because you adapt your writing to the scale of the paper. At the beginning, when everyone was a bit frightened, you'd stand around in groups of four looking at this person writing obscene rubbish on the floor.

HARE: Most of us didn't know each other, you see. The idea came originally from a newspaper clip about fellatio on a lay by on the first day we met.

BRENTON: It was common material from the start.

HARE: . . . as the thing went on, I would say that it got further and further away from the story.

BRENTON: Well, we sometimes retained it to get out of a hole, didn't we? Read the story again, and . . . The schoolteacher scene came out of that, thinking closely about the figures behind this wretched, minimal piece of reporting.

WILSON: That was one of the advantages of the report. It was only 500 words long. There were a lot of spaces to fill in. We didn't make any attempt to find out what was really true, apart from what was in the report.

HARE: It's not something that is generally available to theatre writers, that sort of situation, because it's so much a newspaper story.

BRENTON: The newspaper report was written as a very bland, liberal piece protesting about certain legal aspects of the case. But behind it you saw several worlds described. The people around the M4. The schoolteacher, the married woman in her forties – what was she doing on the road?

HARE: The thing is that it was very innocent theatrically in the sense that originally it wasn't theatrical thinking, and that's why it's shaped the way it is – a sort of cancerous growth that just grew and grew and grew. It wasn't consciously a question of: 'How do we make a play out of this?'

WILSON: It was, actually. We did occasionally try to do that.

HARE: Yes, and always failed. Whenever we planned in advance and said where is this going – you go and write that, and you go and write that – it never worked. It only grew organically from the content, it never grew from the form.

BRENTON: But we did push to get the material public, to get it clear. That created a theatrical form.

HARE: But that only came from thinking the subject through, didn't it?

BRENTON: Yes. In fact, a lot of the formal arrangement was done by Snoo and the actors at the last minute . . .

Hare described to Ansorge the particular brand of 'public theatre' that he and his collaborators in Portable developed:

Portable is on a wave of publicity now. Our shows are successful in London – whereas we used to be screamed at in London, and understood better in the regions. *Blow Job* [*written by Snoo Wilson, directed by Hare*] was called a fashionable show – all the talking in the dark, the blood, the schizophrenic dialogue. But it's only become fashionable because of what we've done in the last three years. We're in the strange position of being fashionable without ever having become popular.

Most of our values come from practical experience on the road. Literary values don't survive on the road. Long, simmering plays can't survive. You must have plays with a strong physical force. You have to find the lowest common denominator for a show . . .

We have a very bad record with working-class audiences – we've hardly played to any. Our weapon has always been a middle-class, middle-brow weapon really. But we used to have a percentage of what we called 'Aggro' dates. The Carnegie Hall, Workington, springs to mind as an example. You knew from the start you were doomed. All you could hope to do was to spread the maximum bad vibrations amongst the audience. We played *Fruit* in Workington – and left the town before the audience had left the theatre. They were waiting in horror for the curtain call while we were driving safely outside the town's limits. You're working in the dark in those places . . .

Our aggressiveness is immensely conscious. I suppose it stems from a basic contempt for people who go to the theatre. It gets worse when we get near population centres. I loathe most people as individuals and, en masse, I find people particularly objectionable. But the aggression isn't entirely spurious. We wanted to pick up the medium of theatre and shake it by the scruff of its neck. A lot of people say we are too arrogant and cynical as a group. It's not the job of theatre to represent every facet of human endeavour. It's specific horses for specific courses. That's Portable's job. With *Lay By* we moved into the arena of public statement. Our plays usually show closely knit social situations in a process of extreme decay. We must concentrate on the issues which all the other media are unable to present. That's why we've been exploring the whole subterranean world of pornography in shows like *Lay By*. But the next writers' group show is going to be about Northern Ireland. If you're on that pitch then various forms of humanity or compassion don't count. The Court are always asking us where our humanity has gone. At the moment, and for some years to come, its absence is stimulating.

England's Ireland, *co-written by Hare – who also directed – and six others, perhaps unsurprisingly ran into considerable difficulties: over fifty theatres refused to take it, as Hare explained to Itzin and Trussler.*

... that was simply a question of fear – fear of being blown up. And partly a feeling that the subject should not be discussed in the theatre at all ... In the end it wasn't just the fear of being blown up that made it unacceptable: also, it was not compassionate. Theatrical producers want plays about how 'this hating has got to stop'. That is the only sort of play the English can understand about Ireland, and it didn't fit the bill.

For much of his time with Portable, Hare also worked as a theatre reviewer and, from 1968 to 1971, as Literary Manager and subsequently Resident Dramatist at the Royal Court, making some much-needed money.

Review (for Plays and Players*) of Giovanni Verga's* La Lupa, *starring Anna Magnani, Aldwych Theatre, July 1969:*

A curious evening. I missed the point of it until the end, when the company took about fifteen curtain calls to a rapturous audience. As I went out of the theatre I could still hear a single strained voice crying 'Anna, Anna'. You realise then that you have not seen theatre as you have come to recognise it, but instead a ritual staged for the international charabanc trade.

If the point of World Theatre Seasons is to represent the variety of, as well as the similarities between, other people's theatre, then well and good. *La Lupa* was wholly vindicated as offering an experience unknown in London theatre (though not at Covent Garden nor at the World Cup) – an emotional rallying point ...

His work as the Court's Literary Manager had been secured through his old school friend and the then Resident Dramatist, Christopher Hampton, and had some influence on his own nascent writing career:

. . . he had been persuading me to try and write a play for a long time, on the basis that I was so voluble about the plays that I had to read, so I ought to try and do better . . . I spent three years at the Court. I certainly read nine hundred plays and saw another two or three hundred. At the end I knew something of what is usually wrong in plays: but that is no help to you at all in the question of what is right.

Writing in 1981 about his time at the theatre in Richard Findlater's book At the Royal Court: 25 Years of the English Stage Company, *Hare acknowledged the vital importance of the theatre to post-war British drama, but was more ambivalent about his own experience there:*

. . . the psychological cost of surviving the constant critical abuse had been very great: the staff were arrogant, touchy, entrenched. And a boy from university, as I was, floating in, scarred from no battles, having seen nothing of the fight, found their prickliness incomprehensible. In a way I was destined never to get on.

I do remember those years as a time of almost perpetual unease, as I had one fight after another in the place. Every project had to be lobbied for by a medieval series of trials, which became more complex and severe in 1969 when a triumvirate of directors – Lindsay Anderson, William Gaskill and Anthony Page – took over the theatre, and developed an attitude to new work which made the championship of new scripts so arduous and humiliating that it's a wonder people stuck their necks out at all. No, they did not want plays from Howard Brenton (one artistic director said he should be taken out and buried in a hole in a field); yes, they *had* promised unconditionally and irrevocably that as an act of faith in the seven writers involved . . . *Lay By* could be scheduled for a Sunday night performance, but now they had decided to *read* it and it was no longer a good idea; yes, I was now resident dramatist, but not for a moment should I take that to mean they had any intention of doing my plays. (All resident dramatists in this period had their plays rejected: it became a feature of the job.)

. . . What then did we have in common, and why did I last even two and a half years in the job? I think what struck and cheered me there from the first day was finding a group of people who assumed, without a moment's self-doubt, that the dominant culture of the day was garbage, because the values of the society were rotten; that, in particular, literary affairs in this country are largely in the hands of a sold-out right-wing middle class who can't write; and that therefore in artistic matters you must, at whatever cost, trust your own experience and believe nothing you read in newspapers. I found this attitude wholly sympathetic, and nothing that has happened to me since has disabused me . . .

The other thing the Court taught me was to value aesthetic excellence. At the time my sole interest was in the content of a play. I thought the political and social crisis in England in 1969 so grave that I had no patience for the question of how well written a play was. I was only concerned with how urgent its subject matter was, how it related to the world outside. As I came to realize that no common beliefs held the Royal Court together, I also slowly appreciated that there was therefore only one reason why writers chose, as they then did in great numbers, to give their work to the Court first, and that was the likelihood that it would be better acted, better designed, better lit, better directed, in short better *presented* than anywhere else, that here the text would be respected, the rehearsals would be serious, the commitment to the project in hand would be real, however bizarre the running of the theatre outside the rehearsal room. And that by encouraging the writer with their great care for the values of presentation, the directors were actually enabling writers to say richer and more complex things than they would have been able to if, like me, they were bundling an exhausted travelling company out of a van and on to an open floor.

The Great Exhibition *(1972)*, *Hare's second play for the Hampstead Theatre Club, came between Portable's Lay By and England's Ireland, and was intended as 'a parody of all Court-type plays'. It was directed by Richard Eyre, who would come to play an important role in Hare's career, first at the Nottingham Playhouse and later at the National. From Itzin and Trussler:*

I have trouble now remembering what the original idea behind the play was. I think it was to do with Labour and politics generally in the sixties. The only political experience I had was believing passionately in the Labour government of 1964, and watching that government sell everything down the river. So the play was about a disillusioned Labour MP . . .

. . . Hammett feels himself to be an exhibitionist both in his public life and in his private life. He feels conscious that he's performing in parliament, and conscious that he's performing in front of his wife.

Hare's comments to Ansorge showed how what were to become key concerns in later plays and films were already developing in his earliest work:

The 'seriousness' of many plays is just another word for self-pity. To me a cultivated seriousness is only so much phoney suffering. *The Great Exhibition* is about people who suffer with a capital 'S' – that area of self-ignorance. I'm fascinated by self-enclosed societies – a very middle-class obsession. There has to be a degree of parody about plays with that theme. My plays are intended as puzzles – the solution of which is up to the audience. People behave in a much subtler and more ambiguous way in self-enclosed societies than literature often makes out . . .

And if, as his remarks to Itzin and Trussler suggested, he remained dissatisfied with The Great Exhibition *as a play, then it is also the case that his own developing understanding of the processes of writing for the theatre was becoming clearer and more certain:*

73

. . . I think people have expectations of plays with one set and a limited number of characters, and I think those expectations are impossible to resist. And although *The Great Exhibition* starts in a room, and then deliberately explodes and opens out to try and confound the audience, I don't think it really succeeded in that. There is something about the ritual of a play in which there is this guy at the centre of the stage with all the best lines, who's being witty at everybody's expense, and whose uniquely subtle psychology we're going to explore over the course of the evening, which is limiting, which is dead. Because it stops the audience thinking – or rather, they imagine they're there to find out what this man on the stage thinks. They're not: they're there to find out what *they* think.

. . . It's really only as a writer that I've begun to think myself straight, work out for myself the answers to political questions. It's a rigorous discipline, playwriting, in the sense that you need to answer questions which are never answered by polemic or journalism or propaganda . . . Playwriting is a ruthlessly truthful medium, and I've come to believe in it much more as I've gone on working. I think the judgements the audience make show up insincerity, reveal the superficial, and more and more I have trouble writing until I've worked out in the greatest possible detail what I think myself about some subject or other, whatever I'm writing about.

Letter to publisher, July 1973 (from the Faber archive):

I read a very funny review of your edition of *Great Exhibition* in the *Amateur Guide to Selecting Plays*. Did you see it? It said the play would be better without the filth, but as the play was all filth, there would be no play without it. Catch 22, I think.

'Whoring around'

... I don't think of it as having a career. I just think of it as following my nose, from one subject to another. It's the subject matter that dictates everything. It's true that I've never had a 'home', theatrically – never had a theatre that regularly did my work – since Portable. But I think most writers enjoy whoring around, actually, much as they pretend to need a home.

A glance at Hare's activities in the years following the demise of Portable shows a considerable range of work in a variety of forms, as his comments to Itzin and Trussler above suggest. He wrote his first teleplay, Man Above Men, *collaborated with Brenton on* Brassneck *for Richard Eyre at the Nottingham Playhouse (where he was Resident Dramatist in 1973), directed Trevor Griffiths's* The Party *for a National Theatre tour, and wrote three major stage plays:* Knuckle, Fanshen *and* Teeth 'n' Smiles. Knuckle *(for which he was joint winner of the 1975 John Llewelyn Rhys Memorial Prize) was his first West End show, and marks the point when, by his own admission, Hare began to believe in himself as a writer, whilst* Teeth 'n' Smiles, *which he also directed, was his first production on the main stage of the Royal Court. However 'homeless' it may have been, this is a body of work which began to establish him as one of our leading post-war playwrights. And, with* Fanshen, *Hare produced what is one of the seminal works of modern British theatre. The play was written with and for the Joint Stock Theatre Group, which Hare co-founded and with which he was to remain closely associated until 1980; one kind of 'home', perhaps.*

The following is taken from an article Hare wrote for Granta *in 1986:*

I've been involved in founding two theatre companies in my life. The first, Portable Theatre, ended for me in the Marylebone Magistrates Court some time, I believe, in 1973. I kept no diary in those days – I was young, and events moved so slowly – so I have no way of remembering. I do know I shook and sweated a great deal, since I'd only learned on the morning of my appearance that Tony Bicât and I would have to appear in court. The charge was non-payment of actors' National Insurance stamps. Since we had relinquished the running of the company some time previously, we were both surprised to find ourselves still legally responsible for its present state – although, to be fair, I had recently seen its administrator at Schiphol Airport in Amsterdam drinking gin at 7.30 in the morning, and might have guessed that the books were not in too solid a shape. The magistrate fined us – was it £35? I misremember – and ordered us to pay all our debts. When the company later went bankrupt, we learned that your debt to the state is the one debt that can never be absolved.

Things have changed a great deal in the theatre in the last fifteen years. In those easier days you needed less money to start a new company, and everyone accepted that theatres might naturally flower and die. The fringe had not been institutionalized to the point where companies fear to relinquish grants from the Arts Council long after their artistic life has been exhausted.

Hare's co-founders of Joint Stock were fringe pioneers Max Stafford-Clark and David Aukin . . .

Max Stafford-Clark, David Aukin and I met among the ruins of Portable Theatre and decided that since we were all freelance members of the awkward squad, we were likely to need our own facility for putting on plays. All our experience had been with the presentation of new work, usually of a modestly controversial kind, and we were all well aware of how producers' expectations then rarely fitted either with our personalities or our tastes . . .

For a while we seemed to choose plays which we rehearsed and presented in the regular way, although our bent was for the pornographic . . . But unknown to me Max had been talking to Bill Gaskill [*former Artistic Director of the Royal Court, and*

one of the British theatre's most distinguished directors] about
doing a period of work on Heathcote Williams's book *The
Speakers*, with no specific intention of showing the result to the
public. I was therefore surprised when I met Bill in the street
one day and he remarked ironically on the fact that, as a member of the three-man Joint Stock board, I was now his employ-
er. Only five years previously I had been the greenest recruit to
his celebrated regime at the Royal Court.

When in 1974 Max and Bill finally decided to show their
work to friends in a rehearsal room in Westminster, I was taken
aback. The directors had re-created Hyde Park Corner by simply upturning a few boxes and asking the audience to wander
freely from speaker to speaker. The evening appeared to be
casual, and yet turned out to be highly structured. There was a
great density of characterization . . . Since the play appeared on
the surface to be plotless, there was none of the usual wrenching
and shifting of gears to which a playwright's ears are especially
tuned. There was nothing flashy or insincere. The evening was
dry, in the best sense, like good wine. I had long known it to be
Bill's aim as a director to achieve work in which the content of
the play was in perfect relief – there was to be no impression of
artifice – and yet often in the past I had felt the very austerity of
his approach to be mannered. Now, perhaps because his talents
allied exquisitely with Max's eye for detail, the audience was
actually presented with the illusion of meeting and getting to
know the speakers at Hyde Park Corner. No more, no less. The
speakers were in the round, unforced, *themselves*.

Six weeks after Joint Stock's inaugural production, Hare's own
Knuckle, *presented by Michael Codron, opened at the Comedy
Theatre in London's West End. Hare discussed the play with
Itzin and Trussler:*

Knuckle is about what morality is and whether it is any use to
us in the last quarter of the century . . . Maybe I am wrong, but
nobody else seems to be writing about these things . . . [It's] an
almost obscenely constructive play! It says something about it

being impossible to live within this system without doing yourself moral damage. That's a huge claim . . . It's a play about knowing, about the fact that there are no excuses, and the fact that people who are damaged by the system know themselves to have been damaged, and are not ignorant of what they've done to themselves. And that is a large claim, because how you feel about capitalists – whether you believe them to be knaves or fools – determines everything you believe and think politically. I felt that in *The Great Exhibition* I'd written a play that was only intelligible to the politically minded, to anybody who cared about the future of the left in this country. If you don't care about that, the play's just a farce or satire – forgettable. So with *Knuckle* I particularly wanted to write a play which was available to everybody – it's about people for whom political rhetoric is no part of their lives. The characters aren't political – or intellectual – at all . . . the reason I don't find the play pessimistic is because it also contains the most admirable person I've ever drawn, this girl who is meant to be a good person. The whole play deals with moral values, and concludes that there *is* such a thing as moral value. That seems to me quite cheerful.

A question from Kate Nelligan, who played Jenny (reported by Hare in a 1989 interview with Kathleen Tynan for Interview*), prompted an answer from the playwright that shed light on his developing sense of style:*

When Kate first read *Knuckle* she asked, 'Why do all the characters talk the same?' I said, 'Well, they feel completely different things, and they do express this in different ways, but the fact is there is such a thing as style'. It's like being a painter. You paint in a certain style. I would regard as a very bad painting one in which each figure was drawn in a different style. I went to see the Lucian Freud exhibition, which influenced me very, very profoundly because I began to understand portraiture. He made me realize what I'd known all along and had never been able to articulate, which is that portraiture isn't anything to do with likeness. It's to do with emotional affinity.

The play, however, was not a financial success, as Hare's new agent, the legendary Margaret ('Peggy') Ramsay had anticipated.

Conversation with Peggy Ramsay, 1974

RAMSAY: This is an incredibly important play.
HARE: Oh, you mean it will be incredibly successful?
RAMSAY: Good Lord, no. Everybody's going to hate it. But that doesn't mean it isn't an important play. You're on a twenty-year burn.

Itzin and Trussler suggested to Hare that its truths were not perhaps 'digestible enough for a West End audience':

That proved to be true. Yet now the discussion of the decline of our society has become fashionable, and society discusses itself obsessively, and uses terms that it hasn't used before. The word 'capitalism' was never used before 1970 to describe their system by capitalists: they called their system 'life', and there was something else called communism. Now our decline is voraciously discussed; but the means of discussion are falling us. That's to say, journalism, however intelligent, will always fail you. It is glib by nature. Words can *only* be tested by being spoken. Ideas can *only* be worked in real situations. That is why the theatre is the best court society has.

Hare's concluding comments here could almost stand as a simple manifesto of the evolving 'Joint Stock method', a method that was catalysed by the creation of Fanshen. *The play was based on* Fanshen: A Documentary of Revolution in a Chinese Village, *a book by American farmer William Hinton, who had spent six years in China in the 1940s observing and documenting the great land reforms instituted by Mao. Itzin and Trussler again:*

Pauline Melville [*the actress*] had read it originally, then Bill Gaskill, and Bill gave it to me. I didn't at first think it was potential dramatic material, but I came round to seeing my way through it, with the help of the Joint Stock actors . . .

We did a five or six week workshop period, during which we explored different ways of exploring the work. The actors mostly dealt with the question of 'how do I play Chinese?' Which to me was a non-question, but to them was very important, and they satisfied themselves with their answers. The way we eventually dealt with it I worked out on my own, and then with Bill Gaskill and Max Stafford-Clark, and the story I found is one of, oh, a hundred and fifty possible narrative paths through that book.

Hare gave a fuller account of the workshop process, and his part in it, in the Granta *article:*

I worked on trying to digest and master the extraordinary complexity of the book, while, in workshop, the actors flung themselves at whatever bit they fancied, more or less in whatever style they fancied. The writer represented reason, the actors imagination. There were certainly masks in the rehearsal room, and there was talk of puppet shows. Stylization was much discussed. At one point, I was asked to play a bird. It was important to the directors that the method of workshop reflect the subject and that it therefore be genuinely democratic. For that reason Bill once insisted as we returned from lunch to our basement rehearsal room in Pimlico that neither he, Max nor I should be the ones to suggest resuming work that afternoon. We would simply wait until an actor suggested it. I think we waited about an hour and a half.

After the workshop I went off by myself and spent four months mining a text out of the book. I threw away a great deal of the more obviously dramatic material, because I was not interested in portraying the scenes of violence and brutality which marked the landlords' regime and its overthrow. In shaping the play, I was very little influenced by any particular discovery in the workshop, but I was crucially affected by its spirit. Although Bill had thrashed about seeking to find a suitable style for the work, often lapsing into long and sullen silences, he never relaxed his basic intention: that we should do justice to the sufferings of the Chinese peasants. This was a matter of the utmost gravity to him. His criterion for examining any scene was to ask whether it was adequate to the experience the peasant had originally undergone. Although the subject matter of the play was political, the instincts of the company were in essence moral. We were not revolutionaries. I think that is why, especially in later seasons when it sought to apply the lessons of *Fanshen* to English material, Joint Stock became confused about whether it was a political group or not. In making *Fanshen*, none of us believed we could duplicate the overturning we described. We knew any form of change here was bound to be different. But we all admired the revolution, and shared an obligation to describe it in a way of which its people would approve. The adoption of a rehearsal process based on the Chinese political method of 'Self-Report, Public Appraisal' might, in other hands and with other material, have degenerated into a gimmick. But here it had weight and was surprisingly quick and effective. The self-criticism was real.

At Christmas I finished, and a few days later was sitting beside my wife's hospital bed when Bill breezed in from two weeks with the aborigines in Australia. He took one uninterested look at our two-day-old son and said, 'Yes. Very nice. Where's the play?' Soon after he arranged a reading with the whole company. It was very long and lugubrious, and at the end people said almost nothing, though one actor shook his head at me and said 'Sorry'. Given the general gloom, I had no idea why I was not asked to rewrite much more. Only the beginning was rearranged and somewhat peremptorily. If I had been more experienced, of course, I would have recognized that moment at which a group of people, expecting everything, are delivered something.

. . . and from Itzin and Trussler:

. . . the play I wrote originally had as its fulcrum an idea that is not in the book by William Hinton. Now that, at the time, was very important to me. Since I've talked to Hinton and since we've done the revival at Hampstead, a lot of that has been removed, and I don't think to the play's detriment. There was a running idea in the text that people needed justice – talking of morality again, that is something I believe, that people have a sense of justice, and that they need justice, and need to believe a society is just. A large claim, but I have found it to be true. Hinton, as it happens, doesn't believe that: he feels justice is a bourgeois concept. Whose justice? And justice in what terms? So he asked me to remove most of the references to justice in the play, which I've done. Also I had deliberately written a text that was as resonant of Europe as was possible, so that people might make their own analogies, about political leadership and so on. And at the very first performance, somebody did come out of the play and say, 'Wouldn't it be marvellous to get Reginald Maudlin [*Home Secretary in Conservative governments of the sixties and seventies*] at a meeting like that, and quiz him?' But that was not what Hinton had intended in the book.

. . . I think like everybody I was sick to death with writing about England – about writing about this decadent corner of the globe. The excitement of *Fanshen* was to write about a society and to cover a period of time in which one felt that people's lives were being materially and spiritually improved, in a culture that was completely different from anything we knew about. We wanted to write a positive work using positive material.

. . . I enjoyed it very much, but, again, the main attraction was the subject matter. Also, the need to do without the things that English playwrights usually rely on – irony, sarcasm, innuendo, all the shadings that make playwriting easy. There aren't many things that make playwriting easy, but the fluency of the English language is a tremendous help. Now if you choose to write in Ur Chinese, you haven't got that, you've only got the meaning of what is being said. And that was bracing, after years of tweedling round with words.

Fanshen *opened in Sheffield in April 1975 to what Hare described in the* Granta *piece as 'a refreshingly intelligent and multi-racial audience'. A later television version was 'something of a fiasco'.*

Subsequently *Fanshen* was revived whenever Joint Stock was in trouble. It became our *Mousetrap*. Once, humiliatingly, I attempted to do a couple of days' directing one of its many revivals and found it to be a lot less easy than it seemed. Although I thought I understood the process whereby Max and Bill had done their work, in practice I was hopeless at imitating even their most casual effects. The spirit of the show was best guarded by actors like Paul Freeman and David Rintoul.

The two directors and I sought many times to work together again as a team. I asked Bill to direct a couple of my plays, but he always turned me down. We all found it hard to imagine material which would suit us as well. In part this was because *Fanshen* describes a period of history in which people's lives were unarguably improved: when someone suggested we do a similar show about the Russian Revolution I pointed out that it was quite hard, in view of what we all knew happened later, to bring the same relish to describing the heady days of 1918. It would have been dishonest . . .

Joint Stock, inspired by *Fanshen*, then chose to go co-operative, and all decisions were taken by group discussion. The actors were brought in to help run the company. Some fine work followed, and for two years they managed both to maintain a high standard of performance and to attract a large and dedicated audience . . . you sensed that the principles of the work were the same as those we had forged when trying to do a play about China. Although the subject matter changed, the ideology became a little stuck. I suppose I reluctantly concluded that an openly political way of working only pays off with dialectical material.

I stopped going to company meetings after a group discussion in which I called someone a cunt. Although I was referring to someone who wasn't present, I was told by one of the group that she objected to my using a piece of her anatomy as a term of abuse. I replied fatuously that it had hardly been *her* anatomy in particular which I had had in mind. Of course she was right, and I have never again used the word as an insult, although it remains the one English swearword with a genuine power to shock. Yet somehow the incident oppressed me disproportionately. An actor made a long speech about how the only purpose of theatre now must be to work for the overthrow of the Thatcher government, then left as soon as his best friend arrived to have a separate conversation in the garden. He had actually cried during the speech. The politics of gesture seemed to have replaced the politics of need. Now we were all to have silly arguments about words.

Despite Hare's reservations, the company survived until the late 1980s. His Granta *article concluded as follows:*

Of all art forms the theatre is most susceptible to fashion. There is good and bad in this. There are times at which audiences seem to respond to an idea, almost irrespective of how well or badly it is expressed, as if it is already in the air, and nothing will now stop them getting to it. All of us sensed that happening with *Fanshen*, and the actors and directors worked to some common imperative. Nobody was frightened. This is not the only kind of theatre I wish to work in, but the feeling has come upon me only twice, and the first time was with Joint Stock.

Letter to the Joint Stock Policy Committee, September 1980 (Modern British Theatre Archive, University of Leeds):

Dear Graham [*Cowley, the company administrator*],

I can't get to the meeting on Sunday, but want you to put my views because obviously it is such an important moment. They are, in brief, that you have to have an outstandingly good reason for continuing a theatre group

---

once its initial impetus has gone; that you cannot just inherit a 'shape' and a 'structure' and pretend it's going to work, because it isn't. The workshop principle suited Bill and Max, that's how it grew up, but it would be silly to go on arbitrarily applying it once its motors have fled. I also bitterly dislike the way the fringe has become a sort of civil service where people are more interested in protecting a certain number of jobs than in having good reasons for making plays. You fight governments with good art, not with trying blindly to maintain old structures. I'd say stop and start again, unless there is someone around with a strong *artistic* sense of exactly what work they want to do, and how they want to do it. No person, or group of people have appeared with an idea yet Richard [*Wilson, the actor and director*] doesn't seem willing to take the company over, and the actors haven't yet contributed a sense of what material they are interested in; and if they don't now, I really think it better to pack it in. Please send my apologies for being away, and I will call you next week.

David

One of the features of Joint Stock's output was that its writers often produced work for the company that was, and remained, quite unlike anything else they produced in their careers; this is certainly true of Hare's Fanshen. Any sense, then, of his personal evolution as a dramatist needs to be looked for elsewhere, in his more conventionally authored work. Hare himself, as he explained in 1993 to Georg Gaston in Theatre Journal 45, has always resisted easy categorization; asked whether his early work was valuable in 'learning your craft', he replied:

Not at all. You see, the question has an assumption behind it which I don't share. You talk about 'learning your craft'. I still can't give a primer on playwriting. You know, I'm asked to go to universities and teach people how to write plays. I haven't the slightest idea how to write plays. To this day, I still couldn't tell you a word about how to structure a play. You just develop, as time goes by, some sort of instinct for the way in which the audience will hear you.

. . . I didn't feel I was a writer for a long time because I was lucky enough to be close to a very gifted generation of writers – Trevor Griffiths, Howard Brenton, Christopher Hampton, who was an old schoolfriend of mine, and others. These were young people who believed in their writing. And I was nervous and hesitant to put myself forward. For a long time I fooled myself into believing that I was a *director* who wrote. I loved the theatre, and I loved its practical aspects. And I loved its unpredictability, which is what I still love. I loved the sense of having no idea at 7.30 how you're going to be feeling at 10.15. But I never until I wrote *Knuckle* felt I had anything uniquely valuable to say as a writer. I felt I was just plugging a hole. The things that interested me I wrote about because there wasn't anyone more talented writing about them. And I cared in those days – which I don't now – about the overall state of the theatre. I used to believe in the word 'should'. In other words, I thought that the English theatre 'should' cover political subjects. And because there was nobody doing it, I kicked a lot of plays into being. *England's Ireland*, for instance, was there to cover the absence of plays on that subject. It may have been a very naïve impulse; but it did mean that the British theatre covered a more interesting variety of subjects than it might have done without that impulse.

Addressing Teeth 'n' Smiles, *Gaston went on to suggest to Hare that 'most playwrights, when they reach their maturity, have developed a recognisably personal thematic voice. Your case seems to be different, however . . . you continue to reveal new approaches and concerns as you move from play to play . . .'*

I think the answer to this is that, yes, there is a great attempt to introduce fresh things into my work all the time. For a time I'll absorb myself in the Church of England, or the Chinese Revolution, or the world of Rock and Roll. In doing that, I've hoped to let some fresh air into my own personal interest. I think that it is plain that there are certain themes in my work to which I do return over and over. I wouldn't necessarily want to tell you what I think they are. But the same interests and certain patterns or themes do recur. Still, I try for something fresh all the time. But when I go for refreshment, it's not to literary influences. It's to the exterior world. And nothing interests me more than to become absorbed in a self-enclosed world . . . I'm always trying to get my own mind shaken up by the assumptions and behaviour of a different group of people. Thus when I wrote about Rock and Roll, for instance, it was terribly exciting for me to find out about the life bands lead on the road . . .

Nor is the issue of any autobiographical content in the plays straightforward:

A writer has two lives. You have your life as a human being and your life as a writer. This is one of the great pleasures of being a writer. I would hate to have all my chips down on one number, so to speak. I'm lucky enough to have two different numbers and two different lives. But, you know, a lot of human beings who don't write and don't have this second creative life nevertheless try to have two lives in their life. Obviously spies have second lives, homosexuals do, various groups of people, you discover, have second lives, perhaps at night, which bear no relation to their first. Nobody really wants just one life. Now in my case the degree to which my two lives, the real and the writing life, mix is very complicated. Pure autobiography in my plays is very rare. I'm not the kind of writer who picks instances from my life and dumps them down in my work. All I meant, then, by my autobiographical comment about *Teeth 'n' Smiles* was that it did have a blatantly autobiographical *context*. Namely, it was about Jesus College in Cambridge, which is the college I went to. So the play is *nakedly* autobiographical in that way, in that I chose something not dissimilar from my own background. Normally, by the time a writer has transformed autobiographical material, it's unrecognisable, which is certainly my case.

. . . I would say that *Teeth 'n' Smiles* is about the fag-end of idealism. It's about utopianism when it turned sour. It's about that stage people reach when they will do anything for an experience, and having originally enjoyed the vitality of the experience, they then become addicted to the experience. So that the central action of the play is that Maggie would rather go to jail than not. I'm not sure that the play finally convinces the audience that Maggie would do this. And so to that degree the play is a failure. However, I hope that meanwhile it was a lot of fun.

National stages . . .

Although Hare had already experimented with writing for television, the later 1970s and early 1980s saw him move into the medium on a grander scale, with Licking Hitler *(BBC, 1978), which won a BAFTA Award,* Dreams of Leaving *(BBC, 1980) and* Saigon: Year of the Cat *(Thames Television, 1983); the first two he both wrote and directed. In 1982, he founded Greenpoint Films.*

The same period saw only two pieces for the stage: in 1978, he collaborated with Howard Brenton, Trevor Griffiths and Ken Campbell on Deeds *(Nottingham Playhouse), and also produced his most successful (and, for some, still his most important) play to date:* Plenty. *Often hailed as a landmark of modern British drama,* Plenty *premièred on the Lyttelton stage of the National Theatre, where Hare had directed Brenton's* Weapons of Happiness *two years earlier.*

Hare recalled the origins of the play in his Programme Note to the 1999 revival by the Almeida Theatre Company:

My starting point for the play *Plenty* was reading a statistic which showed that 75 per cent of the women flown behind the lines for the Special Operations Executive were subsequently divorced during the peace. It was clear that after the exhilaration and danger of their wartime experiences these fine people found it difficult to adjust to the more mundane business of day-to-day living. In my diary I remember writing the simple words, 'A woman over Europe', and then conceiving the vivid image of a woman in a big coat rolling a cigarette over the exhausted naked body of her husband, with light from the high windows falling on her from behind. The picture was so real to me I could touch it.

The play represents a number of the key concerns of Hare's work at this time: the centrality of female protagonists, the importance of recent history, the relationship between writing for the stage and writing for the screen, and the continuing evolution of the craft of his writing. Gaston explored these issues with him:

HARE: Certainly compared to *Teeth 'n' Smiles* I would say that *Plenty* is a much better achieved play, in the sense that the actions of the central characters are presented on the stage, in dramatic scenes. You don't just have claims made from a character's own mouth. You actually see the protagonist do things that are the crucial incidents in her life. It's not a play in which a woman sits in a chair and recollects flying into France. I actually show her flying into France. This is returning to what I was talking about earlier when I spoke of my love for Shakespeare coming from the fact that he doesn't balk at the difficult scenes. He doesn't *recount* the crucial actions; he *dramatizes* them. You know, the weakness of *Teeth 'n' Smiles* is that one of the crucial underpinnings of the play is Saraffian's long speech about what it was like to have been in the Café de Paris so many years ago. It makes me think of the worst *famous* example of this sort, which occurs in Chekhov's *The Seagull*. I've always hated Nina's dreadful speech in Act 4 of *The Seagull*, where she recounts what has happened to her in the interval since Act 3. It's a speech that defeats every actress I've ever seen play the part. The glory of Shakespeare is that he actually demonstrates, shows you the action. He doesn't just describe the action through somebody else's mouth. There is a hideous courage in his writing which sometimes comes to grief; but the fact is, the statue comes to life in front of your eyes. No one tells you about it.

GASTON: *In* Plenty, *in* Teeth 'n' Smiles, *and in other plays as well you have written strong parts for women. Anyone following your career would be bound to be struck by the fact that (unlike most, if not all, of your fellow playwrights) you have quite often placed the major focus on women characters, especially as figures of moral weight. Would you comment on why this is so?*

HARE: I must say, it's easier for me to write about women. I think a leap of the imagination is essential to all fiction. I have no interest in writing about people like me. The first thing I want to do, if my imagination is to work, is to guess. Imagination, in a way, is only a posh word for guesswork. And what greater leap can any man make than to try to imagine what being a woman is like?

Plenty *seems to me a very 'cinematic' play, certainly at least in the way it moves. Did you, by any chance, envision it as a film as you were writing the play?*

No. I remember when it first appeared and Mike Nichols came and asked me if I would be interested in writing a film of it, I said: 'But the whole point of it is that it *is* a play that is like a film. There would be no point in making a film that was like a play.' So, no, it didn't seem to me to be promising material for the cinema. And when I actually started on a script, I found the work of turning a play into a screenplay extremely difficult.

Plenty *also helps locate the precise sense in which Hare could at this point be defined as a 'political' dramatist, as he explained to Summers:*

The plays are about morality. I tend to write about whether there is any such thing as personal morality, and if there is, whether it makes any difference: whether there is such a thing as living and behaving well.

I write constantly about somebody who is in a state of moral dissent. Although the interpretation may be political, I don't write as Trevor Griffiths does about conventional politics. I deliberately don't write about people who don't articulate politics at all. Trevor writes about sentient, conscious, political beings who articulate political ideologies or take part in political debate. I write in much more personal terms about people who don't have anything to do with politics, or very rarely.

I take a figure who says, 'This is not right. This should not be so,' and I try to write about the cost of that way of life. I suppose that what the plays conclude – certainly *Plenty* does – is that not to be able to give your consent to a society will drive you mad, but, on the other hand, to consent will mean acquiescence in the most appalling lassitude. The choice tends to be dramatized within the plays as isolation – sometimes madness – or the most ignominious absorption.

[The play] dramatizes those themes for which I had been seeking ways of expression. That is, it's about isolation or consent. It's about how you can drive yourself mad when you dissent and how you can go mad out of vanity, almost out of arrogance. It also dramatizes the reverse, which in this case is a shabby post-war society. I think that it puts English history since the Second World War in a rather interesting context, something I had been trying to do for a while. It offers the English another way of seeing themselves. It's swift, pointed.

Plenty is formally more successful than my previous plays. I liked the circular movement. Found it profoundly satisfying to have written a play where the end is the beginning and the beginning is the end. I think that the idea of seeing eighteen years of a woman's life in one evening paid great dividends.

But it has its failings. The balance of the scales is not quite right. The play fails because people leave the performance believing that the man's fate – a degraded life in insurance – isn't as frightful as going mad. I was trying to say that his fate is just as bad as the woman's, but I didn't give it as much dramatic weight as I should have. I couldn't make the man's life as upsetting as hers. Although *Dreams of Leaving* is a much lighter play than *Plenty*, it does manage the right balance, and the audience perceives the man's fate to be as bad as the woman's. People always mention how upsetting they found the epilogue.

Also, the war plot in *Plenty* doesn't quite pay off. The play seems to be about the Second World War, then the subject becomes less important as the play proceeds. Consequently, the reunion with the man from the war doesn't quite work.

Hare expanded on what he sees as the shortcomings of Plenty *in a 1994 interview with Hersh Zeifman, included in* David Hare: A Casebook, *edited by Zeifman:*

When we produced the play in London, both Kate [*Nelligan, the actress who created the part of Susan, the female protagonist*] and I were gung-ho for Susan. And because we were so gung-ho for her, we alienated the audiences and we unbalanced the play. Because when I wrote it, there was meant to be a balance between her and her husband [Brock]. She chooses one path and pays the price for that: the price is madness and isolation; he chooses the other path, the path of consent with the society, and the price is inertia and repression. And it was meant to be a classical play offering those two balances – those two tendencies. But because we were so pro-Susan, we unbalanced the play in London.

The first thing I did in New York [*where Hare directed the play in 1982*], unconsciously even, was to put both actors on the poster instead of just Kate. So that in London it was the study of a woman, and in New York it was the study of a woman's relationship and what it meant to be a man. As soon as those two things were balanced out, the play became a much better play. And Susan was less irritating because I, as the director, wasn't trying to rig the play.

In 1978, Hare wrote to Frank Pike (Drama Editor at Faber), concerning the play's preparation for publication. From the Faber archive:

... Now as to research: it has been read and corrected by the Foreign Office, and an expert on the SOE, who say it's accurate, but one or two things I have not had time to check especially

1 When did Charlie Parker records reach England?
2 Did Gucci have shops here in 1962?
3 When does revivalist jazz finish?
4 Was there a Kensington Academy in 1962 (there isn't now)?
5 Would Brock make a Queen's Garden Party? And did they exist in 1962?
6 When did the American Army reach Poitiers? And was it definitely the Americans?
7 What is the correct name for Belgian radio (I've assumed your memory is correct)?

Your starter for ten, Frank . . .

Despite his own perception of Plenty's *shortcomings, Hare was irritated and disheartened by its initial critical reception, and by attitudes to his stage work generally; screen work had become more attractive, as he explained to Summers:*

I was worn down by the criticism, I was fed up with the rudeness I encountered through my work for the theatre. It is disheartening to work in England when every bloody newspaper you open is rude about you. I'd been loyal to the theatre for a long time, and I felt I'd paid my fucking dues. I was exhausted and I wanted a break.

In *Plenty*, I believed that I had written the play I had been trying to write for a long time. I had to find new materials and new ways of writing. I was tired of the theatre and its formal problems, the size of its audiences; I got bored with bringing people through doors; I was weary of dramatic psychology and plays in which people's behaviour is apparently going to be 'explained'. I was sick of the form. I felt free on film.

I felt that nobody cared very much about the 'epic', a form that many of us had worked lovingly in our attempt to write filmically for the stage. Through the work I had been doing, I became interested in the texture, surface and movement of events. Film, therefore, seemed the natural medium to work in. *Dreams of Leaving* is a very new kind of play for me. Whatever its failing, it's not the old 'moral' play, telling people how to live. It's not a finger-wagging play; I like that about it.

SUMMERS: *How much control do you have over the production of your films for television?*

HARE: Total, because I direct them myself. It seems a natural part of the process that the person who conceived and wrote these ribbons of images should also execute them; it seems like one job. When I write a film, I do so with an eye to myself as the director. Although I have also directed my own plays in the theatre for the last five years, it is not important that I do so, whereas in filmmaking, it is essential.

The two arts are complete opposites. In the art of filmmaking, everybody hands in contributions to something that only you can do. Actors don't expect to understand the whole process. If you tell them to pick up a glass more quickly and they ask why, you can reply, 'I can only tell you that it will fit the stream of images that I have in mind. You will understand when you see the film.' Actors will accept that. They know that in film, one eye creates the flow. In theatre, it is different. Theatre is collaborative; everything has to be explained, because in the actors' hands it will have to be re-created every night, independent of you. The act of directing in theatre is handing it over to a group of people who can do it without you. It falls away from you as director.

Have you left the theatre for good?
No, I think that I will start writing for the stage again. What I like best about the theatre is how unfashionable it has always been. In the 1960s when I first started working in the theatre, everybody used to tell me that theatre was a complete waste of time, that the future of culture was in video [*sic*] and rock music. Revolutionaries can't take theatre seriously at all; intelligent people won't give it a moment's thought. I like that unfashionableness.

If you did write another stage play in the next year or two, what kind of form do you think you might choose?
Well, that's the problem. I feel that I got the kind of epic form I had been looking for in *Plenty*. I don't know what I'd do next. I have no idea. I don't know the way around that particular problem of form, yet.

Hare was not unambivalent about his emergence as a television dramatist. Speaking retrospectively to Gaston in 1993, he said:

Television was terribly good for me, in that there is a danger in all theatre that it's designed for a peer group, a danger that obviously doesn't exist in television. I think in my early plays I had a rather smart-ass tone of voice. The danger for a playwright, especially a young playwright, is that he or she isn't willing to be caught out sounding foolish. Such a playwright wants to be clever all the time, wants to be witty and smart all the time, wants to be nobody's fool. Therefore, a brittleness sometimes enters the playwright's tone. I was in danger of this. But when I did *Licking Hitler*, for instance, I was writing under the idea that I would be speaking to eight or nine million – maybe twelve or thirteen million, some astonishing figure, at any rate. And I think the knowledge that I would reach that number of people made me unembarrassed about being sincere.

However, in the 1981 interview with Summers, given when he was more actively engaged in the television work, his views were less sanguine:

I used to let my stage plays be adapted for television but that hasn't worked, so I've stopped it . . . I wrote a film called *Licking Hitler*, which was shown on television two years ago. It's an example of something that would have been a film in the old days. Basically, we have no indigenous film industry left, and the best English filmmakers now work for television. *Licking Hitler* is deliberately made to look like a forties film in the way that it has been shot, cast, and acted, but it uses the conventions of the British war film for subversive ends.

Asked whether the theatre had greater freedom of expression than television, Hare replied:

There are censorship problems in television film. For that reason, I've been involved in various bitter, unpleasant fights with the people running the BBC. There are things that you could do in English television fifteen years ago that you aren't allowed to do now. Certain subjects – particularly sex, drugs, Northern Ireland – can barely be touched upon, let alone treated in serious plays. It's a peculiarly depressing time, mostly because of the depressing crowd who currently run the BBC: narrow-minded ex-journalists, who have no sympathy with people who make plays.

But the censorship battles have been worth fighting, and I think the current trend will be turned around. *Dreams of Leaving* was deliberately written as a film that I knew I could get made. I took advantage of my position as a filmmaker for the BBC to write a play that's at the very limit of what's considered acceptable – that is, it's exclusively about sex. I knew that if I forswore bad language and scenes where people actually made love, I could get a script by, a script that I thought would touch people. While there is no particular virtue in writing about sex for the theatre, because the people who go to the theatre tend to be sexually sophisticated, there is an immense virtue in writing about sex for the television, because the audience is considerably less sophisticated. I have had letters from people of different social classes, saying, 'At last! Something truthful about sex on television.' That's exactly what I had intended.

. . . In the last six months I have been writing a film about the last days of the American presence in Vietnam [*Saigon: Year of the Cat*, 1981]. The film results from a trip to Vietnam that I made in 1973–4, so it has taken me seven years to know how to write about the situation. That's average for me. I write about school seven years after leaving it; seven years after leaving university, I write about university. Not only does it take me that amount of time to achieve some sort of historical perspective, but it also takes time for the material to cool down properly so that I know how to organize it.

History, as both subject and as 'perspective', is a dominant concern in this phase of Hare's career. Summers asked him what had attracted him to writing history plays:

I suppose it was because I found it easier to get a hold on the immediate past than I did on the present. One thing that the theatre tries to do is to explain to people how they have come to their present situation. Shakespeare wrote history plays exclusively. He never wrote about Elizabethan England – not because of censorship reasons, but because he wanted to use the metaphor of history.

Because he wanted a rich texture, Shakespeare chose to represent the passing of years. He showed not just the king but the people around *him*. He chose to represent entire societies, with all their class divisions. Each social group was classed into groups of two or three, so there were movements between the classes and within the classes, and there he had the movement of history: he could show change.

If you don't believe in change, then you can write about rooms. If you believe that what happens in rooms is important, then you don't need to show history. If, like Beckett, you believe that life is cyclical, that the leaf grows and dies and the cycle goes on, then of course you can work with bare stages. But once you decide, 'My subject is how things were, how things are, and how things might be', then that's history, and you've got to show the sweep of things. Change is very exciting in the theatre, which is why I write history plays.

. . . Most people's history is not in the history books. You can show the real underhistory by taking an individual's experience. I did this in *Licking Hitler*, where I tried to show that the official history of the war is lies.

Rewriting history is exhilarating. People have got a model, and you show them an alternative to it. It's tremendously exciting to show that the official version is untrue. It generally stirs up great controversy.

On rewriting 'official history' in Saigon:

I've been having a go at rewriting the account of the American evacuation; to show why the Americans had to bolt, and the process whereby it actually happened. The difference between how the world perceived it and the reality of the evacuation is extraordinary. People should understand what it was in American thinking that led up to that very symbolic event wherein an ambassador was actually helicoptered from the roof.

Saigon is set in 1975, so I do feel that I am nudging toward writing another modern play. *Knuckle* was the last modern play I wrote.

. . . and international perspectives

Even as Plenty *and the television work confirmed Hare's position at the heart of mainstream culture, then, he was raising an increasingly critical voice against the state of theatre, the television industry, censorship and – bearing in mind the election of Margaret Thatcher's first government in 1979 – the cultural 'state of the nation' generally. The extent of his disenchantment with the critics may be gauged from a piece written for the* Guardian *in January 1981, from which the following is extracted:*

I got a bad review from Ian McEwan in the *Times Literary Supplement*, so bad in fact that I couldn't understand the pleasure with which I was reading it, until I realized that I was flattered by its underlying assumption, which is now rare enough for it to be startling.

McEwan assumed that I had intended what I had written. He described the play as if it were exactly the play I wanted to write, as if it were finished and achieved. He plainly believed that because I had spent a year considering its structure and content there was a fair chance that I had thought a great deal about my subject (as it happens, promiscuity – the play was *Dreams of Leaving*) and that, for him, the work was worth taking issue with precisely because it was achieved.

This assumption is now very rare in English arts journalism. Playwrights get tired of being patronized. It is always assumed that they have not anticipated any of the objections to their work. On the contrary, the likelihood is that, having studied their subject for some time, they will already have imagined most of what can be said against their view of it, but that nevertheless, and in full awareness of all anticipated objections, they wish to present it for what it is: personal and considered.

All they will then ask of their audience is that they compare the writer's view of things with their own experience, and decide whether what they are seeing has any value. But from the critic the writer will expect something more: that he puts his own opinions aside for a moment, and takes the intellectual risk of stretching his mind into the shape of another man's. Or woman's. He must try, however briefly, to describe what the object is before passing onto the much easier work of knocking the hell out of it.

Few critics have the daring or the stature to go about things in this order. They don't like the fetching-and-carrying side of their job, partly because it is actually very hard work. But it's also as if they fear losing their own magic by admitting that their work involves describing another man's.

He broadened his attack in a piece written for Plays and Players *in 1981, a piece that significantly takes a view of contemporary Britain 'from the outside':*

I recently spent a year in America, because I was tired of this country. Eventually I came back, if only to see how the story is going to end. The visit made me realize how lucky an English playwright is, for he works under the illusion that what he says may affect people's lives. This may well be an illusion, but it hardly matters. For me it has been an essential illusion. Without it I would rather sell shoes.

Only a fool would maintain this illusion in New York, for there most theatre offers little but the chance for its audience to touch success. They are there to decide among themselves whether the show is a hit, not to embark on the time-consuming and laborious business of listening to what its author is saying. The way of life in the States gives people so much more self-confidence – or at least so much more need to appear self-confident – that only oddballs are interested in spending serious evenings in the theatre. The system, so the thinking goes, *works*. It would be bad magic to go anywhere near an evening of doubt.

Fortunately nobody believes England works. For the country this may be regrettable, but for the playwright it has long been excellent news. The door of self-doubt is already half-open, so it's not hard for the playwright to jam his foot in. Things are so bad that people will listen to any damn fool who comes along to tell them why they're so miserable; and the most conspicuous damn fools of the last thirty years have been the theatre writers.

The usual objection to this line of argument – that uneasy times produce interesting playwrights – is that plays, we are told, should not be addressed exclusively to social questions, but that instead they should be concerned with things called 'the eternal verities'. People go remarkably hazy when you ask them to spit out exactly what these verities are. 'We are all going to die' is sometimes offered. 'Love never lasts' is apologetically advanced as well.

My own view is that by abandoning these bloody verities the British theatre has managed to pass through a remarkable period. Earlier this year a little group of fans revived

Christopher Hampton's early play *Total Eclipse* at the Lyric, Hammersmith [*Hare directed*], and people were generally pleased to find that the play was much better than they had first thought. This argued no special discernment in us, for the truth is that almost at random you could now pick out a whole range of post-war plays that are a great deal better than anyone realized at the time. Any management which mounted a season of, for example, *Occupations*, *The National Health*, *The Soul of the White Ant*, *Events While Guarding the Bofors Gun*, *A Patriot for Me* and *Savages* would be offering a group of plays of some breadth and power. *Christie in Love*, recently staged under the promenade in Brighton by the Sardonic Fish Corporation, looked as smart and funny as ever. Stephen Lowe's *Touched*, a failure at the Old Vic in 1976, revived splendidly at the Royal Court with the original actress in the lead.

I dislike the patriotic argument that the one area in which England still excels is the arts – as if all that Empire-building, nigger-killing energy had now gone into the gouache and the arts centre. It is simply untrue. Anyone comparing standards in the arts between now and, for example, the 1930s would have to deal with the great fact of Auden, quite apart from the lesser facts of Lawrence, Orwell, Eliot. The proposition is self-evidently ridiculous. This is not a specially distinguished period in what is called and taught as 'culture'. But if it has a single feature of any interest it is that from the early fifties public forms became those in which the most gifted writers chose to work. 'Literary' England, isolated, still has no sense of this, still prefers to read and propagate the truly dreadful old novelists and poets who represent the official culture. The best novels now written in the English language are by an Indian. In America and Australia great novelists live and work, while here it is in music, television and theatre that artistic life flickers, not often excellent, but broadly to the point.

Nearly five years after Plenty, *Hare showed his continuing faith in the possibilities of theatre with the hugely ambitious* A Map of the World, *which opened in Adelaide in 1982 and in London (at the National) the following year, both productions being directed by the writer. An American première quickly followed. The play's 'multi-national release' reflects the global concerns of its subject. Another piece for the* Guardian, *written in 1983, offered a detailed denunciation of its critical reception, and is worth quoting in full:*

My new play has opened to quite a furore. Critics have told me how little I understand my subject, how poor my construction is, and – this from *The Sunday Times*! – how perverted my values are. Some others have mercifully been kinder, and to them I am grateful. My biennial run-ins with the British press are no less depressing for being so predictable. But in this case they throw ironic light on the play's themes.

A *Map of the World* takes its title from Oscar Wilde's saying that 'A map of the world that does not include Utopia is not worth even glancing at'. But it also alludes to a line from the play's central character, Victor Mehta, an Indian novelist who complains that we only notice those things which fit in with what we already believe. For 'everything that suits us we place upon our map'. The play's notices provide vivid illustrations of this truth.

Mehta comes to a UNESCO conference in Bombay in order to deliver a keynote address. But first he is asked to read out a trumped-up statement, drafted by a committee, on the nature of fiction. He refuses, citing the writer's absolute freedom to say what he wants.

His position is countered by an African politician who objects that such freedom is frequently abused, and particularly by the Western press in their reporting of anything that has to do with the Third World. He describes the hurt of having the life of your country only ever reported in the political terms of the two great blocs.

His point of view is put by a character called M'Bengue in a ten-minute speech at the centre of the first act. It is acted by

John Matshikiza, a South African-born actor of exceptional power. It is not often in plays that ten-minute speeches go by entirely unremarked. Yet it is as if nobody from Fleet Street has seen or heard of this actor at all.

The whole of James Fenton's long review in *The Sunday Times* does no more than re-state Mehta's position before M'Bengue speaks. Nowhere does he refer to the fact that countervailing arguments exist, whatever he may think of them, nor to the fact that both sides' arguments are extensively modified in a later debate.

John Matshikiza returns as M'Bengue in the last scene – though once more you have only my word for it, for apparently whenever this actor appears the press find urgent business elsewhere. This time he is in a scene with Martinsen, the boss of the conference, who is seen to be pushing aid to Senegal on terms which will effectively destroy the economy of the country.

Throughout the play, the giving of aid has been presented as an apparently good thing in itself, yet now M'Bengue [finds] that not only must a price be paid in terms of political loyalty, but that the World Bank and the IMF both seek to dictate the social policies of those countries to whom they give help. By accepting aid, Third World countries become either political colonies of the aid-givers, or they have to abandon social policies of which the monetarists at the IMF disapprove. This international scandal, which is the climactic reversal of the play, is again something which goes right by the theatre reviewers at the pitch of a dog-whistle.

The critics, in other words, concentrate only on those things in the play which confirm them in their own prejudices, apparently unaware that they are themselves thereby becoming a spectacular demonstration of the play's basic argument. Michael Church, the third member of a Rupert Murdoch formation hit-team, nevertheless concedes in a review of the *South Bank Show*, which discussed the play, that I talk well about cynicism and maturity because, of course, these are the very subjects which most appeal to him. Milton Shulman, in a generous piece in the *Standard*, notes that I give the best arguments to the right-wing figure. He does not consider that perhaps they only seem to be the best arguments to him.

The reviewers also present themselves as thoroughly confused by the device in the play whereby a film is shown to be made from the original events in Bombay. When *A Map of the World* was premièred at the Adelaide Festival, this device caused the Australian critics and audiences no problems at all. Yet for some reason it throws the home team into mass confusion. Shifts in reality, and of time and place, have been so much part of the language of film for so long that only people completely ignorant of modern cinema could find such changes difficult.

Five years ago, with courage, Peter Hall presented my last play, *Plenty*, which opened to what the National Theatre press office assure me were much worse reviews. For a couple of months we were hurt by this. But slowly, by word of mouth, our audience built and the play ran eight months in repertoire. *Plenty* opened in New York last October and is still full. I have no idea if *A Map of the World* is a good play or not, I only know it has not yet been judged.

The audience will judge it, and from an extraordinary mass of letters already sent to me – more, and more various, than I have ever received – their judgement will be rounded. For I still have the unfashionable belief that critics should try to see plays as they are, in their fullness, and not concentrate solely on those parts which flatter their prejudices. In this case, what the press has chosen to report and what to ignore seems to me especially significant.

Like motorway catering, theatre criticism in the main has been so dismal in England for so long that hope of overall improvement often seems to have gone. Higher standards are as likely as a new Trust House Forte sausage. On Sunday I collected £10 from an actor in the cast who had bet on good reviews for the play. The actor, I need hardly say, was not English.

In fact, Hare later acknowledged (to Zeifman) that his play had its problems:

To me *A Map of the World* is a mess. It may be a rich mess – I mean in that there's all sorts of stuff in it – but the formal problems of it are very profound, I think. And the 'Let's go' line is a sort of cheat, in that it's an attempt to pretend that the evening has had a shape which I'm not quite sure it has had.

One aspect of the critical response to his work that has always bewildered Hare is the accusation that it is 'cold'; his rebuttal (in the Tynan interview) is particularly interesting in the light of the cross-cultural themes and casting of A Map of the World:

It absolutely mystifies me. I'm absolutely bemused by it. I mean, it's just a fact that all the greatest performances of my work have been given by foreigners. Kate Nelligan is Canadian, Blair Brown is American, so are Meryl Streep and Irene Worth. Tony Hopkins is Welsh, Bill Paterson is Scottish. Roshan Seth is Indian. I'm often writing about the difficulty the English have with feelings, but the feeling has to be burning away underneath. And English actors do slightly drain my work of feeling. Foreign actors understand that it's very, very emotional. So does the American audience. Also, my work's described as cold because it's about moral things, and anybody who writes about moral things, about what you should do, or whether there's such a word as 'ought', is accused of being cold.

Private feelings, public places

In 1984, Hare became an Associate Director of the National Theatre. A year earlier, he had some harsh – and in tone, not entirely unfamiliar – things to say about the Theatre. Talking to Michael Coveney in the 21–7 January 1983 issue of Time Out, *he argued:*

This place has standards to offer new writers, and a revival in the country should be led from here. The whole place is stricken with inertia, devoid of stimulus. After *Guys and Dolls*, they should have invested in a new musical by British writers; instead Peter Hall is doing something by Marvin Hamlisch about Jean Seberg, for Christ's sake.

In an interview with John Dugdale in The Listener *five years later, he offered a wry retrospective on his initial experiences there:*

I came to the National to start a company with the aim of presenting plays on public subjects, and kicking some into existence. *Pravda* was the first – and it turned out to be the last, because I'm a hopeless impresario, with no gift for persuading others to write.

Nonetheless, Hare's association with the National was, in terms of his own writing and directing, to be a long and fruitful one. After Pravda, *he directed his double bill of* The Bay at Nice *and* Wrecked Eggs, *and directed Anthony Hopkins in* King Lear *(all 1986). Work outside the National included directing* A Map of the World *in New York (1985), where he also directed his opera,* The Knife *(1987), and making a major foray into film:* Plenty, *starring Meryl Streep and scripted by Hare, was released in 1985, whilst* Wetherby *(1985, with Vanessa Redgrave, and winner of a Golden Bear Award),* Paris by Night *and* Strapless *(both 1988) were written and directed by him. He was also, in 1985, made Fellow of the Royal Society of Literature.*

Pravda *(a 'Fleet Street satire', co-written with Howard Brenton, directed by Hare and starring Anthony Hopkins) was a great success, and offers a useful opportunity to reflect on Hare's views at the time on politics, theatre and, first, collaborative writing. His experience of such work, of course, began with Tony Bicât in 1968 with* Inside Out, *and moved on to a grander scale with the Portable work. Although he had come to*

Leabharlanna Fhine Gall

feel, as he told Gaston, that multiple-authored pieces had their limitations –

I learned that there was a limit to how far you can go in a group. You can get a burst of energy, specifically a burst of comic energy. And *Lay-By* was a wonderfully anarchic and comic show. Working in a group, you can succeed in getting people aroused in the theatre, because something of the energy that you've had in creating the play spills over into the auditorium. And that's terribly exciting. But in the end, I wouldn't compare one of these group plays with the work, let's say, that Trevor Griffiths or Howard Brenton achieved writing on their own.

– it is interesting to note that his comments on 'comic energy' apply equally to Pravda, *as well as to his earlier collaboration with Brenton,* Brassneck. *There is a sense in which the commitment to an 'anarchic public theatre' that was a key impulse behind Portable found a new form in the work with Brenton ... the mainstream theatres. The two writers spoke to John Wyver for* City Limits *shortly before* Pravda *opened in 1985:*

Hare is quick to correct any preconceptions I might already have formed. 'The play is *not* a study of Fleet Street working practices,' he says. 'If you want,' and here he can hardly contain his laughter, 'a sensitive, detailed study of the moral tensions of being a journalist, that's not what we're concerned with. It's a play about what it's like to *read* the newspapers every day.'

'We started with the idea of putting Fleet Street on the stage,' Brenton adds. 'But then we became more interested in England now, and in the nature of power.'

'It's a comedy about power,' Hare says, 'and about how people behave when power enters their lives. And obviously it's about a climate in which people are encouraged to do whatever they want in the interests of power.'

During the writing of *Pravda* they both spent time observing journalists at work but they are not worried that they will be attacked for lapses of accuracy. 'That will be a totally irrelevant charge,' Hare says. 'Our concern is the relationship between the newspaper and the reader, and why people who work on newspapers allow themselves to be moved about in certain ways. And *that* is to do with guesswork, not research.'

Brenton agrees. 'We were interested in the cast of mind of journalists working for these shitty papers. What it must be like to know that you're writing shit, to know that you're writing a ruthlessly exploitative load of rubbish, and how you accommodate that with your life. And that's a matter of the imagination.'

Pravda is Brenton and Hare's second collaboration. The first, *Brassneck*, was written for the Nottingham Playhouse in 1973 and later seen on television. A sprawling comedy of Northern post-war politics, *Brassneck* details the rise of a family who move from property speculation into heroin dealing. They are both amused by the similarities between *Brassneck* and *Pravda*, and by the differences from the plays they write separately.

'It's what we call the third man syndrome,' Hare observ 'When we write together neither of us is the writer, there is th third man. And the funny thing is that *Pravda* is in almo exactly the same tone as *Brassneck*, in spite of them being sep-arated by almost twelve years. And that's not just stylistic, it is that the people and the concerns, namely business, power, men in suits, things about which I never write, and Howard never writes, this third man writes.'

Hare said more about the 'third man' in the Gaston interview:

With Howard Brenton, I would say that what I did was write satire, with the limitations of satire that I've described before. What the experience was like was immensely comic. I mean, he and I would make each other laugh, and the purpose of both *Brassneck* and *Pravda* was to make the audience laugh. And by and large we laughed at each other's jokes, and when we didn't, the jokes didn't go into the play. When we both laughed, in they went. I think comedy is a wonderful thing to write with someone whose sense of humour you trust – not necessarily share. We had different senses of humour, Howard and I. His was perhaps blacker than mine. But the two of us together were a good test of what should go in. The most interesting thing about collaboration, then, became the creation of a tone which is neither his nor mine, but which is a third person's, who is sometimes laughingly called Howard Hare. And Howard Hare's interests aren't really either mine nor Howard Brenton's. I don't normally write plays, for instance, about men in grey suits in offices. I don't normally write about men. I don't write plays whose subject is primarily power. But those are the plays that Howard Hare writes. And he writes in a tone of caustic, abrasive, satirical confidence, a tone without doubt, if you like. Whereas when I'm writing as myself, my work is marbled with doubt.

He acknowledged the importance of Pravda *to his career generally in a Profile by Nicholas Wroe in the* Guardian *in 1999:*

Those weeks of argument with Howard about how we could satirize this nihilist [*Lambert Le Roux, the central character*] were incredibly important. From that I began to get an energy that then produces *The Secret Rapture*, and then I'm away with *Racing Demon*, *Murmuring Judges* and the rest. I also made a series of good decisions at the end of the 80s: stop doing cinema, stop directing, do adaptations of great works . . .

He touched further on his sense of the differences of approach between him and Brenton in his interview with Wyver . . .

'It does sound arrogant,' Brenton says, 'but I think that plays which celebrate the opposition in this country, which celebrate the socialist tradition, the great radical England that has never really come to power, such plays should be at the centre of our national theatre, our national culture.

'That politics and that England should actually be at the centre of our country, and in power. So I've no hesitation at all about trying to nail down, bang in the middle of the theatre, irreversibly, a whole stream of work that speaks for or belongs to that England.'

Hare is a little more tentative about the relationship between theatre and politics. 'The political objection to most of what I have written,' he reflects, 'is that it does not ascribe to some political programme or other. I think I'm saying such and such, but I usually find it wasn't, I was saying something else. And that's called imagination, and for that reason artists and political folk rarely see eye to eye, simply because you can't write to a proscribed programme.'

. . . and more fully spelled out his particular political position to Dugdale:

As a socialist, which for me is simply a matter of social justice, I've never felt that people's ultimate happiness could be achieved through politics. It's just always struck me that 95 per cent of the population are disenfranchized and that the education system, the public health system, and the whole rigging of the capitalist system is so against the interests of the people at the bottom of the pile. But politics for me has never meant profound moral questions about what sort of life you should lead, your relationships with family and friends, how your work is structured. I've often as much in common on those issues as people on the Right or on the extreme Left. I suppose what I'm saying is that I don't feel a lot of angst about my politics. If you choose a job like mine, 'what to do' is very clear – you write about today as truthfully and as much from the heart as possible.

As to the role of theatre in political life, he had this to say (to Gaston):

I feel that the theatre is uniquely valuable, however. I have actually written an essay on this. I'm referring to an essay that I gave in King's College in Cambridge in 1978 [*variously published; see Bibliography*], and which I wouldn't really wish to change in any way. In the essay I said that the theatre seems to me to be the unique forum in which a society can discuss itself, in a way which is infinitely more profound than journalism and more public than the novel or poetry. The central paradox of the theatre, which is as paradoxical as making ice cubes in the desert, is that we are trying to have very private feelings in a public place. When theatre really works, when it happens, when you forge feelings in your mind which are yours, and seem to be yours and nobody else's, and then you look around you as the lights come up and you realize that they are common feelings that everybody in the theatre has shared together . . . I don't know any experience to equal it. So, I think the main value of the theatre is that it's a place where society can go to take a sober account of itself, and see itself truly . . .

. . . I didn't say the theatre dramatises lies, exactly. I think what I was trying to talk about was the theatre's unique political power and its power to tell the truth. It does stand for that. In the theatre you can see the difference between what people say and what people do. That's what theatre is. Something comes out of people's mouths, which are the words, and which often are what the characters claim to believe, or claim to think, or claim to feel. And then by counterpointing all this with the action of what the characters actually do, you get a complex picture of the relationship between what we claim to be and what we truly are. And I noticed that in an age where politics is marked by mendacity, then obviously the theatre is very well suited to talking about politics as they're really practised. But more than that, what I love in the theatre is that great sense that we are so much more than just the words that come out.

Hare's comments here are particularly interesting in the light of his move into film – as opposed to television – work. He told Dugdale:

I suppose I fell in love with the 35mm camera. You can't get that wonderful sweep, that breadth, on television. And I feel that feature films are so difficult to finance that whenever you get the chance you should grab it. But I have a feeling that may be over now, as I find directing less and less to my taste. Watching Bruno Ganz and Blair Brown act in *Strapless* is the most profound satisfaction I get from it, but the other side of directing I find ever more frustrating.

Hare discussed Strapless *further with Tynan:*

It's about romantic love. Blair plays a doctor in a cancer hospital in London who loves and loses a man, played by Bruno Ganz, who can't deal with ordinary life at all. So he leaves. He loves this woman from the bottom of his heart. But what is the point of love? The point of love is the overturning . . . the overturning of everything, of all your feelings. The rest is the bit where you have to go on living . . .

I'm trying to write something in which you know that it's all about sex but you never see any. Well, it's not *all* about sex, but sex is surely the thing that carries the spiritual charge, isn't it? You see, the reason I've had great difficulty with the screenplay is that it was basically about a woman who opens the box and then finds these feelings coming out. Then, because the man disappears, she puts the lid back on the box and says: 'Well, that's romantic love. It's everything, but it's nothing. It's totally sublime, but it also has no relationship to the rest of your life.'

It's taken me months to work out that I don't believe that I actually think that love changes everything. I think it's the only thing worth having. And also, what I've been fighting to get right is the sense that you're changed by it. Now, to show that in a film is fantastically difficult – to show that you *are* changed by it, and so are your relationships with other people. I want her to come out of it better off, in spite of the fact that the man has vanished . . .

I believe love opens people up. Picking up the bill, after all, is part of feeling. If you feel, then you've got to pick up the bill. That's what we come to understand.

Later in the same interview, he had this to say about Paris by Night:

It's about a member of the European Parliament . . . It's about the old things, what all my work is about. It's about the soul.

. . . Are we just what comes out of our mouths? Or are we more than that? It's about a woman who seems to be nothing except whatever thought is ever passing through her mind. To me the most frightening idea is that we are only the stuff that's going on – the inner dialogue and the words. So I try to give the audience the fright of their lives by saying to them 'Now, do you really think this is all life is?' *Paris by Night* really is a thriller. It's about death. It occurred to me that the thriller was a really profound form. I realized it because it plays with the idea of when you will die. It's inevitable that you will die, so the only question is when. The great thrillers are the moments that play and tease with the question 'When will it be?'

From Gaston:

HARE: My interest in film goes back to when I was a child and I loved going to the cinema. I loved being in the dark, I loved dreaming in the dark. I think that the films of mine that I have liked most are those that depend most heavily on the element of dream, that have an ethereal quality of something that is printed from inside the human imagination, that seem to happen as if under a glaze. I think that *Wetherby* works because it's a film that most relies on dream – in addition to memory, reality, fantasy, all mixed up in a suitable way for cinema. I think *Strapless* also works suitably.

GASTON: *Just how different do you find writing a film script is from writing a play?*
HARE: Completely different. To use the crudest generalisation, it's impossible to think of a film whose appeal is not primarily to the heart. It may have some ideas in it as well. But if a film doesn't move you, it's a very hard thing to sit through. A play can present an argument, which can be the riveting thing.

Zeifman questioned Hare further on the relationship between his film and stage writing:

HARE: The claim that was made about my plays from the very beginning was that they were filmic. I was much more nourished by the cinema when I was young than I was by the stage. And when I grew up, the stage was the prisoner of the closed set, the one-room play, the psychological drama, etc. – which has never been my interest. It was from the cinema that I got all the richness, the sense of life's passage, history on the hoof, you know, that you went to [François] Truffault or Louis [Malle] himself or [Jean-Luc] Godard for.

ZEIFMAN: *So it was European films you were attracted to more than American films?*
HARE: Yeah. And British. When I was a kid, war movies and *Doctor in the House* and everything – the whole pageant – was at the cinema. So, yes, when I started working in the theatre, yes, I thought, why shouldn't it have the same freedom as the cinema to move where it wants to, to show the passage of time boldly? Why shouldn't it? Why shouldn't you tell stories that are just as melodramatic as the stories the movies tell? Why shouldn't the fun of the cinema be on the stage? Certainly I felt that. But that also coincided with a way of looking at things which was not suited to box sets. You know, I've never wanted to put three characters in one room and let them get at it.

So my plays have always been fluid; they always had that movement. In fact, the reverse is what usually people want or ask for – namely, to make a film of *Pravda*, to make a film of *Secret Rapture*, to make a film of *Racing Demon*, all of which people want to do. And I am lost for any way to – I just don't know how to adapt things for the cinema that so depend on the live audience. In every case I've drawn a blank.

Reproduction of part of a page from the Catalogue of Hare's papers, held at The Ransom Center, University of Texas at Austin (available on-line: see Bibliography):

Transit of Venus—Unproduced screenplay based on the book by Shirley Hazzard

3	Clippings, agreement, and holograph notes, 1980–1

The Unseen Enemy—Unproduced screenplay based on the novel IL FASCISTIBILE by Giulio Castelli

4	Typescript and holograph notes, nd
5	Typescript with holograph revisions, nd
6–7	Mimeograph typescript, nd. Two copies, one incomplete
8	'First Draft Work,' discarded original and carbon copy typescript pages, some with holograph revisions, nd

WETHERBY (No, Go On, Say) (O! Solitude) (In Harm's Way)—Screenplay

9	Photocopy of typescript with holograph corrections, nd
10	'Drafts and First Finished,' typescript draft, nd. With typescript draft fragments and character analyses, nd
11	'Revised,' photocopy typescript with holograph notes and revisions, bound, nd

26	1	Photocopy typescript, bound, nd
	2	Photocopy typescript, with some holograph revisions, bound, nd
	3–4	Photocopy typescript, bound, nd. Two copies
	5	Photocopy typescript, 4 May 1984, with holograph revisions and typescript insert pages, 29 May and 9 June 1984. With shot list, list of voice tracks required, call sheet, and other production material, 17 Sept. 1984, nd
	6	'Rejected Scenes,' original and photocopy typescript draft pages and notes, nd
	7	Memos from Simon Relph and Sally Jenkins, 2 May 1984, 13 July 1984
	8–9	'Post Production Script,' photocopy typescript, nd Press Kit, 1985

WHAT HAPPENED TO BLAKE—Playscript

27	1	Mimeograph typescript, nd

WRECKED EGGS—Playscript (see also THE BAY AT NICE)

	2	Photocopy typescript with holograph revisions, nd
	3	Photocopy typescript with holograph revisions, nd

4	'Rehearsal Script,' 'Control Script,' original and photocopy typescript, with holograph revisions, nd
5	'The Second Half,' original and photocopy typescript note and draft pages with holograph revisions, nd
	WRITING LEFT-HANDED—Book
6	Incomplete composite of original and photocopy typescripts and photocopies of printed texts, with holograph revisions, nd
7	Composite of original printout and photocopy of printout with holograph revisions, with additional holograph revisions, nd. With typescript list of corrections, nd

What has begun to emerge here is some sense of the variety and interplay of influences at work on Hare's evolution as a dramatist and theatre and film-maker: between writing individually for the stage and collaboratively, adapting for film, writing for film, directing his own work and that of others on stage, directing his own films ... What is important are the demands of the present and 'density of effort and imagination', as he explained to Zeifman:

In a way, playwriting is a craft. I can weigh a play in my hand like sliced meat: I know how much effort it's cost; I know, within fifteen minutes, how much the playwright's put into it; I know what it means to him or her; I know the density of the effort they've made. Those people who make that density of effort, and it's very clear who they are – well, it's not true to say that I don't mind what they're saying, but it's true that you can't not respect people who go on struggling with form, struggling with the real problems of the day, who stay writing contemporary material. And this I do feel very, very strongly about – that this whole retreat into historical romanticism which has beset the modern theatre is just a cul-de-sac. To keep writing about the present day is the job. And anyone who goes on being engaged with the present day, and who goes on putting into it that density of effort, as I would call it – density of imagination, even – of course you respect them.

ZEIFMAN: *Are there contemporary playwrights you care to mention whose work you feel reflects that density of effort and imagination?*

HARE: Well, Fugard obviously, Mamet goes on trying to be involved in the real day. Christopher Hampton, I would feel very strongly; Caryl Churchill, certainly. Now, Christopher's politics are very different from my own. Caryl's politics I'm sure are completely different from my own. But you can't not know that Caryl is serious. She's fantastically talented: everything she writes is very, very interesting. She's just the real thing. You don't go saying, 'Ooh, I hope they toe the line. Ooh, I hope they say something I agree with.' Caryl's a great mind, so you go to find out what Caryl's thinking now. And it's exciting to find out what Caryl's thinking about. Even if you don't like a particular play, you want to find out where she's going next.

Take her play *Ice Cream*. I mean, plainly *Ice Cream* is not Caryl's greatest work; Caryl would not pretend it was her greatest work. But she's someone who's going on evolving, and will evolve to something that you know will come out of *Ice Cream*. And sometimes, like with my play *The Bay at Nice*, you just have to say, 'I'm sorry, I need this play to go on. I just actually need to see this play. I know it's not the greatest play ever written, but we'll look at it and I will learn, and only by writing that will I be able to write the next one.'

ZEIFMAN: *Do you mean* Bay *specifically, or are you referring to the double bill with* Wrecked Eggs?

HARE: I don't like the second play at all; I still haven't really cracked it . . . But it had to go on. I would have felt very unfulfilled if it hadn't gone on. But it plainly is there to lead to something else.

Hare had more to say about The Bay at Nice *and* Wrecked Eggs, *and their particular place in his writing career, to Tynan:*

In *The Bay at Nice* and *Wrecked Eggs* I had to sort out various things. I cared very little about whether the public came to see these plays. We deliberately presented them in a very small theatre and for a very short run. We put them on because I couldn't grow up unless I worked out some things I felt . . .

The Bay at Nice is a play, set in the fifties in Leningrad, about the authentication of a Matisse by a woman who has lived in Russia all her life. The character, played very brilliantly by Irene Worth, has to decide whether this Matisse is authentic or not. It's set against the background of her daughter's divorce. In the second play, life in Russia is contrasted with life in America, where people, although theoretically free, lead lives as rigid as the lives in Russia. It's an East–West evening . . .

The American half of the evening is not as strong as the Russian, so I've been nervous about presenting the plays in New York . . .

Mrs Thatcher . . .

The year (1988) of Strapless *and* Paris by Night *also saw Howard Davies's award-winning production of Hare's* The Secret Rapture *at the National. Hare, of course, had long been a vociferous critic of Thatcher and Thatcherism (at one point wondering aloud on BBC Radio 4's* Desert Island Discs *what had happened to make her so 'angry'), and did not confine his opposition to the stage. In particular, he lent his support to a 'socialist philosophy group' formed by Harold Pinter, Lady Antonia Fraser and others, about which he spoke to Tynan:*

You could tell they were all going to fall out before they came into the room. You can dragoon right-wing journalists, who will simply say what they're told to by Thatcher or by representatives of Thatcher. But getting left-wing people to agree with anything is very, very hard. They don't like lying on behalf of a cause. Whereas right-wing journalists will say anything. One of the depressing things in England at the moment is the total orthodoxy: the law is handed down from Downing Street.

. . . what politicians want and what creative writers want will always be profoundly different, because I'm afraid all politicians, of whatever hue, want propaganda, and writers want the truth, and they're never compatible. For a politician, the means to power is paramount, and the ideology, in a way, can look after itself; I'm afraid a writer can't think like that. A writer has to think that it's more important to be right than to be popular.

Hare went on to talk about his own politics as 'a socialist and a libertarian' in the Thatcher years:

If you do the things that Britain needs to do – namely, withdraw from NATO, get rid of the bomb, and stop being aligned with one side of the Cold War – then presumably the run on the pound, the result in the stock exchanges of the world, will be fairly catastrophic for the economy. But some sort of political realignment is plainly what this country needs. I've absolutely no doubt that the state ought to do a great deal more than it does to help the lowest, the worst-off members.

. . . [Mrs Thatcher's] got the smallest percentage of the electorate of any prime minister since the war. She's the least popular prime minister, and actually the people who dislike her actively make up the highest number since the war. But these facts simply don't appear in the official version, and she's universally admired by the press. She has television cowed, so her control of the media is very powerful.

But when a statistic appears – as it did in *The Sunday Times* last week – saying that 48 per cent of the electorate would like the country to be more socialist in its outlook, this statistic is simply glossed over. It's suppressed. It will never appear again. And the official propaganda version keeps being pumped out from television stations and the press. They simply lie about her popularity. It's disorienting to foreigners, who can't understand it.

. . . This whole thing of the Thatcher revolution – I don't feel that she's truly transformed the country in any direction different from the direction that Edward Heath would have liked to take it in. What she wants to do is what all Tories have always wanted to do, namely, take away from the poor and give to the rich. That's what she's done.

Earlier, in April 1986, Hare had contributed (along with fellow playwrights Brenton, Griffiths, Hampton, Edgar, McGrath and Frayn) to 'The Theatre-Going Public', a discussion hosted by Tom Lubbock for BBC Radio 3, in which he described what he saw as the role of political theatre at a time when it was under great ideological and economic pressure:

I suppose that I still feel that the stage is the place where ideas best enter the bloodstream. It may be an illusion that you believe that people are listening, that some sort of national debate is going on through the theatre, but to me it's an essential illusion. I mean, I couldn't be bothered to write for the stage unless I imagined that I was contributing to the way England saw itself . . . I go to New York, and I greatly enjoy having plays presented [there], and it's a thoroughly exhilarating experience, and there's an extremely intelligent audience . . . but I could never enjoy the illusion that by writing about America I could in any way affect America's destiny. But I do enjoy the illusion that by writing about England I can at least slightly affect the way it sees itself. I don't think I can have any effect at all on its destiny or its policies or the mass of its people, but I can alter its image of itself – a little. And the existence in this country of a strong socialist movement in the theatre has no doubt focused public argument about socialism . . .

. . . [The theatre] is one of the few areas in which socialists are strong – you know, you don't look to Fleet Street for a successful socialist newspaper, but there are socialists running theatres.

The Secret Rapture was Hare's theatrical reponse to Thatcherism. It was a play he conceived partly out of a sense that 'playwrights have gone quiet about the times we live in'. He cited Pravda *and Caryl Churchill's* Serious Money *(Royal Court, 1987) as amongst the most important oppositional plays of the decade, but where those plays revel in the 'malign energy' of their Thatcherite protagonists,* The Secret Rapture *is 'about people who are corrupted by the age'. He discussed the play with Dugdale:*

DUGDALE: *What's the meaning of the title of your new play?*
HARE: In Catholic theology, the 'secret rapture' is the moment when the nun will become the bride of Christ: so it means death, or love of death, or death under life. But I understand that in Protestantism it has something to do with the coming of the Antichrist, so we're having a bit of a problem with that.

DUGDALE: *Was there any personal experience that led you to write about death and grief?*
HARE: I was passionately in love with somebody who at the same time was coming to terms with the death of her father, so in our lives love and death were incredibly mixed up. That certainly sent me spinning; but if that was the starting point there's no trace of it in the play, apart from a couple of lines.

DUGDALE: *Do you see the Isobel character as a kind of modern saint?*
HARE: The play's about someone who's lumbered with being good, and if it's a tragedy – which it may or may not be – that's her fatal flaw. What's been obvious about the most popular plays of the eighties is that they hitch a ride on the malign energy of characters who the author ostensibly disapproves of: the real estate salesman in [Mamet's] *Glengarry Glen Ross*, the crypto-fascists in [Shawn's] *Aunt Dan and Lemon*, the financiers in *Serious Money* – and the characters, obviously, in *Pravda*. In this play, I've sought a way about writing about the present that doesn't rely on the form of theatrical vitality.

DUGDALE: *But won't audiences be drawn to Marion rather than Isobel?*
HARE: Well, yes, probably. Marion is actually one of two, because *Paris by Night* is also about one of the post-Thatcher women in the Tory Party. Infuriatingly, I wrote the script four

years ago knowing that they would rise to prominence, but by the time I'd arranged the financing the name of Edwina Currie [*the former controversial Conservative MP, now novelist and broadcaster, who in 2002 revealed her past affair with Conservative leader John Major*] was already on everyone's lips.

DUGDALE: *So are you worried that audiences will identify Marion with Currie?*

HARE: Greatly worried, because, you know, Edwina Currie belongs more to my *Pravda* mode that to this mode. Both my Tory women are much more complex and sensitive and self-confident. I went to the Tory Party Conference with Charlotte Rampling, who plays the Euro MP in *Paris by Night*, and we were both shocked by how stupid the women made themselves appear in order to ingratiate themselves with the men.

To Gaston:

As far as I'm concerned, *The Secret Rapture* is a play about the intractability of goodness. Now, the play is political in the sense that it's set in the present day, and into the room, I hope, comes the atmosphere of what it is like to live in Britain at the moment. To me that has to be the political atmosphere, because one of the effects of Thatcherism has been to introduce politics into every aspect of people's lives. And I don't know how you can write truthfully about what it's like to be alive in Britain today without some reflection of what the political atmosphere is and how ethical attitudes, moral attitudes, and even, I would say, emotional attitudes have been changed by a very polarizing government.

GASTON: *The Secret Rapture was met with great acclaim in England. But it had a very short run when you brought it to New York. Why do you think that happened?*

HARE: One thing was the difference in productions. In England there was a Chekhovian production, which mediated between the audience and the action of the play. It was a very, very beautiful production. It was done in an elegiac tone, which was entrancing, but which suggested that in some way I yearned for an England of decency that existed before the time of the play. And I think that elegiac quality the audience found very attractive, and I think that quality made them accept a play which is perhaps in the writing harsher than they realized in that particular production. In my own production in New York, I tried to make it much more a play about the difficulties of living in the present. My production was a tougher one. I'm not saying that either one of the productions was necessarily the one right way to do the play. But that was the difference.

The main reason why the play had such a short run in New York is pretty crude. I think it was because the *New York Times* didn't like it. That, unfortunately, makes it impossible to get access to your audience. You can't get your audience to listen to the ideas in your play without overcoming the power of a monopoly newspaper. That newspaper is dishonestly prescriptive and badly staffed. So it's a problem.

And with Zeifman:

ZEIFMAN: *I'm curious as to how you respond to criticisms of specific dramatizations of goodness in your plays. Did you see the profile of Clare Higgins [who played Katherine in the original NT production of* The Secret Rapture] *in the recent* Plays and Players *(November 1991)?*
HARE: Yes, I did. It was very interesting.

ZEIFMAN: *She mentions that a friend of hers, after seeing the play, commented that the 'good' sister Isobel was the most fucked-up and evil woman on the stage, and that that kind of innocence is dangerous.*
HARE: Well, that's right. I mean, it's right in the sense that I've always thought that, in the first half of the play, Isobel has no theory of evil. She doesn't realize that people are doing her harm, and for that reason she's not able to fight evil. But then in the second half, by the time she comes to fight it, she's

trapped: she's in a situation in which whatever route she takes leads to trouble. So yeah, she has an inadequate way of dealing with the world, just as I think Lionel in *Racing Demon* has an inadequate approach to the world. It isn't good enough to wander around pretending that everybody means good; they don't.

ZEIFMAN: *But there's still an important difference here, isn't there? Because finally Isobel is a character one senses you admire –*
HARE: No, I don't think that's true. No. She's a character I love, and that's different.

ZEIFMAN: *OK. She's a character you love, whereas a lot of audience members find her irritating.*
HARE: Absolutely. I'm way out of key with everybody else. (*Laughs.*) But then that's always the case. I mean, it's my experience that people are never going to take from a play what you intend. That's different from 'misreading'. They don't misread it; what they do is run the play by their own life and experience and then they come to a particular conclusion. There's nothing I can do about that. I know where the balance of *my* sympathies lies in the play, although it changes with the years.

The trilogy

The period from 1990 to 1993 saw Hare produce more screen work, for both television and the cinema. Heading Home, *with Gary Oldman and Joely Richardson, was written and directed for the BBC in January 1991, and shown the following year on the American A&E channel (the* Hollywood Reporter *rather unhelpfully found it 'curiously inert but strikingly passionate').* Damage *('a cold, brittle film about raging traumatic emotions' – Variety), Hare's adaptation of a Josephine Hart novel, was released in 1992, directed by Louis Malle and starring Jeremy Irons, Juliette Binoche and the Oscar-nominated Miranda Richardson.*

However, the period was dominated by the production of 'the Hare trilogy': Racing Demon *(1990, winner of Olivier, Plays and Players, Critics' Circle and Time Out Awards);* Murmuring Judges *(1991) and* The Absence of War *(1993, televised 1996). All were produced at the National Theatre under the direction of Richard Eyre, with designs by Bob Crowley and lighting by Mark Henderson; a number of the same actors appeared in two of the three plays, whilst Michael Bryant was in all three. The première of* The Absence of War *on 2 October 1993 saw revivals of the first two pieces played on the same day.*

Taken together, then, the plays amount to a deliberate and concerted examination of the three institutions that so define public life in Britain, three institutions in crisis: the Church, the Law and the Labour Party. As with Pravda, *the earlier treatment of 'the fourth estate', the overriding concern was to identify what Hare saw as the moral and social cost of Thatcherism.*

From Zeifman:

The main reason for a trilogy is that I felt able now to do an English canvas. I wanted there to be three plays which could be played together, which would present a whole canvas of British life. And which were researched, in that I went to pay my dues to real life by finding out what was actually going on on the ground, but which were not in any way documentary. They are works of fiction – the stories are made up, the characters are made up, they are works of the imagination. But they're works of the imagination which I hope are enriched by trying to find out what people's real lives are like.

The basic idea that it came out of was realizing that we have had, for the last ten years, sort of ideological prima donnas who are dancing on the top of the society, producing an ideology which they say the society is meant to believe in – as it happens, an entrepreneurial ideology. And at the bottom or in the middle of the society, we have all the people who are actually dealing with the tensions that are created by that ideology. It seemed to me that Thatcher's survival and prosperity had actually been guaranteed and ensured by clergymen who were willing, for £8,000 or £9,000 a year, to act as surrogate social workers, dealing with all the problems of society at the grass-roots level. And in the same way the police, although they are much better paid (they earn £20,000 a year), are the people at whom all the criticism for what is wrong with the society is being flung. All the grave divisions that have been created by this very self-indulgent philosophy at the top, all those tensions that have been created by that philosophy, the police are having to mop up. So I wanted a trilogy about the people who do the dirty work. You know that line in *Murmuring Judges*, the very emotive line Barry has: 'Let's hear it for the guys who keep turning up' – it's a trilogy about the guys who keep turning up.

Hare spent five years undertaking first-hand research for the plays, interviewing a range of figures from each institution. A selection of the interviews, with Hare's commentary, was collected in Asking Around, *which appeared in 1993. Hare, however, remained adamant that the pieces were not documentaries. Zeifman again:*

Racing Demon originally came out of an idea that I would create Synod, which is the Church's parliament, in the Cottesloe Theatre. And I think the original plan was that I was going to work with Max Stafford-Clark, and that we were going to create a Joint Stock kind of show where we researched. Similarly, at the beginning of *Murmuring Judges* I was going to send the actors out into different parts of the legal system. But then I realized I'm no longer, if I ever was, a classic documentary writer. I'm not interested in documentary as a form at all, and I find the vindication of work by the fact that it actually happened really depressing.

You know, people send me documentary stuff all the time. They think that I'm an expert on the Church. What do I feel about women priests? What do I feel about homosexual clergy? Should gay priests be allowed to marry? I don't have any views on these subjects. I'm not a journalist; I'm not a polemicist. But I *can* try and show you what it's like to be a gay priest who daren't come out of the closet in a South London parish, and I hope I can make you feel for him. But I don't have any sociological brief at all, any polemical or political belief. What inflames my imagination is character, character and narrative. All I'm doing in researching, in fact, is being led to characters and people who interest me, and so I have to have people called research assistants because they're people who lead me to other people.

He talked more about the origins of Racing Demon *in a 1990 interview in* Plays and Players *with Graham Hassell:*

I began researching the play because I was fascinated by the CoE – the state it found itself in and its peculiar problems as they reflected on other institutions in Britain. Since *The Secret Rapture* I'd been interested in the nature of goodness, what it constitutes in the present day. I found the Church's people in the inner cities devote themselves, perhaps fourteen hours a day, to doing what is effectively social work, yet drained of a great deal of the religious content it used to have. And they're doing this work which nobody else is willing to do, being paid miserably to do it and they're doing it from the best intentions. And what powers them is a belief in God's love. I found the idea of these men – whose values were not the current values of society and who would not have any of the conventional rewards – their commitment to their work, terribly moving. I also found the dilemma of the weakness of the institution they serve rather illuminating . . . I think the eighties have raised some profound questions in this context. How do the good guys fight? The Conservative government, which has never been particularly popular, has profited from a divided opposition. The liberals, the socialists, the anarchists, the greens etc., the so-called good guys, haven't been able to agree on anything. So how does good fight evil without it acquiring the characteristics of evil? Especially when a liberal institution, which the CoE is, is obliged to turn the other cheek and put up with all the blows dealt it.

... There was a time when all plays were about religion, but for some reason that has completely disappeared today. And yet the most oversubscribed subject at Oxford University now is theology ... not because people are believers, but because they're interested in comparative theology. It's one of the effects of having a very materialist government – everyone concentrates on what the opposite of materialism is. Perhaps a new play should reflect this.

And from Gaston:

... once *all* plays were about man's relationship to the gods. It's only recently the subject has fallen out of fashion. When *Wetherby* won various religious medals, my friends were amused. But I wasn't very surprised. I knew before *Racing Demon* that religion is a subject in which most people are interested. I was very pleased with a critic who neatly described the subject of the play as being about whether it's possible to have religion without a supernatural element. It's really about whether the moral and the spiritual have anything to do with each other. It also exemplifies some of the things we've been talking about today. As epic, I hope it's more accomplished than *Knuckle*. But more than that, I hope Richard Eyre's excellent production demonstrates the power of writing about a group of people: it's about four vicars, any one of whom might be said to be the play's central character, and the sense of tragedy in the evening comes not from any one individual but from a sense of common loss in the whole group and, by implication, in so many well-intentioned people who find themselves living in an England where good intentions count for nothing.

From the Spectator *'Diary', 18 May 1996 (*Racing Demon *was nominated for a Tony award following its American production at the Lincoln Center):*

People have been ringing about Julie Andrews. They want to know if, as a fellow-nominee, I am going to express solidarity with her by withdrawing myself from the New York Tony awards ceremony on the grounds that the nominating committee has outrageously overlooked the part played by, let's say, the hat-check man in the Broadway production of *Racing Demon*. Outstanding contribution, and so on. In my view, Julie Andrews may be well out of it. Earlier this year, Lloyds Bank, without permission, entered me for some new award no one had heard of. When I declined to take part in the usual humiliations in a London hotel, they said it was their right to enter me whether I liked it or not. A letter arrived, making lawyers' threats. They don't understand. No sensible playwright likes to be entered like a rat in a trap opposite their colleagues. The ideal theatrical award is the one given by the *Evening Standard*. It's a model, because they ring winners up a few weeks in advance and tell them they've won. An award becomes what it should be: a gift, not a competition. For this reason, in the theatre, the *Evening Standard* award is the one people actually want to win.

He went on, in the Zeifman piece, to explain how Murmuring Judges *evolved out of* Racing Demon:

Having done the Church in *Racing Demon* – I suppose that the Church was a sort of metaphor for other British institutions. *Racing Demon* was about how liberals fight, when the essence of Christianity is to turn the other cheek – how Christians organize themselves to fight evil, so to speak. Also, how do liberal institutions function without rules. And then I wanted to take some British institutions where power is the only reality – where the rules are very, very strong – and examine the way they connect or rather fail to connect. You know, the most striking thing about the British judicial system is that the various parts of it – the police, the Bar and the Bench, the prisons – don't relate to each other. And so *Murmuring Judges* is a study of the way Britons are more interested in their own peer groups than they are in the reality of what they're actually doing. At the centre you have somebody who is being mashed by this process, and then you have a group of people who are only interested in their own part of the process.

Zeifman pointed out that the 'conscience' of Murmuring Judges *again resides in its female characters, and went on to ask Hare about his reaction to recurrent criticism that the women in his plays are stereotyped, albeit 'positively':*

The thing is that you're damned if you do and damned if you don't. In *Murmuring Judges* it's simply true about the police and the law that they are male professions, and that women tend to be one step back from them. And given that they're one step back they maybe look at them with a slightly more critical eye because they don't belong to the club. That's not a piece of imaginative fiction, that's just a fact about how those male clubs are organized, and any policewoman will tell you that it's not an easy line about whether you fall in with the sexism. You are offered stereotypes as a policewoman: you can either be flirtatious or you can be hatchet-faced. To just be a woman in the police, particularly at the lowest level, is not easy. And so it's not only justifiable that those characters would be the people one step back, it's also realistic. The general run of feminist criticism seems to me that you're criticised either because the women are too good or because they're villainesses. If they're villainesses you're called misogynistic, and if they're not villainesses – if they're good – you're told you're stereotyping. So frankly I find most academic feminist criticism of my work completely inane; it's never struck me as anywhere near the mark. But the only thing that annoys me is when that criticism becomes censorious, because it implicitly becomes a 'you shouldn't'. In *Licking Hitler*, for instance, a woman who has originally been raped goes on enjoying sex with the man who has raped her. It is then put to me, 'You shouldn't show this'. And I say, 'Well, do such things actually happen?' And the feminist answer is, 'Yes, they do happen, but it's undesirable to show them'. Right? I say,' Where do you think all the imaginative sympathy of the work is? Do you think it's with the man?' They say, 'No, it's quite clearly with the woman. But sexual stereotypes are reinforced on television all night long; therefore you, the progressives, should sort of clean up when your hour comes on. You should counterbalance. So although such things do happen, they should not be shown.' Now that to me is censorship, and just as insidious as the Lord Chamberlain's blue pencil. Because if we're really saying that you can't show what actually happens, you can only show what you would like to happen, then I don't know how a playwright can operate. That's the only feminist criticism that touches me; it annoys me in the way all censorship annoys me.

Zeifman also asked Hare about the use of music in the play:

ZEIFMAN: *The literal use of music of* Murmuring Judges – *the use of Mozart – is wonderful. Presumably you chose* The Magic Flute *deliberately, in that it too portrays a closed and 'secret' society.*

HARE: And the play has a triangular structure, while of course *The Magic Flute* has the famous three chords. Also – I aim, I don't know if I succeed – the whole structure of the evening is meant to have the grace of a Mozart opera, so that it has choral passages, it has ensemble passages, then it has duets, solos, arias. The prison scene – the love scene (what we call the love scene) between the prisoner and lawyer – is intended to be like a long duet in a Mozart opera, before the play does indeed become a Mozart opera. We worked very hard on satisfactions of form.

ZEIFMAN: *There's that breathtaking moment at the end of both acts when the separate parts of the triangle suddenly come together, accompanied by the music of Mozart – it's a fabulous moment.*

HARE: Well, those are the things that theatre can do. You know, in the last ten or fifteen years we've all been on the defensive about theatre in this country, and certainly in the United States. We've been going through a period of enfeeblement, and when these periods come then people start asking 'What can theatre do at all?' And what theatre can do are those extraordinary collisions of the kind that you get in *Murmuring Judges*, which only theatre can deliver. I'm trying in the trilogy to be as flamboyant in the use of form as I possibly can be. *Racing Demon* is quite austere, but it is in a very bold style, namely direct access – people coming out and praying directly to God. I was very struck by a brilliant remark of [*the literary critic William*] Empson's, where he says that the English theatre died when the subplot died. What he meant was that with nineteenth-century scenery, with the arrival of rooms with walls, all that stuff, plays just became one story in one room. What I'm trying to do with epic narrative, with subplot, is to create a theatre that goes back to Elizabethan ideas of plot and subplot. I was very, very influenced by going to see three Shakespeare plays at the RSC [*The Plantagenets* – the three parts of Henry VI conflated into two, followed by *Richard III*] all in a day. And the aim of this trilogy is that eventually you'll be able to see in one day an entire canvas.

The Absence of War *was in many ways the most controversial, and in some ways the most difficult, of the three plays; despite Hare's intentions, the piece was – perhaps inevitably – seen as being 'about' Neil Kinnock and the 1992 Labour Party's lost general election campaign, to which Hare had been granted priv-*

ileged access for his research. The publication of Asking Around *only exacerbated the problem: 'KINNOCK AIDES ACCUSE AUTHOR OF BETRAYAL' (Daily Mail, 23 July 1993).*

Hare tried to 'set the record straight' in an interview with Mark Lawson in the Independent Magazine *in 1993:*

There's such a prejudice against plays about politics that, obviously, what you hope is that people are not going to say, 'I'm not interested in politics,' or, 'Isn't it a play about the Labour Party? I'm not interested in Socialism' . . . So, I'm trying to write a play that isn't just about any of those things. It's a play about leadership, a play about the group and how the thing of groups works . . . As far as I'm concerned, the play will fail if people see it as just being a play about the Labour Party . . .

. . . [but] I made a rod for my own back in publishing this book (*Asking Around*) as well. Looking back, I obviously regret that, because the play is not documentary, but to try to explain this complicated thing – that there is a documentary book about the research of the play but the play itself is not documentary – is almost impossible. So the Labour Party's hostility is, on the whole, not to the play, it's to the book, and as for the play itself . . . there could be no worse way of convincing people something is not documentary than to simultaneously publish a documentary book. So this has been my own mistake . . .

Lawson pointed out that making the play's protagonist, George Jones, a keen theatre-goer like Neil Kinnock, was 'asking for it':

Yes. I didn't really mean it to be taken like that. That's unfortunate. I did it because I wanted to get the sense that Jones is aware of his tragedy, and trapped in it. You know, it's very rare that tragedies are tragedies of self-ignorance. Most of us, if we're involved in tragedies, we're all too well aware of it . . .

. . . To me, George Jones makes a tragic pact, and the pact is with respectability. He becomes convinced that to be elected he has to convince the electorate that he's a good manager. And, to do that, he has to adopt certain attitudes and, as he says, he's in a corset. I believe he's too good a man to survive that process. I can't think of a politician who successfully fools the public about what their natural instincts are. So, for me, the play is a tragedy: a classical tragedy . . .

Has Neil Kinnock seen the play . . .?
He's read it. He will see it . . .

What was his reaction . . .?
His reaction was what yours or mine would be if a play was written about someone who was confusable with us . . .

Well, I would feel angry and anxious . . .
I've said all I'm going to say about this . . .

In fact, according to the Independent *(21 March 1998), Kinnock's response was 'It shows me as an arsehole . . .' Hard, then, to imagine his response to a piece Hare wrote for the* Sunday Telegraph *in April 1995:*

Nothing has annoyed Neil Kinnock more in the past few years than to be driven round London by taxi-drivers who tell him that they have only just realized what a wonderful bloke he is. Opponents will say that everyone's retrospective eagerness to vote for Kinnock is coloured by the certainty that they will never again be offered the chance. But if, as is so often predicted, John Major finds himself having to ride by black cab within the next twelve months, then my guess is he will also be driven mad by drivers telling him that he was one of the best prime ministers this country ever had . . . in the way that he has dealt with a three-year campaign of personal abuse, John Major has shown exceptional resources of character and good humour way beyond the abilities of any of his tormentors . . . My own hope, of course, is that when Tony Blair finally stops fiddling with his rear-view mirror and tells us what direction he proposes to drive in, then he will offer a Labour programme for which all intelligent men and women will be able to vote. But meanwhile, for the first time since I became an adult, I am ruled by a man who appears to be fundamentally decent and honest. Having a prime minister I am not ashamed of is a feeling I like.

Hare's piece was received with some incredulity by fellow socialists, but they need not have worried: a year later, Hare was by his own admission 'eating crow', having witnessed the Tory Party Conference of October 1995, where he found Major a 'soured' figure, characterized by a 'demeaning crudeness which was not there before'.

Satisfying the thirst

The middle 1990s showed no diminution in Hare's output; indeed, if anything, his work over the decade as a whole offered a greater variety than that of any previous decade. Original stage work included Skylight *(National Theatre, 1995, and winner of Olivier and New York Critics' Circle Awards), and* Amy's View, *with Judi Dench and the trilogy production team of Eyre, Crowley and Henderson (National, 1997). He also developed a strong association with the Almeida Theatre, for which he was to produce a series of adaptations. A version of Pirandello's* The Rules of the Game *(1992, Hare's second adaptation of this play) was followed by Brecht's* The Life of Galileo *(1994). Hare's work as a director of his own and other writers' work also continued, notably with his production of Wallace Shawn's* The Designated Mourner *at the National in 1996, and a subsequent film version of the same play.*

Despite the reaction of some in the party to The Absence of War *(which was televised in 1996), Hare received a knighthood from the Labour government in 1998, having been appointed Officier, Ordre des Arts et des Lettres, by the French government a year earlier.*

Richard Eyre's production of Skylight *opened at the National in May 1995, before transferring to Broadway and then returning to the Vaudeville Theatre in London (with a new cast) in 1997. The play provided Hare with occasion to ponder (in the* Guardian, *June 1995) the differences between British and American theatrical culture:*

Some years ago, when the American playwright Wallace Shawn had the opening of his play *Marie and Bruce* at the Theatre Upstairs in London, I asked him, after a couple of highly impressive previews, how long he would be sticking around. 'Well,' he said, 'I had been planning to go home today, but now I am wondering if I should stay for the acclaim'.

Anyone who has ever worked in the British theatre will understand why, at this point, I let out a hollow laugh. Talk to any of my play-writing colleagues, and you will find that on the morning after what may pass here for a reasonable success, they find themselves with nothing more than a silent phone, and the prospect of sitting down to write another play. Acclaim, you may say, is something they do better abroad.

The return of *Skylight* to the West End after its recent Broadway season – it previews tonight at the Vaudeville Theatre – gives me the chance to make a fairly direct comparison between our two theatrical cultures. The British affect to disdain New York as a place of horrible vulgarity, where spurious sentiment and spectacle win out all the time over high seriousness. The city is caricatured as a place where plays are prized not for what they say, but for what fame they can bring to their creators.

Wendy Wasserstein and Tony Kushner are represented as spending as much time addressing Congress and going through the strange American rites of celebrity, as writing. Yet my own experience is that, should you be lucky enough to survive the arbritrary power of a monopoly critic at the *New York Times* [*Hare famously fell out with Frank Rich, the paper's theatre critic, over a show-closing review of the Broadway production of* The Secret Rapture], then waiting for you in New York is a formidably intelligent audience quite as discerning and various as those we have here.

Skylight is a love story about the re-kindling of a passionate relationship between a carefree London restaurateur, Tom Sergeant, and his ex-girl-friend, Kyra Hollis, who has chosen to forsake teaching in the private sector and work in an inner-city school. In our slightly naïve way, all of us working on the production had imagined that an American audience would approach the play through its instinctive sympathy for its swashbuckling entrepreneur. Tom (played then by Michael Gambon and now by Bill Nighy) was someone they would understand. But in performance we found that the social critique presented by the East End teacher (then Lia Williams, now Stella Gonet) and her contempt for capitalist excess was received with a silence which made clear that the nuances of the play were not passing anyone by . . .

Hare's version of Brecht's Galileo *at the Almeida was followed by a version of the same writer's* Mother Courage and her Children *at the National (1995). His comments on Brecht (taken from a piece entitled 'Brecht is There for the Taking' – see Bibliography) hold a particular interest, given that Hare's own* Fanshen *is perhaps the most 'Brechtian' of British political plays:*

When the Berlin Wall fell, the *Daily Telegraph* took the opportunity to delight that one of the side-benefits of the collapse of communism would be that it was no longer necessary to perform the plays of Bertolt Brecht.

Since Brecht remains the world's fourth most-performed playwright, we must assume that the *Telegraph*, in this matter at least, is not getting its way. Yet, if we are to be honest, those of us who love Brecht's work will admit that it presents a particular challenge. When Tallulah Bankhead was asked why she went onto the stage, she replied: 'To get out of the audience'. All too often Brecht belongs to that special category of playwrights – others are Webster, Büchner and, I fear, Chekhov – who seem to give more pleasure and interest to those of us who put them on than they do to the people who come to see them.

Mother Courage and her Children has a uniquely uneven production history. It is a play more honoured in the study than on the stage. Even if you are 50, you are too young to have seen the author's own legendary version for the Berliner Ensemble. Yet its reputation as one of the great twentieth-century productions still casts a long shadow over anyone who attempts the play. If, as has often been said, *The Threepenny Opera* survives however badly you do it, then the unhappy converse has also seemed to be true: that *Mother Courage* empties theatres, however brilliantly it is performed.

When Jonathan Kent and I first discussed the idea of an intimate *Life of Galileo* at the Almeida Theatre a couple of years ago, we were both convinced that it was the stale trappings of so-called 'Brechtian' productions that stood in the way of the audience's access to the play. When I had seen John Dexter's faithful staging of *Galileo* at the National Theatre in 1981, I had admired Michael Gambon's excellent performance and Howard Brenton's supple text. But I found the elaborate paraphernalia of Brechtianism – the placards, the announcements, the forties German music – an impediment to my enjoyment rather than an enhancement to it. Self-conscious mid-century modernism did not help me to the Renaissance. You did not need to travel through Berlin to reach Rome.

For this reason, Jonathan commissioned new music from Jonathan Dove, while I tried, in the stage language I used, to rid the text of all its most Germanic traits. But if we were both sure that Brecht's plays did not need to be mediated through the aesthetics of a particular period in theatre history, we were equally certain that the last way to make them work was by ditching their politics. Pretending Brecht is some kind of 'universal' writer – just one more humanist among many – is not just wrongheaded, but inevitably doomed. The purpose of sandblasting away some of the layers that now cover these plays is not to soften their politics but to reveal them.

Mother Courage and *Galileo* are twin plays, both written by a man as far away from the dogmatist of popular caricature as you could get. Conceived during the period of his enforced exile in Scandinavia, they both draw on the profound sense of compromise that comes to be at the centre of his increasingly uneasy and disturbing art. Both take place at the beginning of the seventeenth century. One is set in Catholic Europe, the other in Protestant Europe. Both concern that moment in history where man first realizes that he is alone in the universe. He ought to find hope, but instead sees that hope betrayed.

In both, the central character does terrible things, then tries to learn to live with the consequences of what they have done. If we can present these plays as portraits of people struggling with the devastating effects of bad faith in a fast changing society, how can we doubt they will survive . . . yes, even the eventual fall of the *Daily Telegraph*. The subject of both is silence and survival. What on earth could be more timely?

. . . 'the devastating effects of bad faith in a fast changing society' might almost stand as one statement of Hare's own concerns as a writer; his views on the continuing relevance of Brecht in the 1990s are certainly useful to set alongside an article he wrote for the New Statesman *in 1997, three months before* Amy's View *premièred:*

. . . if you examine the current repertory, it seems remarkably little changed from the middle-brow selection that attracted so much contempt 40 years ago.

It is not just the plays that haven't changed much; neither, truly, has the audience. If one kind of post-war energy went into changing what was seen, another movement, pioneered by Joan Littlewood, was intent on changing who saw it. The early part of my own theatrical life was dedicated, typically, to taking violently contemporary plays to army camps, villages, prisons and schools in order to introduce a new audience to the special pleasures of the medium. Yet as the years go by, I think I may also be typical in coming to see that the artistic benefits of playhouses which enable me to say complex and sometimes delicate things may outweigh the satisfactions of what were only temporary gains in the constituency for theatre.

The danger in admitting this is that I begin to sound defensive. But I do not know anyone who has endured the fashionable onslaught against theatre in the past decade who has not occasionally sounded a little bewildered and rueful. This has not been an easy period. The once serious business of cultural commentary has been adjourned to a sleazy motel room, where newspaper and magazine writers have been conducting a fullblown love affair with pop culture. Supposedly up-market journalists have been heard rending the night with their piercing shrieks of 'Give-it-to-me-baby' at every American stud who has happened to pass. Fans of live, rather than mechanically reproduced performance, have been branded elitist.

In Britain practitioners of literary culture have long looked down on the performing arts. They may imagine them vulgar and in some way suspect, compared with the rarefied business of writing novels and poems. But lately the snobs, as you might say, have made common cause with the populists. Theatre's value has been persistently questioned by a generation of graduate writers who regard the form as too difficult and too cumbersome to bother themselves with. It achieves effects too slowly. It goes too deep. At the same time, the theatre's own confidence has suffered a definite internal decline, perhaps from learning that the fight to convince governments of the ultimate value of art can never finally be won.

As the author of a recent trilogy of plays about three British institutions, observing the audience had taught me that, whether these plays were any good or not, there was, in the quality of the audience's attention and the variety of their response, a palpable need for the public to have a place where they could see the currency of modern life set before them.

To judge from our audiences, the throats of the young seemed to be quite as parched as those of my own generation. If we failed to satisfy that thirst, we had no one but ourselves to blame. If the theatre appears – as it often does – to be drifting from the centre of many people's interest, the likely reason is that not enough good writers are writing enough good plays.

Obviously this is a hard view, and you might well object that it is a highly privileged one. In Britain, after all, it is impossible to disentangle the subjects of culture and education, and it is only the occasional appearance of an exceptional playwright such as Shelagh Delaney or, more recently, the brilliant Andrea Dunbar – who wrote *The Arbour* and *Rita, Sue and Bob Too* in exercise books from the Bradford council estate where she lived – which reminds you of the massive untapped creative potential among people who would never normally think of going to the theatre, let alone writing a play.

For all the superficial changes in the British class system, the single greatest scandal in our national life remains the imbalance in the way we are educated. The quality and nature of our plays does finally depend on who in the society is empowered to write them. But it does trouble me that the younger generation of playwrights with which the British theatre is richly blessed seem unable to work their way out of the studio theatres and on to the bigger stages where they might make some more general impact.

That this new generation exists at all may be seen to be a matter of wonder and surprise. When Stephen Daldry at the Royal Court and Nick Wright at the National Theatre tell us that for the first time in years they are receiving plays from young unknowns that merit immediate production, we may conclude that all the easy cultural theorising of the past ten years has turned out to be a load of nonsense. Young writers are turning, unexpectedly, to the poor beleaguered theatre – in particular to places such as the Bush, the Traverse and the Royal Court's Theatre Upstairs. However, none of the younger writers has yet provided that kind of rallying point which every theatregoing generation needs to provide a focus for its own wishes and dreams.

The ability to hit your time is of course not the only thing a playwright needs. And it may one day be the reason your work is superseded and forgotten. Who, in a hundred years' time, will read the most interesting plays of our period without exhaustive footnotes? But surely we all sense some essential fun, some vigour goes out of the theatre unless it displays writers who have the special gift for making the form topical and urgent.

Often it seems that we are living through less urgent times. When the cold war was at its height, liberalizing playwrights were attacked with open hostility. Now, in a less overtly ideological era, they seek to destroy us with neglect. I have no complaint about this, for it may well do us good in the long run. The spotlight is not always the best place to work. But what will be less forgivable is if the cause of the living playwright is abandoned by those who work in the theatre themselves. Like everyone else, playwrights live in uncertainty. We can never be sure that ten years ago we did not all board the wrong boat. But let the waves take us, not the idleness of the crew.

> *From Hare's 'Campaign Diary' for the* Daily Telegraph *(kept during the run-up to the 1997 general election). 12 April, Leeds:*
>
> Real courage is rare in politicians. It is commonly attributed to Margaret Thatcher, and nobody can take away from her the extraordinary bravery she showed on the night of the Grand Hotel bombing. But one of the things you noticed about her politically was that she tended to take on enemies whom she knew she could beat. She rarely wasted time on fights she knew she was going to lose. Faced with the power of the legal profession, she backed off her reforms of the Bar pretty fast. Clare Short, with her campaign against the ugliness of the gutter press, is, by contrast, one of the few politicians to ha ve spat in Rupert Murdoch's eye and got away with it.
>
> Also greatly to her credit is that she argued, rightly, for the innocence of the Birmingham Six while herself repre-

senting the Ladywood constituency in which some of the families of the bomb's victims still lived. That required guts. Far from being, as the press paints her, Old Left ('I hate that term, with its connotations of Trotskyism and hatred, of a revolution that was never going to happen'), she belongs instead to that broad, enabling strand which created the National Health Service and full employment.

So, inevitably, it was disappointing to walk round a couple of key marginals in Yorkshire with her and to find that she is fighting this election with six rolls of sticky tape wrapped round her mouth . . .

On Amy's View, *from 'The Idea of Amy', written as a Programme Note to the original production:*

Everyone always wants to know how a playwright starts work. In my own instance, it has generally been with an image or a memory. Although plots, ideas and characters may eventually become more important, I seem unable to begin a play unless, first, there is some sort of significant picture in my mind, almost like a painting. The play *Plenty* . . . came to me because I was moved by the idea of a woman sitting in a wrecked room, among packing cases, rolling a cigarette over the inert body of her naked husband. *Skylight* . . . started similarly in my head with the powerful vision of an isolated young woman rubbing her mittened hands as her gas heater flared uselessly on a cold winter night in Kensal Rise.

Amy's View has an interesting history for me, because the notion of the play is tangibly mixed up with my own memory of first coming upon a genuinely Bohemian household . . . I shall never forget the almost visceral excitement of a New Year's Eve party in 1966 when, fresh from making my way to university, I first entered the Berkshire home of a working painter. It was here for the first time that I met adults for whom Art very definitely had a capital A.

Anyone who has seen any of the three plays I have mentioned will remember that they all then developed in very different directions. But the opening image remains crucial. *Amy's View* starts in a widow's sitting room which is casually littered with the work of a dead artist, Bernard Thomas. It is Thomas's spirit which then presides over the whole play. The story that follows, about the relationship between a leading West End actress, Esme Allen, and her loving daughter, Amy, is played out over a sixteen-year period, starting in 1979. It describes an era in which it becomes more and more difficult for an actress to make a living in the theatre alone. But, throughout, it is the memory of her dead husband which provides Esme with the lasting principles of her life.

Since I was young, I have adored work in the theatre and cinema which is set over a long period of time. There always seems to be something specially heartbreaking about watching the way the years treat us all differently. But, beyond that, while I was planning *Amy's View*, I particularly relished the challenge of realizing a four-act play. This subtle and difficult form was used by groundbreaking writers like Ibsen, Chekhov and O'Neill to make interesting elisions and connections between separate events, and to work careful shifts of style. But recently, it has been more or less abandoned by the modern theatre in favour of more fractured techniques, often borrowed from film and television. I also treasured the special neatness of writing this particular play a full thirty years after I first walked into an artistic environment. Doggedly, I remain today just as star-struck by the transforming power of art as I was then. I am more passionately convinced than ever of its potential importance in giving shape and purpose to our lives.

In saying this, and in writing a play which is, at the last, a testimony to art's dignifying importance in the life, at least, of one individual, I am pleased that so many people have spotted the fact that the play aims to use all the armoury of theatre to defend theatre itself. Since the play opened at the National Theatre six months ago, I have also been amused and sometimes taken aback by the sheer variety of people's responses to it. It is not unusual for an author to believe he or she has written a play about one subject, and to find instead that the audience sees it as being about something altogether different. But I have never known a play where the letters I have received have been so diverse. To some people who write to me, *Amy's View* is, primarily, a family play, the study of a relationship between a mother and daughter (often painfully reminiscent of the correspondent's own relationships). To others, it is a tragedy, centred round the deeply mysterious question of why we can never make amends with people we need to, but instead always choose disastrously to put reconciliation off to another day. To others again, it is seen primarily as an attack on a generation which regards art itself as old-fashioned and elitist. To a last, substantial group, *Amy's View* has appeared principally as a political play, showing how the spoilt British characteristically dream their way through their lives, hopelessly trusting to their own superiority, and never really bothering to come to terms with a reality which has changed beyond recognition.

I hope it will ruin nobody's fun to say that I recognize all these interpretations, and intend at least three-quarters of them. But beyond all of them, my purpose in writing *Amy's View* was to do something blindingly simple, and yet still distressingly rare: to put modern women's lives on the stage in a way which I hope women will recognize. Since my first play *Slag* was presented at the Hampstead Theatre in 1970 with an all-woman cast of Rosemary McHale, Marty Cruickshank and Diane Fletcher, then revived the following year at the Royal Court with Anna Massey, Lynn Redgrave and Barbara Ferris, I have always aimed to give equal voice to women at a time when so many plays have been dealing exclusively with the concerns of men. The result is that I have watched my work being played by Vanessa Redgrave, Helen Mirren and Irene Worth; by Clare Higgins, by Meryl Streep and by Kate Nelligan; by Charlotte Rampling, by Penelope Wilton and by

Lia Williams; by Stella Gonet, by Zoë Wanamaker and by Joely Richardson and now by Joyce Redman and Samantha Bond. Over the years, Judi Dench, happily, has appeared twice before in work I have written – first, as the expatriate Englishwoman Barbara Dean in my television film about the American evacuation of Vietnam, *Saigon: Year of the Cat*, and secondly, as Marcia Pilborough, the nosy and insensitive neighbour in the feature film *Wetherby*.

Years ago Harley Granville Barker, the prime mover of the British National Theatre, wrote that 'the art of theatre is the art of acting, first, last and all the time'. The great pleasure of being a playwright in this country is being able, from experience, to agree so wholeheartedly with this sentiment.

Still adapting

Hare's association with the Almeida Company – created by joint Artistic Directors Jonathan Kent and Ian McDiarmid as one of the most exciting and innovative British theatres of the last decade – continued after Galileo *with adaptations of Chekhov's* Ivanov *(1997) and* Platonov *(2001), as well as with his direction of Shaw's* Heartbreak House *(1997), and a revival of* Plenty, *with Cate Blanchett. The production there, too, of his original treatment of the life of Oscar Wilde,* The Judas Kiss *(1998, with Liam Neeson), suggests the theatre was at least as much of a 'home' to him as the Royal Court and the National had been. Another, 'freer', adaptation, of Schnitzler's* La Ronde, *achieved a certain silly notoriety: press coverage of Sam Mendes's production of Hare's* The Blue Room *(Donmar Warehouse, 1998) seemed overly concerned with Nicole Kidman's brief nude scene. The multiple-award-winning* Via Dolorosa *(Royal Court, 1998) marked a radical departure for Hare: he performed his own monologue, in a production by Stephen Daldry that played both in London and on Broadway. Another original play,* My Zinc Bed *(Royal Court, 2000) completed the decade.*

The adaptations of Chekhov first, from 'Hot and Young', the programme note to Platonov:

The four familiar masterpieces [*The Seagull, Uncle Vanya, Three Sisters, The Cherry Orchard*] have been played in the international repertory more or less ever since they were written, sometimes giving more pleasure to actors who relish their ensemble qualities than to audiences who, in second-rate productions, find them listless. But few meanwhile take time to study the playwright's younger work, whose special impact is always patronized and overlooked. It is time, I believe, to see these vibrant and much more direct plays for what they are – thrilling sunbursts of youthful anger and romanticism – not just for what they portend.

. . . When I adapted *Ivanov* for the Almeida Theatre in 1997, I observed that it was an inconvenient fact about the man generally credited with abolishing melodrama from the modern stage that he had once written a rather brilliant melodrama himself. Immediately after *Ivanov*'s opening, the company's artistic director asked me to look next at the adolescent sprawl that is known to English-speakers as *Platonov*. (Russians call it *Fatherlessness*.) It was, he argued, the logical next step. *Ivanov* had been a tough case. It had hitherto been ignored by audiences and academics alike. Chekhov had intended that its self-absorbed, self-hating hero should represent a critique of solipsism. But in performance, its hero had all too often come across only as a tiresome embodiment of its indulgence. It was Ralph Fiennes who finally played the part the way the author wanted, surprising audiences both in London and in Moscow. Fiennes revealed Ivanov not as a man lost in useless introspection, but rather as someone who found the whole Russian tradition of introspection and self-pity humiliating. Fiennes was not a stereotype. He was a man fighting with all his willpower not to surrender to a stereotype. The play was no longer propelled by despair, but by honesty.

Watching *Ivanov* become accepted in Jonathan Kent's excellent production as a play worth reviving for its own sake was one of the most rewarding experiences of my writing life. But I admit that it has taken me a further three years to adopt Ian McDiarmid's suggestion and find my way towards a version of the even tougher *Platonov*. Up till now, the most successful adaptations of this play have, significantly, tended to be the freest. When Michael Frayn wrote his popular comedy *Wild Honey* for the National Theatre in 1984, then he admitted frankly that he treated the text 'as if it were the rough draft of one of my own plays'. When Mikhalkov made his 1985 film *Unfinished Piece for Mechanical Piano*, then similarly, he re-allocated lines, banished half the characters, abandoned the substantive plot, and shoehorned in ideas and images of his own. But my conviction, both more and less radical than that of my two gifted predecessors, has been that I should once more stick as closely as possible to Chekhov's original structure and plan. Working from a literal translation, I would clear away massive amounts of repetition and indulgence, I would re-coin and re-balance much of the dialogue, I would hack determinedly through acres of brushwood; but my final aim was that the audience should see the work in something like the form in which Chekhov had left it.

It is undoubtedly a risky undertaking. *Platonov* may appear an odd-shaped play. It can seem like a man who sets off for a walk in one direction, but who is then lured by the beauty of the landscape into another destination entirely. The First Act has a gorgeous breadth and sweep that leaves you expecting a finely nuanced evening in the company of a whole community. The Second centres on a long, almost Godot-like meditation between two lost souls. By the time the Third is underway, you are witnessing a series of extremely painful and funny duologues, all with Platonov himself as the common partner, and by the Fourth you are, with a bit of luck, adjusting yourself to a climax of feverish hysteria. No wonder commentators have dismissed this ambitious story of steam trains and gypsies for what they call 'uncertainty of tone'. A faithful version of *Platonov* will test to the limit the idea that an evening in a playhouse needs to be held together in one dominant style.

. . . Chekhov sets off to give us a broad-brush view of a society rotten with money, drink, hypocrisy and anti-Semitism. The brutal practices of capitalism, all too recognizable in their modernity, are sweeping aside a privileged class which no longer knows its function nor how to maintain its way of life. Ruling-class attitudes have survived long after ruling-class influence has gone. But then, once he has established the context of his vision, Chekhov goes on to embody the contradictions of this superfluous class in one single individual.

The schoolteacher Platonov is a man who has squandered his inherited fortune. Again, critics usually say that the character is a small town Lothario, seeking bored amusement in the aimless pursuit of women. But if we ignore the play's reputation, and instead examine what Chekhov actually wrote, we will find a hero who is, in fact, surprisingly reluctant to consummate his relationship with at least one of the beautiful women who are in love with him. Far from being a determined seducer, 'the most interesting man in the region' is, on the contrary, a person to whom things happen – sometimes at his wish, sometimes by accident. In his relationships, he tries not for any easy conquest, but rather to discover in love a purpose and meaning which eludes him elsewhere. Should we really be surprised that this is Anton Chekhov of all writers who breathes humanity and contradiction into the tired, traditional figure of the provincial Don Juan?

. . . In the interests of artistic neatness, it would be satisfying if my project could be rounded off with a new version of the great play in which the romantic playwright merges into the classical. For me, *The Seagull* is the apex of a triangle whose lesser-known points are *Ivanov* and *Platonov*. However, a play which has already been served by so many expert translations hardly has the need of any more advocacy, no matter how urgently conceived. If *Ivanov* and *Platonov* have, by comparison, been neglected, then we have the Almeida Theatre to thank for their prominent revival. In performance, *Platonov*, like *Ivanov*, is simply too good a play for its status to depend on the foretelling of some other, better-known work which is not being offered tonight.

More on adapting, from the 'Preface' to the published text of The Blue Room:

It was never Schnitzler's intention that his loose series of sexual scenes, *Reigen*, should be publicly performed. When he wrote them in 1900, the author called them 'completely unprintable' and intended only that they should be 'read among friends'. It was no surprise when the eventual première of the work was closed down by the police in Vienna in 1921. Similarly, the actors in its first Berlin production in the same year had to endure a six-day trial on charges of obscenity.

For years the sketches enjoyed an underground reputation . . . [but] it was only when Max Ophüls made his famous film in 1950 that the work escaped its provocative reputation and became associated instead with a certain kind of enchantment . . . Few people knew the original work well enough to notice that Ophüls had, in fact, adapted the text with extreme freedom, even introducing a figure – not in Schnitzler – of the all-seeing ringmaster, superbly played by Anton Walbrook . . .

After the success of the film, the play became better known as *La Ronde*. For myself, I first heard of it when my father told me that only when I was grown up would he allow me to see what he called his favourite film of all time. Since 1981, when the theatrical rights fell temporarily out of copyright, there have been a good many stage versions, and in many different languages. Some of them choose, as *The Blue Room* does, to re-set the play in a contemporary world. Mine is also not the first version to allocate the ten parts to just two actors.

Over the years audiences have continued to argue about whether the idea of the sexual daisy-chain that is at the centre of Schnitzler's conception is profound or over-neat. Whichever, it is wonderfully malleable. When I have put plays by Chekhov, Brecht and Pirandello into English, I have never considered anything but a fairly strict fidelity to the original. But when Sam Mendes asked me to adapt Schnitzler, I instinctively chose to follow Ophüls's example, licensed by the knowledge that the author himself never put the material into a form where he foresaw it being performed.

The hundred years that have followed the writing of *Reigen* have seen a supposed upheaval both in social attitudes and in sexual morals. But the fascination of the work is that its treatment seems hardly dated at all. Schnitzler was not only Freud's almost exact contemporary. He was also, like Freud, like Chekhov, a doctor. His essential subject is the gulf between what we imagine, what we remember and what we actually experience. You have to wait years (in fact for Marcel Proust to stop partygoing and get on with his great novel) before you find a European author having the prescience to chart this treacherous, twentieth-century territory of projection and desire with as much longing and insight as Schnitzler.

Completing the 'Almeida plays' is the original The Judas Kiss. *The production transferred to America, where Hare gave an interview to Michael Kuchwara (available on-line: see Bibliography):*

'Don't go to *The Judas Kiss* expecting the stereotypical stage portrait of Oscar Wilde: a languid fellow, wearing a velvet jacket and a green carnation, with mascara running down his face,' warns playwright David Hare.

'What we are trying to do is radically reinterpret the myth,' says Hare of the man who personified the idea of sacrificial love – being true to his idea of love whatever the cost.

The play, now on Broadway for a limited run through Aug. 1, deals with Wilde's loyalty to Lord Alfred Douglas, the young man who, in the world's eyes at least, caused his downfall.

'I find it an incredibly moving story,' says Hare of the play-wright and poet who, 100 years ago, was lionized by London society as a brilliant raconteur and author of some of the best comedies in the English language, including *The Importance of Being Earnest*.

Married and with two children, Wilde fell in love with Douglas, nicknamed Bosie. Publicly chastised by Douglas' father, Wilde sued for libel. The suit failed, and Wilde became liable for prosecution under British law for 'acts of gross inde-cency'. Convicted, he spent two years in jail before leaving England in disgrace, never to return.

In *The Judas Kiss*, the conventional effete image of Wilde goes out the window with its casting of the lead character. Wilde was a 6-foot-3 Irishman. So is strapping film star Liam Neeson, best known for his roles in *Schindler's List*, *Michael Collins* and *Rob Roy*.

Hare finds Wilde's Irish heritage politically important, too. 'He was someone who had a certain view of the British estab-lishment, who was outside that establishment and was pro-foundly critical of it,' Hare says.

Hare's Wilde doesn't speak in a steady parade of witty epi-grams either. 'I didn't want him making sparkling jokes all the time,' Hare says. 'Yet this man was one of the greatest conversationalists who ever lived, so you do have to rise to a certain level of invention whereby the audience believes, "Yes, this man is Oscar Wilde".'

'One thing about Wilde, which Liam captures so wonderfully, is his open-heartedness, his extraordinary generosity. Wilde was a man who never passed beggars on the street without giving them money. Servants, as is shown in my play, remarked on the fact that he was the only upper-middle-class person who ever talked to them as if they were human beings. He treated all people equally.'

'I hate it when others make Wilde into a cynic,' Hare says. 'He was not. On the contrary, he was someone whose genius was for love. Wilde actually was quite an innocent in the sheer intensity with which he loved. Yes, he was critical of hypocrites and he was brilliant at exposing hypocrisy – not from a deeply cynical position but from a very loving one. That's what I am trying to show, too.'

In *The Judas Kiss* Hare doesn't attempt docudrama – 'other people have done that, and they have done it wonderfully well,' he says. What Hare is after is more elusive, capturing the spirit of the man through what he calls 'stage poetry'. The playwright takes two of the most obscure and difficult moments in Wilde's life – why he didn't leave England to avoid prosecution and why, after getting out of jail, he went back to Bosie. He then speculates on them in a way which, he says, 'doesn't claim to be true, but which claims to be truthful' . . .

'Wilde really believed what he says in *The Judas Kiss*, that you only really see a person through love. It's only when you love somebody that you really see the true person. When you cease to love, they become obscure again.'

Shortly afterwards, the transfer of Via Dolorosa *from the Royal Court meant that, with* The Blue Room *and* The Judas Kiss, *Hare had three plays showing on Broadway at the same time. His 1999 book* Acting Up *includes his experiences in New York as part of a very full account of the production of* Via Dolorosa *from the earliest rehearsals in London through to the eventual television version.*

Just before the play opened in London, in 1998, Hare gave an interview to Michael Billington for the Guardian, *in which he explained that the Royal Court* . . .

. . . wanted someone to write a play about the British mandate for Palestine, which expired 50 years ago. I soon realized the British question didn't interest me at all. What I did feel was that it was very bad that there should be a passionate argument going on in the Middle East largely confined to the Israelis and the Palestinians. A good argument is one where the generality of people share views.

So I decided to write a classic, old-fashioned, Joint Stock show, the kind of thing I did for Bill Gaskill and Max Stafford-

Clark in the seventies with *Fanshen*, where the writer distils mountains of research. On a very basic level, the play exists to inform people about something that's a peculiarly interesting point. Originally, the idea was to have a triptych of monologues from an Israeli, a Palestinian and myself. But the Palestinian refused on the grounds that it might be perceived as a gesture of reconciliation to Israel . . . I discovered my show ran an hour and a half. So I said: 'Let's do one for now'. Maybe, in the long run, the idea will build. Who knows?

I could have written an article . . . but journalism just doesn't stick. I know far more about subjects I've seen plays about than those I've read about in newspapers or magazines. There was, as it happens, a brilliant piece in the *New Yorker* recently about the apocalyptic tendencies among religious Jews but it only hit me because I'd researched the subject. Of course, reactions to this play will be diverse, and I'll be fiercely attacked by Middle East specialists. But my claim has always been that people think more deeply when they think together. That's what theatre does.

At the same time, I hope the play will be seen as a meditation on art. I talk about my visit to Yad Vashem, the museum of the Holocaust, and the sense that its sculpture and painting seem superfluous when set against the bare facts. I also understand the feeling of a Palestinian poet who wishes that a play could be half a poem and that you didn't have to worry about the audience. Stephen Daldry, who is directing, says that the play only starts cooking when you forget it's about Israel and Palestine. In the same way *Pravda*, which I wrote with Howard Brenton, wasn't just about the British press, and I suppose the test of this play will be whether audiences respond to the questions that certainly intrigue me. What does art add to this situation in the Middle East? How, if at all, does it illuminate?

I just had no clue that the arguments in each community appeared to be – I'm not saying they are – as profound as the arguments between the two communities. That for me was a revelation and what, more than anything, I wanted to tell the world about. It's a very fundamental argument that is going on.

The Palestinian territories are being run by a corrupt, implicitly capitalist, quite nasty regime, which is balanced by a trace of Arab idealism on the other side of the community. There are those who wish to deal with Israel and those who don't, and personal advantage is being served as much as national aims. But there is an equally strong split on the Israeli side between the religious and secular arms of society with [*the then Israeli Prime Minister*] Netanyahu in hock to the religious right and desperately needing their votes. Until you visit, you don't understand the divisions and the depths of despair on either side. The reason the play is called *Via Dolorosa* is because I'm saying I come from a different Christian tradition as a total outsider. It's always claimed that in the West we don't believe in anything and so the initial impulse is one of 'Let's go to a place where people do believe and see how we like it'. I come back asking, 'Is it true we don't believe anything in England?' I've never felt that. I've always thought we believed in lots of things. We're just out of touch with our beliefs.

Speaking the following year, after he had performed the play in both London and New York, Hare offered a retrospective view of his experience in an interview available on the world-wide web at http://www.pbs.org/viadolorosa/davidhare.html

As Stephen Daldry said, the play is not about Israel and Palestine, it's about you, and what he meant by that was that I was seeing two societies . . . in which everybody has to think very deeply about what they believe. In the West, we can say we believe things. We can say that we're Socialists or Capitalists. We can say that we're Christians or not Christians. We can say that we are convinced about this or convinced about that, but we're not tested.

And I went to two countries where what you believe will determine where you live, which street you live in, who your friends are, what school your children go to – everything in these two countries is about faith and belief and everything is something you are going to have to argue with your near neighbour. And so the subject of the play is what is it like for somebody who has, as it were, no faith or at least whose faith is never tested to go to a place where faith is absolutely everything. And so in that way I was drawing attention to the similarities between the two communities, the Palestinians and the Jews, as much as the differences between them and I think it's that which stopped people finding it unbalanced.

The only objections – literally in a year of playing it – the only objections that I had were occasionally from supporters of the settlers who felt that I was unfair to them. And I have had two Palestinians only who have complained about aspects of the way Palestinians were portrayed. But those have literally been the only complaints about the portrait of either community that I have had in a year.

Acting Up, of course, offers a much fuller account of the play, but it's worth quoting this interview a little more, especially from Hare's comments on acting his own work:

I'm not an actor and so, you know, I was fifty-one and making my stage debut. *Via Dolorosa* is the only thing I have ever acted in my life, professionally, and I'll never act again. I'm a playwright and I did it purely and simply because it was the only way to convey what I wanted to say about the region.

But I had to play thirty-three characters and so plainly I'm not Peter Sellers, I can't impersonate people. And so through the work of the director, Stephen Daldry, I hope I became a sort of medium for these people. And I did give them intonations or characteristics perhaps which is the most I could hope to do, but we both realized pretty quickly that for it to become the kind of 'putting-on-one-hat-and-then-another' show would not actually . . . it would honour neither the people nor me. It wouldn't play to my strengths.

But what I could give them I hope is the emotional reality and the passion and the humour and all the vitality that I felt of them. Because . . . one of the characteristics that everybody remarks about *Via Dolorosa* was that – I don't meet anyone of . . . the thirty-three people who isn't both opinionated and full of life. I think one of the reasons for the extraordinary reaction to the play was that Westerners found it refreshing to meet people who felt so strongly and who expressed themselves so brilliantly.

. . . And I think with the great – the very, very important – subjects you have to be careful what you are doing by fictionalizing them at all. In the play, I mention that when we go to the Holocaust museum, paintings of the concentration camps are so much less powerful than photographs. The art in the Holocaust museum seems gratuitous and stupid. You just think why is an artist interposing himself between you the viewer and the experience that you can get from the records, the objects, the photographs, and art in that sense seems gratuitous.

And the effect of *Via Dolorosa*, I hope, is to bring people as near as possible to the subject matter itself without a whole load of gratuitous, interpretative gloss from me. The one thing that *Via Dolorosa* has is no opinions. To me curiosity is fifty times as valuable as opinion. There are enough opinions about the Middle East, whereas there is too little knowledge.

. . . The idea of the play is that I step in and out of the play all of the time. And that meant that we were always trying to throw the focus either on to the events or on to my reaction to the events. And Stephen gradually produced this wonderful path through the evening whereby the audience slowly realized that I was both in the events and describing them. And I think one of the effects of one-man shows is that you feel that at the end of the play you know the person on the stage terribly well. And there wasn't a night where there weren't lots of people waiting for me at the stage door.

At first this alarmed me because I'm not used to that as the playwright. The playwright's an anonymous figure. But the reason they were waiting for me was they felt they knew me because they'd spent an hour and a half or more in my company. So they wanted to give something back. They wanted to tell me what they felt because they had listened to me talk about what I felt.

. . . It was quite educational for me, that twenty minutes at the stage door every night.

From Hare's Spectator 'Diary', 15 April 2000:

Other people's court cases are as interesting as other people's babies, but last week the Royal Court Theatre enjoyed a welcome victory in a Manhattan court. A New York judge threw out a claim by a Los Angeles playwright that the invitation to send me to the Middle East to write my play *Via Dolorosa* had been prompted by one of the Royal Court's play-readers happening to see the litigant's own unsolicited manuscript on a similar subject two years previously. The claim was so far-fetched as to be preposterous, but typically it took ten months to reach the court, where it was immediately thrown out, at a cost to the theatre of $40,000 in legal fees.

The case raised important issues of principle. Vexatious litigation has provided movie studios and a good many American theatres with a convenient excuse not to read anything which is submitted from an unknown source. The Royal Court argued that it could not fulfil its role as the country's most important theatre for new work if it wasn't free to read unsolicited manuscripts. The discovery of unknown writers depends on a theatre's ability to open the post without fear of litigation. Anyone who cares about freedom of speech is invited to send money to the Court's beautiful new playhouse in Sloane Square to help defray its legal expenses.

In July 2002, and in the context of a situation in the Middle East that was deteriorating yet again, Hare revived Via Dolorosa *for a seven-week run at the Duchess Theatre in London. He explained why in a piece for* Guardian Weekend *in the same month; see Bibliography: 'An Act of Faith'. The* Guardian *interview also allowed Hare to explain what Billington described as his 'obstinate, quasi-religious faith in theatre':*

. . . At the moment something is definitely going on. The habit of theatre-going as a social ritual is more or less dead, but there is still an enormous appetite for plays. You don't see it because you only go to first nights, but I've recently encountered the best audiences I've seen for years – [*Patrick Marber's*] *Closer*, [*Conor McPherson's*] *The Weir*, [*Alan Ayckbourn's*] *Things We Do For Love*, [*Kevin Elyot's*] *The Day I Stood Still*, *Amy's View* and *The Judas Kiss* all sold out and all, when I saw them, were playing to young audiences. Something is definitely happening.

But I also made a conscious decision about ten years ago that my life was in the theatre. It seemed to me no coincidence that in the Thatcherite period there were these sustained political attacks on theatre or dreary articles by sub-literate journalists claiming that theatre was dead. It provoked me into thinking that I really believe in it and wanted to spend my life in it. I also felt I didn't have enough years left to do the amount of work I wanted to do in other media and to fight all the necessary fights. If you talk to someone like Stephen Frears, you realize the intense difficulties in trying to do serious work in the film industry. I also see, in the cinema or on video, about 165 movies a year, and I swear there's been nothing recently that sets your mind singing in the way *Closer* does or that is as purely accomplished as Howard Davies's production of *The Iceman Cometh*. In theatre, you have a regular turnover of work through which you grow and learn. After all those years of being fashionably beaten, theatre is suddenly healthy again.

From an obituary for Diana Boddington (National Theatre stage manager), Guardian, *21 January 2002:*

When we came to work together in the early 1980s, I had, like everyone else, picked up anecdotal scraps of her mythical reputation, but nothing prepared me for the pudding-basin haircut and the flowing pinafores – she

---

always looked as if she had been drawn rather hastily by Raymond Briggs – nor, more important, for the salty, affectionate mix of warmth and truth-telling that made us best friends on sight. Seeing her puzzling over my text in the first days of our acquaintance, I asked her what was troubling her. 'I can see this play works,' she said, 'but I'm buggered if I can see why'.

. . . For someone of her religious convictions, Diana's language was paint-strippingly coarse, though never blasphemous. A nautical blast of force 10 obscenity awaited any actor or director who was late or ill-prepared. As I entered a third day of round-table discussion of some of the finer points of interpretation and nuance in one of my plays, I was surprised to find myself impatiently interrupted by the scornful woman beside me: 'John Dexter would have this fucking staged by now' . . .

A conversation with David Hare

This interview with Hare was recorded by the present writer in London in March 2002. At the time, he had just completed a new play, The Breath of Life, *and was working on his film adaptation of Jonathan Franzen's novel* The Corrections. *He was also writing a memorial lecture on the playwright John Osborne for the* Guardian Hay Festival *of June 2002.* *

I began by asking him whether there was any significance in the fact that much of his more recent work has taken the form of adaptation:

* A report on Hare's lecture appeared in the *Guardian*, 4 June 2002, 8. The lecture itself was printed in the same newspaper, 8 June 2002. Hare had also spoken at Osborne's memorial sevice in 1995; his speech is available on-line. See Bibliography for full details of all these.

I've largely given up directing. In between original plays I used to work on the floor in the theatre, now I adapt.

Is there a particular attraction in adapting?
I don't think of myself as deeply influenced by other playwrights, but I can see that when I was young I was so determined to break with what I saw as the continuum of British theatre, to try to create a *new* theatre, that it didn't seem worth spending a lot of time thinking about Ibsen and Chekhov and Brecht. I think it's a mark of an increased confidence that I now find working with these writers rewarding. I'm in a private dialogue with them about the way they write: I'm having an intimate dialogue with a whole lot of the world's greatest playwrights. More than that, I think the act of adaptation is a way of doing a production 'in your head'. When I hand over a new adaptation to a production company, I've already directed it in my mind; that's what I've done by putting it into English, and I've done it without the messy business of actually having to get actors to perform it in exactly the way I anticipate.

What about the two most recent adaptations, both of novels into films?
I just did the film of *The Hours*, which is the Pulitzer Prize-winning Michael Cunningham novel about Virginia Woolf. It is a sort of tribute to Virginia Woolf, set in the present day. Because I did that with Stephen Daldry, I've now been asked to do Jonathan Franzen's *The Corrections* with him. It's a hugely ambitious social chronicle of present-day America.

I enjoy the leap of the imagination into something that I know comparatively little about, something that is far away from me. To me the American novel represents a kind of vitality which is parallel to what we find in the performing arts in England. Michael Cunningham and (particularly) Jonathan Franzen write about novel-writing in the way that we – meaning my generation of playwrights – thought about play-writing. Before he wrote *The Corrections*, Franzen wrote a wonderful essay called 'Perchance to Dream', in which he simply asked:

'How do we re-engage the American social novel with the American public, and how do we do it in a way that will reach beyond the small academic readership to which most novels are addressed?' A great deal of my own professional life has been concerned with a similar question: how do we break theatre away beyond its traditional audience? Both Michael and Jonathan try to do with the novel in America what we try to do with the theatre in Britain. For me, that kind of 'social canvas' work – those novels, and also the work of Philip Roth, like *American Pastoral, I Married a Communist* and *The Human Stain* – are the parallel in America to what I wish to do here in the theatre. I take it as a given that the English novel is of almost no interest to people of my age and of my disposition.

So, to put it simply, you are still attracted by the idea of working on that big canvas, dealing with social engagement on a big scale.
Yes, completely. *The Corrections* is about a period of American history, and it takes a political view. Jonathan describes how it was the Gulf War that made him want to write the book. It uses the word 'capitalism', and it uses it as a familiar word, not something that you have to be ashamed about using. It talks about a particular period of boom before the 'correction' that is the bust; it's about the nineties. So suddenly you get an American novelist who has a political perspective, which is almost unheard of in the British novel. Of course I'm drawn to that, and I'm drawn to the energy as well: I'm attracted by the sheer narrative energy of both books.

How does that notion of grand scale square with your recent original work, which seems more 'private'? My Zinc Bed, after all, has just three characters which seem to materialize out of the air . . .
I don't know what to say about these plays – either *My Zinc Bed* or *The Breath of Life*, which I've just written, and which is again what you would describe as two people 'materializing'. *My Zinc Bed* for me has never happened: we ran it at the Royal

Court for seven weeks, but one of the actors didn't want to transfer, so I feel I haven't yet fully experienced it. I don't yet know what it is.

My Zinc Bed was deeply influenced by *Via Dolorosa*. I felt that what people were drawn to in *Via Dolorosa* was *portraiture*. People waiting at the stage door after the shows appeared to feel they knew me. Everybody who's been in a one-man show has this experience, and yet it's an illusion: Stephen Daldry and I had created a character called 'David Hare' who wasn't actually me, but the person that they spent the evening with. But they felt very close to me, and responded much more intimately than they had with certain of my plays. They had the illusion of having met a real person, and I wanted, with *My Zinc Bed*, to see if such profound portraiture was possible with three people, so that you'd leave the evening not judging them, but *knowing* them. That's what I was after, and I think it's also what I'm after in *The Breath of Life*. Contemporary consumer culture makes us feel that people don't run very deep. The whole endeavour of advertising, newspapers, television, cinema, is to make it seem that people are no longer very profound and mysterious. It's to make us seem all more alike: in other words, we all dress the same way, we all dress from 'Gap', we all watch the same things, we all consume the same stuff. We are reduced in some way to less than what in our most searching moments we know human beings to be. The theatre seems to be the place where you go back to be reminded how deep and dark human beings run. It's some sort of retrieval of the deepest things in people that I could feel happening in *Via Dolorosa*. I felt people come and think, 'I'm going to be bored by this – I'm not interested in Israel and Palestine,' but then I could feel them connect to the importance of the material. I wanted to do the same in *My Zinc Bed*. It's about addiction. It asks if we are doomed to act out patterns from which we can't escape and if we are simply running around like rats along a course which our addictions commit us to. Or is there such a thing as a free act of will any more in a consumerist, capitalist society? Is there such a thing as an authentic action any more? Can you escape your own addictions? It seems to me one of the most important and profound subjects I've ever addressed. Yet at the end of it, having had a wonderful run – for seven weeks I played to the youngest audience I've ever played to, people of my own children's age – it felt like unfinished business.

It's an interesting connection with Via Dolorosa. *Are you suggesting that the fact that that play was a monologue was in itself a political statement? That culture and politics now are so fragmented that a passionately political personal statement is almost the only form open to you? And that that sense of the personal, the private, was what you were trying to work with in* My Zinc Bed?

Yes. I'm having to think about these questions at the moment because I'm writing a John Osborne memorial lecture. It seems to me that the generation before us were romantic individualists: I'm thinking of figures such as John Osborne, David Mercer, Dennis Potter, Simon Gray, and to a degree Harold Pinter as well. What do we know about these people that they have in common? They are all difficult, bolshie, bad-tempered, rude, offensive, violently charged-up people who scream and shout! They are people who are almost proud of behaving badly. It seems to me with the benefit of hindsight that what is happening in their work is a kind of prescience about the reduction of the individual by consumer society. They scream because they sense that society is going to try and reduce the importance of individual emotion.

I believe that whenever history comes along with difficult circumstances (as it may, with Bush's foreign policies), circumstances in which you are forced to *choose*, in which people may be faced with agonizing questions about what they believe, then the individual will discover that his own particularity is as deep as ever. If you talk to Israelis and Palestinians, they don't have problems with a sense of identity, of being different from other people, because they are making the most profound choices

about their own lives all the time. With *Via Dolorosa*, I wanted
to go somewhere where the place you live, the person you have a
cup of coffee with, whom you know and whom you don't know,
is an expression of what you believe. I think it's very important
to know what you believe, because one day it is going to be tested. But we all live in a world where we think that won't happen:
as Osborne said, 'There are no good brave causes any more.'
When there are no brave causes, there is only yourself, and this
thing called truth and honesty whatever the price. If that means,
as it were, spitting on your wife's grave, as Osborne did, and saying that she was a bitch and you hated her, then of course people
are shocked – and John intends to shock, because he's saying:
'Everyone's telling us not to feel, well, damn you all, *I* feel.'

Now that sort of extreme romanticism was abhorrent to my
generation of playwrights. We had a different project, and we
are by and large more easy-going. You'll never meet nicer people than Howard Brenton or Caryl Churchill. We don't see the
playwright's job in such a romantic and individualist way as
the previous generation did. But, as the years go by, I suppose
I'm becoming more and more like the previous lot, and I'm
coming more to their point of view. I now feel a tremendous
affinity with that generation that I didn't feel at the time. I feel
that they are more like me than I did when I was young . . . or
maybe I'm becoming more like them.

*That idea of prescience is fascinating. It's the notion that
Chekhov's plays were unconsciously picking up the vibrations
of the Russian Revolution years before it happened.*
It's so true. I went to a reading of *Teeth 'n' Smiles* the other day.
It was written before punk, and it was about a bunch of hippies, but everybody in the room said, 'Was this about punk?' I
said, 'No, punk hadn't happened when I wrote this,' and yet
everything that created punk was in the air and it seems now
like a punk play. If you're any good at the job at all, that is
what happens: you pick up something before it happens rather
than after it happens.

Are you saying that, very simply, it's part of the territory as a playwright?
Completely. I think that's what good playwrights do. We were talking earlier about what Osborne represents, and *Look Back in Anger* represents some extraordinary acuteness about what people in the audience were feeling at that time but couldn't articulate. Then along comes the man who can articulate it. It's the same in America with *Catch 22*: Joseph Heller puts into writing what people have been silently feeling about the Vietnam War. I suppose it's a gift that I stress among dramatists in particular because it's something that I aspire to myself, the ability to 'feel the time'. I think we did it in *Pravda*, which is why *Pravda* took off: I think it put its finger on the spirit of the time before anyone else did. Afterwards, what *Pravda* – and *Serious Money* – had had to say became a so-called conventional analysis of Thatcherism, but before it wasn't really the press, or the novel, or even television that produced the critique, it was the theatre. I think that's why the theatre came under such attack in those years: it was a political attack. It may have been masked as an aesthetic attack, but actually it was a political attack on the idea of theatre itself, which a whole lot of Fleet Street journalists were very happy to join in.

Many people have commented on your ability to catch the zeit-geist; *is that a function of the particular way in which you approach the business of making work? Your plays, even from the earliest days, seem to me often to have worked in terms of clearing away what isn't true, what isn't of value, in an attempt to pinpoint what is true and of value ...*
Yes, I think that's right. I think there's a lot of correcting misapprehensions – of what you might call 'cleaning the gutters' – of what it isn't.

So it's rather like the story of the artist who, try as he might, couldn't draw a chair, so he tried drawing the space around the chair, and was left in the middle with ... a chair?
David Edgar argues that the scene in *The Absence of War*,

when, primed to speak about what he really feels and believes, George Jones *can't* speak, is the archetypal moment in modern drama. Just as, when Tony Blair was asked what he believed, he simply couldn't answer the question. I think most people can't – don't know how to – answer that question. But the sheer scale of what is at the centre of us is my subject and my interest. The claim of *Wetherby* – that beneath the surface of ordinary life lie huge, operatic dramas and issues – was much attacked, and people resented it, and wrote ferocious denunciations saying that 'Yorkshire people are straight and simple' and all that stuff. Yet whenever you actually see into a cross-section of people's lives – for example, when someone is caught, almost accidentally, in the glare of publicity, such as Diane Pretty [*the terminally ill woman who took her campaign for her right to be allowed to die to the High Court*] – you suddenly get an insight into how deep and complicated are the moral and spiritual lives of the most (apparently) ordinary people. That's what interests me as a writer.

That perhaps brings us on again to the sense in which your work is 'epic', of how by following the thread of a private, 'ordinary' story you can begin to unravel the big social tapestry. I think so. The writer that I most admire is Wallace Shawn, who I think is the greatest living American playwright bar none. He has a wonderful metaphor about a man sitting down to enjoy a cup of coffee, but the dog's barking outside, and if only that fucking dog would stop barking he could enjoy his coffee. That's exactly what our lives are like now. In the West, everything is set up for us. Optimum conditions are produced for us to be happy, yet for some reason we can't be happy; either because when we look out of the window we're not very pleased with what we see and have to turn our eyes away, or because 'happiness' doesn't turn out to be quite what was expected. As Wally says, the problem with satisfying your need for pleasure is that there's almost no limit to it: once you start saying, 'I'd like to stay in a more luxurious hotel, or live in a bigger house,' all that's left is a permanent sense of dissatisfaction. I think that's one of the things we caught in *Pravda*. That figure of the driven businessman, and that phrase about 'the melancholy of business', strikes a very deep chord: it's to do with the restlessness and anger that comes with great power and satisfaction. That sense of restlessness you can see clearly in Western life.

The critics seem to me often to misjudge your work, or at least to misread its intentions. Do you simply have to trust that your audiences will pick it up?

Yes. Certain things that you hope they are going to understand, they don't understand: you have to trust your own instincts that something is interesting and that it will resonate, and often you're wrong. A character that you thought would be instantly recognized, and whose dilemma you thought would seem very important, doesn't seem important. I felt this about Oscar Wilde. In advance, everyone said, 'Oh, Oscar Wilde, it's a very modern story,' but afterwards I was left unsure. It may have been my own failure in *The Judas Kiss* to make the subject seem urgent or contemporary, but I didn't feel that 'thing' happen in an audience, where they completely identify with something that they feel is common to them.

It's a difficult thing. You're talking to an audience that's just had Stephen Fry playing him in the movie aren't you . . .?

Yes, but there's no faking what goes on in an auditorium. The wonderful thing about the theatre is that the experience of sitting with other people in a room is unfakeable; you know if it's happening, or you know if it's not. In fact, there was an Australian production of *The Judas Kiss*, directed by Neil Armfield, with Bille Brown playing Oscar Wilde, which was (I don't think I would be betraying anybody to say so) a much better production than ours, and the Australian audience *did* connect with it. One of the fascinations of being a playwright is that you see what works in certain countries and not in others, and certain situations which seem terribly important in one country don't matter in another.

You've been to America often and had lots of work done there, and of course elsewhere in the world. Does that perspective feed into how you look at British society?

Oh yes. Again, quoting Wally, it was the sheer chance of his plays being played in England, and his English relationships with Caryl Churchill and Howard Brenton, which made him realize that America was just one more society: it wasn't 'Society', it wasn't how people ought to be, it was just one culture among many. America is so insular. I never for a moment after 'September 11' thought that America was seriously going to ask itself the question, 'Why do people hate us?' They asked it through their official organs for about three days, and then the question was banned. Now you're not allowed to ask it. 'September 11', apart from anything else, is a shocking indictment of the official American media: in the *New York Times*, in the *New Yorker*, in the *New York Review of Books*, it is impossible to ask serious questions about the effect of 'September 11' – even in the so-called liberal organs. The universal silence in the media is shocking. The only place you can ask questions is in the theatre.

Now yes, I've travelled a great deal, and obviously my generation was marked by the Vietnam War, too. Vietnam is the place that taught us how to think how we now think, or at least it's the place we set off from. And so going to Vietnam in 1970s, and seeing for myself that the price of the society in which I lived was being paid on the other side of the world in a very different kind of society, that has stayed with me. So I do have a sense of relativism between cultures, and it's been very important to me to see the plays performed abroad.

I greatly resent this idea that I'm a very 'English' writer. It's said only in England and I think it's absolute nonsense. Anybody who goes to see my plays in Paris, or in Cape Town, or in South America, can see that the audience is not responding to what is called their 'Englishness'. What it's responding to, always, is this area you're talking about, which is the area of 'What are we and how should we act?' That's what works when the plays work abroad – they don't say, 'Oh, it's so English'.

This is the problem, isn't it, with the way you are critically pigeonholed into a particular English tradition –
Exactly.

– and I think you say somewhere that one of the pleasures of having Skylight *on Broadway was the way in which the very different expectations of that American audience flooded into the play and discovered new things in it.*
That was a very interesting example of what I'm talking about. We went to New York thinking, in a very patronizing way, that the audience would respond to the character of the entrepreneur, but would struggle to make any sense of this woman who felt that she was on the social front line doing her best. On the contrary, the American audience knew Tom too well: he was too like everybody they already knew. They responded to the dilemma of Kyra, because they recognized their own lives in it, and that was a shock to us. The New York theatre-going audience said, 'That's what our lives are like, not like his'. That was fascinating.

Can we talk about your sense of the style of your writing a little?
To me, it's like a musical score. The previous generation's plays were more robust, I think. However badly you do Osborne's *Look Back in Anger*, it works. However badly you do *The Caretaker*, it works. But if you do *The Secret Rapture* badly, it doesn't work at all; I'm more performance-dependent than the previous generation. The usual explanation for that is that the previous generation began as actors and were in 'reppy' plays, so they built these sturdy vehicles that worked however badly you did them, but my plays are very performer-dependent. It's not that they need famous actors, or greatly gifted actors, but they do need actors who are willing to learn the score and get every single word in place musically. Judi Dench says that my stuff is the most difficult to learn that she's worked on, and, as she says, unless you get it absolutely word perfect, it doesn't feel right. I demand that it be learned in a particular way, and if you go off it for a second you lose the feeling. To me it is

musical, so it's very unsatisfactory to me when the music is wrong – and I think it's subtly unsatisfactory to the audience.

It sounds like jazz.
Exactly, but like the jazz musician, you've got to know the tune before you can improvise. The great performances of my work have been the ones where the score has been mastered, and off they go: in *Skylight*, for example, Michael Gambon and Lia Williams, and later Bill Nighy, got it. You always felt the beat underneath, even when they weren't playing the beat. But, as they say, you need fifty performances under your belt before you can reach that freedom. I have a very Germanic phrase, where I say to the actors: 'Beyond discipline, freedom'. That's it: you have to get the discipline first, and then you're free. But my plays only benefit by being played and played and played. The more they're played, the better they get. *Amy's View*, at the end of two years of being played, was much, much better and fresher than when it opened. The more Brendel plays Beethoven, the better he gets, and it is like music in that sense.

It is also like jokes, isn't it? Now obviously you write jokes . . .
Loads of jokes.

But not 'just' jokes – I'm thinking in particular of the cross-word joke at the beginning of the second half of Map of the World, *where the joke not only carries unexpected weight of meaning, but also sets through its delivery the dramatic struc-ture of the whole sequence. Is there a sense that, even when you're not writing specific jokes, the structure, the rhythm of the writing, is like a joke?*
Yes. I can't explain style. I just know that . . . I think Virginia Woolf says somewhere that meaning is conveyed as much through rhythm as it is through sense. This is what you learn as you go along, and it's what you work at more and more: the *sounds* of words doing a job as much as the words them-selves. You get to a point where you become almost unhealthily obsessed with it. When I'm writing dialogue, I have a very bad

thing happen to me: I can't make sense of the *Evening Standard*. I start reading a sentence in the *Evening Standard* and find myself saying, 'But that sentence has no rhythm.' It dismays me! I know that the plays I've been writing recently are more worked as poetry than the much looser stuff that I wrote years ago. Now every word has to be in place or I go nuts.

Again, huge discipline for the actor . . .
Yes, huge, and some actors feel constricted by it. They feel, 'Where's the freedom?'

Moving on, can I ask how you now see the relationship between your politics and your writing?
I think that I'm a political writer in two senses.

One is that I always have to know in advance what my own thinking is about my work. A lot of writers will say that they don't really know what they are writing about. I don't. I have to get the analysis first. I've often said that going to the Synod of the Church of England for me was a blinding moment of inspiration: that's when I got my politics straight. I didn't know that I was going to write three plays, but the three plays that followed [*the trilogy*] came out of my beginning to understand what the after-effects of Thatcherism were going to be. I came up, rightly or wrongly, with an analysis which argued that a load of intellectuals caused all that damage: right-wing intellectuals, with a series of madcap ideas about welfare dependency and monetarism. The effects of them being allowed to play in Downing Street were then being dealt with by a group of professionals: namely the police, the Church, lawyers, and Labour politicians. These people became my heroes. I stopped producing critiques of society and instead wrote plays in praise of those who sought to bandage society's wounds, of the people left to clear up the disastrous mess made by Thatcherism. Kyra in *Skylight* is that kind of person, as is Lillian in *Strapless*.

The second way in which I'm a political writer is simply that I believe in politics. I believe in social change and I believe in

the social view – in other words, that who we are is not determined by what we are born with in our heads, but by the historical circumstances by which we arrive on the planet. The
place, the time and the things that we do to each other have a
social effect. *The Caretaker* is a good example of what I call a
'bell-jar play'. It's a play that can take place in any time and any
place, always in a room, usually with walls. The drama is psychological and between people in that room. (Harold now
argues that his intentions were political; I don't believe him. I
think he's retrospectively ascribing politics to his early plays,
though they can undoubtedly be seen by the audience as political – *The Birthday Party*, especially.) I could never write a play
in which the engagement was purely psychological, because to
me, who people are is affected by time and place and the nature
of the society they live in.

How do you see yourself compared to other political drama-
tists? What about Brenton, your most frequent collaborator,
for example?
I always felt that Howard and I were completely different writers. The confusion between us was one we made ourselves, by
having worked together at Portable Theatre and by having
written plays together. The limits of what we could do together were that we could only write about what we thought
wrong. When two writers get on to the subject of what is *right*,
they're never going to agree, and Howard and I in particular
were never going to agree. I think Howard is much more scornful of social democracy than I am. To me social democracy is
the embodiment and expression of people's confusion and contradictions, so that I don't find it contemptible. I don't find
Tony Blair contemptible. He does a whole lot of things that I
disagree with and don't like, but I don't find him ridiculous. I
find the mess that he's now in our mess. It's a mess that I identify with. His confusion is not so different from my own.
Whereas when I've talked to Howard about Tony Blair, he sees
him as almost intrinsically absurd and doomed; I don't – unless

Howard sees us all as intrinsically absurd and doomed. He's us, Blair. We may not like it, but that's what he is.

Trevor Griffiths once said, affectionately, that 'the trouble with Howard is that he's a bloody Utopianist'. What about the utopianism in your writing? It seems to me your characters often achieve snatched moments of a kind of grace . . .
Exactly, but those moments distinguish our lives, don't they? I always used to say that it was about romantic love, because it's the most intense feeling people have. A lot of people live lives in which they sense that what they feel towards their partner is the most intense feeling they experience on Earth. I don't now tie it to romantic love. In *My Zinc Bed*, for instance, Paul's entry into Victor and Elsa's world, the enchanted evening when he sits there and decides to start drinking again, is for him one of the greatest moments of his life. And yes, I do try to write about that, and that lyric sense that human beings can suddenly have when they feel fifty feet high. It's so important to remind people that that's part of living.

So it's not the case the romantic love in itself is the subject?
It's one of the means you happen to have to go through to produce those kinds of moment.

The same thing is true of language, isn't it? There's an eroticism to your writing. In something like Saigon, *even leaving aside the romantic scenes between Barbara and Chesneau, there's a kind of teasing erotic play to how characters test, explore, try to define each other, that's nothing to do with sex or romance . . .*
Yes. Actually, I wrote a very successful (I felt) erotic scene in *Saigon*, which the actors refused to perform because they said it was too dirty. There were only two words in it, neither of which was obscene, but that was absolutely the feeling. Sensuality. I felt Julia Ormond had it in *My Zinc Bed*: you could feel the whole audience sensed it. It wasn't that it was erotic, it was sensual. You felt that with Elsa, and Julia Ormond's playing of her, that there was this wonderful, sensual

play about the character, that made every man and woman in the audience want to spend time with her. It's an almost painterly thing; the sensuality of paint is exactly what I love to summon up in the theatre. I have gone through profound jealousy of painters.

It's that sense of wanting to touch?
Yes: wanting to touch, and feel, and be with, just to remind you of the richness of life. I love that in the theatre.

There is an even greater sense of eroticism then: you're saying to the audience, 'You want to touch this, but you can't – you've got to sit there'?
Yes, absolutely, because that's what I loved as a child when I went to the cinema or the theatre: the *feel* of the world that was on the screen or stage. I'll never forget it. The things that made the deepest impressions on me seem to be the deepest worlds. Hitchcock had it in the Technicolor period: in something like *Vertigo* you feel how incredible it must be to inhabit that universe he creates. That's one of the things I like to do on the stage: to make you think that it's part of a wonderful world. Vietnam before the fall did have an incredible sensual dazzle to it, and I wanted to write about that in *Saigon*.

An obvious question to conclude: how do you see the theatre now? Its role, if you like, the part it plays in where we are now, politically, socially, culturally . . .
I don't know how to talk about it. As [*the film director*] Stephen Frears says, one day he's rung up by a journalist who asks him about the state of the British film industry and he says 'Disastrous', and the next day he'll say 'Terrific', and both things are true. The fact that the theatre, in any form, has survived the incredible battering that it's taken over the last thirty years is wonderful. The battering has been not entirely from politics, but also from the rise of reproduced entertainment and from a particular way of looking at the world that is not suited to theatre (plainly, the growth of celebrity culture is not a

means by which you can usefully discuss the theatre, unless it's Nicole Kidman and *The Blue Room*). In other words, to survive at all in this climate is miraculous. On the other hand, you might say that, given that the climate is the way it is, the opportunity for a different culture is so much the greater. People argue about whether it is possible to make an impact with a play now in the way that *Look Back in Anger* did in 1956. I would say, 'Well, twenty years ago, Alan Bleasdale's *The Boys From the Black Stuff* made exactly the kind of profound social impact that we know a work of art can make on a society'. I think it's still possible. The work just isn't good enough, and that is a failure of the writer to make theatre seem sufficiently important. However, is it a climate in which it is easy to do it? Plainly not. I do think that the sort of handing-over of the National Theatre to operetta, or to musical comedy, is a tacit way of saying, 'We do not believe that there can be a contemporary playwright of sufficient importance or urgency to write for these huge theatres on contemporary subjects.' Now, as I was doing precisely that ten years ago, I take the change of direction as a grave personal insult. I think it's an abdication of policy: I don't think it's a policy at all. I don't see that reviving American musicals of the mid-twentieth century is a policy for a national theatre. Does that then filter down into the attitudes of theatres throughout the country? Yes, there's a very great danger of it. Do I see a revival of the kind of theatre that I think is important? Sporadically, yes, but I think it's fitful.

3

Working with Hare

Bill Nighy

Bill Nighy is one of our most respected stage and screen actors, and has a long association with Hare's work. He played William, the narrator and leading character of the 1980 TV play Dreams of Leaving, *Stephen Andrews in the British première of* A Map of the World *(1983), Eaton Sylvester in* Pravda *(1985) and Edgar in Hare's production of* King Lear *at the National in 1986. He also played Tom Sergeant in* Skylight *in 1997, winning 'Best Actor' in the Barclay's Theatre Awards.*

I began by asking about his views on the style of Hare's work:

Whatever the demands of individual plays, it's true that there is an overall style to David's work, which – probably almost subconsciously – leads you to approach it in a way that is unique. I admire his writing as much as I admire anybody's, the beauty, elegance and power of it. You don't, for instance, have to concern yourself with authenticating it in the terms of naturalism: there is a 'spin' on it, to put it clumsily, that helps you, once you've become accustomed to his work. Stephen Moore [*the actor who played Brock in the first production of* Plenty] once said that in order to perform David's plays, you have to know five hundred different ways of saying the word 'well'! One of the things David achieves is to write dialogue that recognizably reflects ordinary human speech and human exchange, but which is poetic in a modern way. It has great beauty, eloquence, is tremendously witty and deals with profound things.

How do you approach that as an actor?

It's difficult to put your finger on. It's your job as an actor to make dialogue appear authentic within the convention of the play: to make it appear as if the words you're speaking are occurring to you for the first time. With David's work you have an extra yard or two to go to honour its poetic quality. It's not a struggle, in fact. Great art, however else you feel about it, gives you a feeling of familiarity with it; it's as if the words were something you were about to say if you'd have got round to it, or as if it was something that you were born knowing. You only get it with great writers. The problem with 'great art', though, is that there can develop an over-respectful, even awestruck way of performing it: when I first saw the script of *Dreams of Leaving*, I mistook it in a way that I think people sometimes mistake Pinter or Shakespeare, for instance. Harold Pinter's plays used to be produced in such a way that the actors seemed to have inherited a particular tradition of performing them. Every time they opened their mouths it was as if to say something terribly important; the plays were performed, as it were, in church, with nobody laughing, the jokes going for nothing because they were all delivered as if something deeply symbolic were being said. I think that is probably the opposite of what is required. Harold has made it plain enough that there is a complete absence of symbolism in his work: what you see is what you're supposed to see, and what you hear is what you're supposed to hear. 'That's all she wrote,' as Hank Williams once famously said. Similarly, when I first read a David Hare script, I thought that something other than naturalism was required of me, and I was confused because I was not used to seeing such successfully achieved writing. But once I'd done a couple of his plays, new scripts started to become more familiar and comfortable, and I couldn't wait to speak them. So it *is* 'naturalism', but there is a kind of extra muscle required. There are eloquent people in his plays, who say some of the most beautiful, profound and funny things that I've ever seen written on a page, but it never betrays the convention, it never betrays 'naturalism'.

Skylight, for instance, which is one of my favourites, is so marvellous because it deals with one of the central facts of our lives: what do you do about the poor, about being more wealthy and powerful than the people around you? How do you live in the world when it's so unbalanced? Yet it is shown in the form of a love story, with, most of the time, just two people in a room. But it's a love story which exactly mirrors the larger struggle outside. It's that thing that everybody tries to achieve: to make a story, a play, which incorporates everything you want to express, and on several levels at the same time, all completely and beautifully integrated. It's a magnificent achievement.

With a figure such as Tom in that play, are you conscious of working off and against an audience expectation of what it is to be a Thatcherite businessman?
Yes. One of the things that I admire about David's plays is that I have been encouraged from an acting point of view never to make moral judgements about the character I was playing. You have to allow the audience to do that. And as an actor, and as an audience, you do not necessarily believe how the other characters describe you, behave around you, judge you, either. I'm very interested in plays that reveal the world to be a place that is not easily dividable into right and wrong, or into heroes and villains. For an actor playing Tom it gives enormous satisfaction to go on in a cashmere overcoat, with a bit of a tan, and present this brash figure in surroundings which seem rather unlikely, with a young woman whose life plainly isn't the same, knowing that you are about to present a complete human being and not just a device to illustrate just how bad people can be. This is a real person, his name's Tom Sergeant, and in a moment he's going to show you just how confused he is, and how, if money really helped, we'd have heard about it. Similarly with Kyra, you see that things aren't simple in that way either. I think the world needs as many of those reminders as possible. It's too easy to stereotype on stage and in life.

Tom's a wonderful part to play, because from a comic point of view he's so blissfully and sublimely pleased with himself that he's got all these *things* – a private beach in the Caribbean and a lovely house and so on – and he finds it incomprehensible that Kyra *doesn't* want them. To swish around in a cashmere coat in that flat is a beautiful and very pointed image. As well as being a wonderful writer of words, David is also very particular about how everything looks, and he's very, very good at finding accurate, beautiful images that tell parts of the story without words. The final image of Kyra and [*Tom's son*] Edward enjoying a boot-legged five-star-hotel breakfast in her modest flat before she goes off to work again is enough to send you out sword-fighting down the street with hope in your heart.

When you act Hare, does the writing push you towards starting to work with the inner psychological life of a character, or with its place in the story, or argument, of the play?
'Inside out' or 'outside in'? It's a question that actors are often asked, and the answer is both yes and no. We could talk all day about this: there has always been a huge debate about psychological acting. Performance takes place in a kind of altered state, brought about by adrenaline and terror, so it's a bit hard to report back from there. Melvin Bragg once asked David Mamet: 'If an actor's playing a plumber, does he have to go and do a six-month plumbing course and then come to rehearsals?' Mamet replied that he didn't mind what they did as long as when they arrived onstage they communicated. He then added, 'They may as well wear a necklace of garlic around their necks to ward off self-consciousness.' Bragg said, after a rather stunned silence, 'Am I to take it that you are dismissing seventy years of psychological acting?' There was a long, rather wonderful pause, and then Mamet said, 'Yep.' In my case, if you had a gun at my head I would scream 'outside in', at least in terms of the rehearsal process.

There are parts of David's work that require great emotional turmoil, or at least you have to *resemble* someone who is undergoing great emotional turmoil. If you are playing, say, someone who is grief-stricken, you don't have to go back to when you were a child and your dog died, because the thing that you have been asked to present is *in itself* terribly affecting. For people who don't act, acting is seen as a matter of all the 'feeling' involved. For an actor, it's often the case that he is too busy for all of that. He's at work. There are so many things moment to moment that must be achieved. He doesn't have the time. The audience can't know what's going on inside him, and it remains therefore beside the point.

Sticking with this notion of 'inside out/outside in', how aware are you, when you play Hare, of the politics of the work? Or is that something you let happen?
I was thirty-two when I was given the chance to do *A Map of the World*, and I had unfocused political feelings. But I had the pleasure, particularly in the second act, of delivering speeches that were everything I wanted to say out loud in front of that many people. It drove me to make it as clear as possible, and I was also driven by a desire to win the debate with Mehta – and David always said, 'On any given night, it's up to you or Roshen Seth [*who played Mehta*] to win it.' Really win it, not act winning it. But also I felt excited about saying the things that I, personally, had to say. The thing about sophisticated plays is that everybody gets to say the good stuff. You don't have, as in less sophisticated plays, a character who comes on finally and tells you how the author thinks you should live or think. That's what's marvellous about David's work: 'good' characters sometimes get to talk tosh, as well as what the audience might think are 'bad' characters. The devil doesn't get all the good jokes, and sometimes unlikely people get to say the most profound things, which is the way life is.

It's that old theatrical convention that audiences tend to believe that the character who speaks most is representing the playwright's position, isn't it? In Dreams of Leaving, *the part you played had a particularly great authority: you had his voice-over, it was his story, we saw it from his perspective, yet his authority was undermined. The convention leads us to trust him, but then we realized that this was a weak, untrustworthy character – who was nevertheless absolutely right about certain things.*

Yes, that's the case, and that's what's radical in terms of story-telling – it's fabulous, and I love it. But I have always been aware of the politics. I was politicized by [*the ground-breaking BBC drama flagship*] 'Play for Today': Dennis Potter was my education, along with other people. I've sort of been educated in the theatre, and I've been very lucky in that I've had the opportunity to do plays that were in tune with things that I felt. You're trying to tell the story and you're trying to serve the text, so you do whatever's required, but your own feelings inform the way you do it. I've been spoiled: I've had the deep satisfaction of performing David Hare plays, and there have been moments where I have been required to deliver lines that rang in my heart and in my head.

What about something like Skylight, *where the politics are much more 'submerged' (Hare calls it a 'submerged epic')? Can you play the politics in that?*

You don't have to, because it's so beautifully made. You don't play the politics. I don't mean to suggest by anything I've said that you play politics. You can't play politics. In *Skylight*, for instance, you don't have to do anything except deliver *Skylight*. That is, you impersonate, in my case, a man who has this particular experience on this particular evening, and if you achieve that as well as you can, then the audience goes away having received everything that David intended. It *is* an epic: it concerns itself with just about the most central fact of our lives. It's about something that everybody thinks about several times a day in one form or other. Every time you think about your sense of your own status in the world, you are touching upon what *Skylight* touches upon; every time you check your wallet, every time you look across the street and see someone who is disenfranchized or lonely or ill, and every time you pick up a newspaper and read that children have been abandoned, by the government or by individuals . . . it's everything. That's part of what David's work offers us: you get a close look, a proper look, a respectful look at different kinds of people, and you discover that no one gets anything out of this present system. Except that's not entirely true, of course: some people get to live, some people get to be very, very comfortable, some people don't. Some people get to die, some people get to live in despair and shit. The solution doesn't lie in individual blame, but in understanding how the whole system works to produce that inequality, that injustice, and in examining our own behaviour and relations with people trying to lead decent lives.

We're straight back to the end of Dreams of Leaving, *where he talks about the quiet desperation of people's lives and their misery . . .*
'Our lives dismay us. We know no comfort. We have dreams of leaving. Everyone I know.'

On a very different tack, what about Pravda?
It was an enormous pleasure, and it was one of the happiest professional times of my life. We'd rehearsed for nine weeks at the National, doing jokes that people ceased to find funny after about the second week because we'd heard them, and then we went out in front of about a thousand people for the first preview, and had to worry about their health, they were laughing so much. You had to give the audience time to recover from the last joke because they were having trouble breathing. It was also great to see the wonderful reception Anthony Hopkins received on what was his return to the major British stage, and to have done something about Rupert Murdoch. To go to work every day, and get paid, and be given the opportunity to do something about Rupert Murdoch, was in itself deeply satisfying, because, as the play tells you, nobody else was doing anything about Rupert Murdoch except rolling over and taking the money. And the play turned out to be this comic epic. It was

one of the first modern plays ever to be produced in the Olivier theatre (which caused much consternation to the people on the top floor, because that stage had never been associated with a modern work), and it was beautifully directed by David. Again, it's epic. I do think David has a taste for emptying the stage – you get it in *Pravda*, and you get in *Map of the World* – and I love those empty spaces. In *Map of the World* he emptied it right back, to make it like a film studio, and then in *Pravda* we had the Yorkshire Moors.

Anthony Hopkins was brilliant: he based Le Roux on a mixture of David O. Selznik (the Hollywood producer), Stalin and a lizard. He did most of his performance on tiptoe with his tongue hanging out. Playing his sidekick was as near as I'll ever get to [*the comedy double act*] Morecambe and Wise really: I used to have these wonderful feed lines for Tony. It was most satisfying: they all came, the people we were supposed to be satirizing – Lord Goodman came with his lawyer, Reese-Mogg sent his lawyer – but they couldn't touch anybody. It was a great opportunity to *do* something, because the world can drive you mad, and one of the things then, and still now, was Rupert-fucking-Murdoch. But the brilliant thing about David and Howard's take on him was that he was a great nihilist: he was a kind of blind force. He's just better at it than anyone else. There was the great black joke about 'In my lovely home in Limfontaine I have a million books. I don't have to read them, my mind is made up'. It's a fantastic thing.

What so angered and motivated David and Howard was that the establishment just rolled over. *The Times* newspaper, for instance. Murdoch came along and lowered the tone and the standards of a whole nation, and we continue to suffer from it now. He abandoned manners, and it eats away at us still. Nothing has ever been done about it, presumably because it's too scary and that man can destroy you. David and Howard come from sterner stuff: they come from a radical tradition, and I was so proud to be in it.

*Pravda, obviously, is a comedy. What about the comedy else-
where in his work?*

David writes brilliant jokes, but they're often more than jokes.
One of the most beautiful examples is in *Map of the World*:
what happens straight after the interval in that play is in my
experience one of the most beautifully constructed comic
scenes ever written. It's the crossword joke, where Martinson
thinks the answer to 'It's the plague of the earth' is 'Zionism';
pages later, M'Bengue points out the right answer is 'Slavery'.
At that moment, the whole moral frame of the play switches:
through a joke we're made to see the world differently, like
M'Bengue sees it. And David delays and delays the punchline:
the whole of the first part of the scene is this long, beautiful
joke, but it contains all these 'depth charges', *and* it tells the
story, makes the argument.

*Brenton once said that he only learned to write plays when he
learned how to write jokes, because of the absolute discipline
that jokes demand, and because the structure of a joke is like
the structure of an argument . . .*

Well, jokes are constructed like clocks, as precisely as anything
you can imagine. It's true that the quality of laughter you will
receive is proportionate to how carefully you follow David's
instructions – the instructions within the writing. If there's one
'I don't know', or 'well', or even '. . .' not observed, you *might*
get a laugh, because it's funny, but it won't be all it could or
should be. If Howard says that learning to write plays was
learning how to write jokes, then with David you could almost
say the same is true for acting, because the same disciplines are
involved. It's absolute, as you say, and you have to work out
how to do it, and maybe to delay it, or when to pause, or when
to ring the consonants a little tighter than you would normally
do; you must always make sure that if there is a consonant on
the end of the last word of the punchline it is unnaturally
stressed, because if the audience don't hear it in unison, you
won't get the laugh – simple stuff. It's almost always an audi-

bility problem, or an ill-judged intonation, if you don't get the laugh – it's usually something terribly simple.

Lia Williams

Actress Lia Williams has appeared in a number of feature films, including Firelight *(1998) and, most recently,* The King is Alive *(Dogme95, 2001); television work includes* The Uninvited *(1997) and* Imogen's Face *(1998). Since winning a Critics' Circle Best Newcomer's Award (1991) for her work in Alan Ayckbourn's* The Revengers' Comedies *(1991) she has worked extensively on stage, most notably in the plays of Harold Pinter, with* The Lover *(1998),* Celebration *and* The Room *(2000) and* The Homecoming *(2001). She created the part of Kyra in Hare's* Skylight, *for which she was nominated for Olivier and (following the production's transfer to Broadway) Tony Awards.*

Richard Eyre directed the play; was Hare involved in the rehearsal process much?

Yes. After the audition (where both David and Richard were present, and very much like a double act), Michael Gambon and I were invited to read the play through in an office with them and some other people from the National, just to hear it out loud. That's the first time I started to get an idea of David, and the most extraordinary thing about that occasion was that from that first reading – and the original copy of *Skylight* was as thick as the telephone directory – he went home and instantly cut thirty pages from the script. I found that extraordinary, that a writer could so willingly say, 'No, no, no, get rid of it'. It's a very healthy thing to be able to do. From that one reading he managed to cut it back to its quick, which I always remember as being very brave.

Did that go on? Was he making cuts and changes through the process?

Very much so. As we went through the process of rehearsal, David would be in and out the whole time. He worked very closely with Richard and with us. The other startling thing was that we were into the second week of rehearsal – as far as that – when we all sat round a table and said, 'This ending doesn't work: it doesn't feel right'. We felt that Michael Gambon's character, Tom, desperately needed to leave with some kind of dignity, or that the ending of the play needed something more purposeful. We talked this over for a while, and David left, and came back a day or two later with the most passionate ending I think he's probably ever written. It was very, very personal, and very surprising to him, I think. For him to go away with the thoughts that we'd all shared, and to come back a day later with the most extraordinarily different and beautiful ending, which felt as if it had been wrenched from the heart, stunned everybody.

It's Kyra's speech really, where she says something along the lines of 'I love you, I've always loved you, but I can't be with you' [*the ending of Act Two, scene one*]. They both give each other great dignity, and they are deeply and utterly in love with one another, but there's an understanding that they can't be together. That simply wasn't there before: Gambon's character left too easily. David said, 'Just read it. Read it out loud, I don't know what it's like'. So we read it, and there was silence. We read it as if we were reading a dictionary or something – without any invested feeling – because we didn't know what we were reading, and yet these exquisitely beautiful last five pages came out of our mouths. We all sat in silence afterwards, and then Richard Eyre said: 'Yes. I think that'll be very good'. And that was it.

Would you say Hare understands actors particularly well?
I think so, because he directs; though I also think it's a dilemma. He does work, he does communicate with you, as an *actor*, as opposed to a character (something that's two-dimensional on the page, as it were) but often his intellect will disrupt that. He's got a fierce, laser mind, and he can get frustrated: he often wants things to happen instantly, and that's not how *Skylight*

worked. The play unpeels like an onion, until you get to the core of it; it strips itself back as it goes through the past to reveal the 'now'. That's a fantastic technique, because you're stripping it away to a bare nothing. That's what we did in rehearsal: we stripped back the layers, and that took time. It was a difficult process which David would sometimes get frustrated with, because I think he wants answers 'now', he wants things to be 'now' . . . He could often be quite abrasive, but it's simply his artistic frustration, his intellect and then this very volatile, passionate soul, all working simultaneously. Sometimes those qualities hit up against each other – and that's what creates terrific writing at the end of the day. But it's often difficult for things to be smooth.

Do you think Hare's writing is in any way like Pinter's?
No. Not really. I was about to say that their structure, their 'scaffolding', is absolute and rock-solid and lethally correct, but I think that's the only area. I think they approach their work in very different ways. I suppose there could be a comparison between him and Pinter, because Pinter writes jazz – most of his plays are 'jamming sessions' really – and David, too, has a great sense of musicality about his writing which I respond to instinctively and love.

There's a frustration when you begin to rehearse David, because when you first read it on the page, it seems to be naturalism; then you start speaking it out loud, and you realize that it is not. It is a unique style, which only belongs to him, and it becomes an enormous battle once you've made that discovery. You battle away to try to make that style inhabit you; you're trying to 'tuck it into you' and make it your character.

That was really one of the most frustrating things we found about *Skylight*: it had to appear to be totally naturalistic, but in essence it wasn't. That, for both Michael and for me, was extremely frustrating, until David came into rehearsal one day and said, 'One day, you will just fly. It will happen; it's just a matter of time and familiarity.' And that's what happened. It's just like riding a bicycle – you can suddenly say, 'Hey, look – there it is, I'm doing it!' His language, the way his phrasing is, is unique to him, and it's not behaviouristic at all: it's strong, clear dialogue, and totally theatrical.

It's interesting you say this, because Kate Nelligan made a similar point when she played Jenny in Knuckle *(much earlier in his career), asking Hare why all his characters 'sounded the same'? He said – 'Because there's such a thing as style. We expect that of a painter, why shouldn't we expect that of a playwright as well?'*

I totally agree with him. I identify with what Kate Nelligan said, and I agree with it completely. His characters often have the same phrasing and the same use of certain words ('Oh sure' – he'll use 'sure' a lot) and *all* his characters would use this . . . and then finally you listen to it, and it's great. It's very much its own style: the characters within that work totally independently, but it's within the framework of a David Hare play. When I played Ruth in *The Homecoming*, Pinter's punctuation became very important. I discovered how to play her by looking at the way she was, the way her sentences finished or didn't finish, by the way she was silent, by the way she was phrased, and I realized that she had a totally separate 'music'. I think that is essentially different from Hare, although Pinter, of course, still has a very defined sense of overall style.

What about the non-verbal aspects of performing Hare? In My Zinc Bed *he makes clever use of particular objects in a largely empty space, for example – though in* Skylight *you were working on a much fuller and more naturalistic set, weren't you?*

Very much on a set, and also for the entire first act I was cooking a meal, and that had its own 'music'. I worked very hard to use the preparation and the cooking of the meal to punctuate the emotional drive of the scene, or the point that the character was trying to make at the time, so I'd tip the pasta into the bowl at a very specific moment, for example. I used the cooking as punctuation – as percussion, if you like – so that the final moment – when she throws the tray of cutlery about the place, that was very much 'clanging symbols' [*sic*]!

Do you think the nature of Hare's writing requires a particular discipline of his actors in terms of how they move, the space between them, their gestural vocabulary?
That's true of any stage acting. I think David would find that crucially important, but then I do as an actor anyway, because it informs the audience of certain things. He's absolutely right, and he is meticulous about that, but I don't see how it could be any other way. It *is* true that if one was less specific, one could be telling a different story with any given moment, and he wouldn't like that: he's fairly rigid and perfectionist about his work. There's one through-line, and he likes that line to be played to the hilt. He can get quite gruff if one isn't presenting the thing that he is imagining.

Do you think that's a good thing?
I think he has a right to it, because he's such a fine writer. I think lesser writers should be able to let go more, and open up for greater interpretation, but he is such a fine writer that one trusts his knowledge. He has an odd mix between an extraordinary innocence and an intellectual, political fierceness. He's at conflict with himself, I would imagine.

Out of which the writing comes, as you suggested earlier . . . He's known, of course, as a political dramatist. To what extent did you feel in the performance or the rehearsals that the politics were present?
Quite rarely. He did move away with *Skylight* from a lot of his polemic. Because it was essentially a love story, first and foremost – or I believe it was, anyway – and because I could understand Kyra and immerse myself in that, I didn't feel like her character was trying to sell a political line to the audience; neither did I feel that Michael Gambon's character was. I think in some plays he does like to do that: he has some urgent need to tell us what he thinks in quite a passionate way, and he's loth to

throw up an alternative argument to it, or *not* provide answers. He likes sometimes to tell us what he thinks and then tell us what the solution is. That is totally opposite to Pinter, who doesn't provide any answers: he's completely amoral, and has no sense of judgement whatsoever. I think David's characters are much more judgemental of each other, which people are in life, but I feel as if he made a move away from that in *Skylight*. It was there, it added an interesting layer, but not profoundly so.

But isn't Kyra one of those decent, ordinary people, who strug-gle on against the odds trying to do the right thing, whom he celebrates in the trilogy?
Yes, absolutely, but I'm not convinced . . . I think, for me, it was more about the human condition. She's a very flawed person, which is great because it didn't place her on a pedestal. The way she behaved at the end was desperately lonely. If she was more of a grown-up she might have turned to him and said, 'Let's try again, let's see if we can work this through; I'm sure it's possible in some way.' I think that would have been more adult. I don't think she was making any plea for what you were just describing; I think she was just – well, I'm less fond of her at the end than I think you might have been. I think she was willing herself to be determinedly independent and do good . . .

In a self-destructive way?
. . . and in the process destroy her happiness, yes. I do like play-ing characters that aren't perfect, and if a halo appears to be developing over their heads, then I more often than not try to rub it out. I don't think people are like that and I think that the human condition is much more fascinating to watch with all that crap.

Hare has always been known for writing central parts for women, and associating with those characters some quality of goodness – old-fashioned goodness. Do you think he writes female parts well?

He's been accused, hasn't he, of making angels out of women; but I think that's all dependent on interpretation. I think Kyra is an essentially good person in that she's not a bad person! I suppose he's in danger of making them appear too moral in some ways, of being the moral centre of his plays.

Tom does accuse her of being self-righteous at one point.
Oh yes, and she is, and there's a marvellous self-righteous political speech that she makes at one point, saying, 'You people can fuck off, 'cause I'm doing something worthy . . .'; but that knocks her off her pedestal. Although it's interesting because I would get letters from people – from men as much as women, and particularly from teachers – who really believed the character held the key to the future.

How did the show change when you took it to Broadway?
We had to make it bigger. It was very intimate at the Cottesloe (and probably it was best there), although when we took it to Wyndham's, in the West End, we had to make it a bigger performance, and we had to project our voices. In the very simple process of doing that, we realized what a big play it was, that it was taking on huge, 'Greek' subjects. We realized that we were dealing with something that could crack the templates of the earth if we wanted it to, because it was about big emotion – quite a removal for David, in a way. Then, when we took it to New York, it had to become bigger still, because it was a bigger theatre and the audiences demanded the love story. Interestingly, too, they much preferred Kyra in New York: they loved her dry humour and her sense of irony. On the opening night there, I got a lot of laughs that I've never experienced in London, and I was quite taken aback by it. I absolutely relished it. I'd always thought that the laughs should be there, and felt that it was my failure that they weren't; but actually I think that the New York audience 'got' Kyra much more readily. They loved her passion and her fierceness, and her sensitivity with this love; they saw it as a great love story, and really ran with it. There's nothing like a New York audience when they decide they like you.

Hare's success in New York always interests me: in Britain, he's often seen as a very English figure, all repressed emotion and coolness . . .

That's why *Skylight* is so extraordinary: it's as if for a moment in time he cut himself open and let out this extraordinary stuff, and then zipped it back up again. And that's what an actor does. That's what I responded to in the play. I remember reading it, and by page five I was terribly excited and I felt as if he had really cracked something open – for himself.

I always say to him, when I see his plays and drop him notes, that I'm knocked into the back of my seat by his bravery. He could be firing on all cylinders in all sorts of crazy directions, and you'll be saying, 'No you can't do that!' or 'No, your voice is too loud – I can only hear your voice, I can't hear the actor,' but I have nothing but admiration for a writer who can be so bold, and so brave, and so much on the balls of his feet, and so able to make mistakes and to wear his emotions on his sleeve as he does. I find that very un-English, and very admirable.

Rick Fisher

Rick Fisher is currently Chair of the Association of Lighting Designers, and is one of the leading practitioners in his field: he has worked extensively in dance, opera and musical theatre, as well as in the 'straight' theatre. His portfolio includes work for the National and Royal Court Theatres as well as on Broadway, and he has won a Tony and two Olivier Awards. He has worked with Hare on The Designated Mourner, Via Dolorosa *and – the first topic of our conversation –* My Zinc Bed:

What hit me immediately about the play is that it's almost made out of light, isn't it? It 'materializes' out of the air . . .

When David approached me about it, he said, 'I've written this play, and I'd like you to do it because I've written a lot of light in, so I think you'd find it interesting'. And indeed I did. I was quite surprised – a bit dumbfounded, almost – at how much light he *had* described in the play. I was moved by that because I thought maybe because we've worked together he's become more conscious of what light can do during a production. Some of the lighting notes that he described in the printed text we realized onstage, and others we chose not to, as is ever the case. Working with him as a director, we chose not to make all the choices that he chose to make as an author.

I think it's a piece that he always saw being staged in a fairly non-naturalistic way (maybe because he also had a bit of his director's hat on). He felt the play should be conjured out of *things*, out of the air. He wanted things there that were *suggestive*. I looked at one model of an early design for the show (some of which stayed and a lot of which went), and entered into the process that he and Vicki [*Mortimer, the scenic designer*] were going through. Almost all the real, literal allusions to things went. It became much more as if it were smoke and mirrors that created the world of these people. I think that is so appropriate for describing somebody – Victor – whose world is the world of an internet company. And what is that? Is it something real or something not real? What *is* the net? Is it real information or is it just electronic information? The difference between those things became echoed in the physical representation of the space that we chose to set the play in, and I think light and electricity were part and parcel of that.

One of the things that is said about Hare's writing – often critically – is that it's 'cold' in its 'objectivity'. Did that translate into the way you thought about the lighting at all? Did it translate into which gel you put in a lantern?
In the end there was a lot that was quite cool in the environment that we chose. There were those cool frosted glass (or frosted Perspex) surfaces that reminded me of that nice quality, that green edge, you get on plate glass, so I was very much conscious of those colours, as well as greys and steel, and that kind of very modern feel that an internet tycoon might surround himself with. Those very cool, smooth surfaces that don't have

much detail on them . . . One thing you have to say about David, though, is that he's absolutely passionate about the theatre. Any coolness that one might perceive in his writing is wonderfully counterbalanced by the importance to him of people speaking in front of an audience – them telling their story. And so in a physical staging of *My Zinc Bed*, trying to get that balance was one of the challenges that we strove to achieve. These people were all in their own worlds, but all interacting. I don't know if we completely got that right the first time, but a lot of it did happen. There's a kind of energy between these people: they are all adrift in their own very cool worlds, but when they come together something sparks; there's a heat generated even in the 'misfiring' of people coming together, or people *not* making the connection.

So it's not just 'atmospherics', but the dynamic structure of the play and how light can help that?
Light in any theatre production can offer a number of different qualities to help in the staging of it. One of them is just by providing illumination, of course, so you can see people – that's its most basic form. In addition, it can offer atmosphere and location, place-setting, time of day, those sorts of things, which are the standard kinds of information light is used to help convey. But as more and more people write plays that have multiple settings, or 'cross-cut', or have asides, or characters going in and out of settings, light is used in a way that is much more filmic: it can show different realities, add punctuation, pull something out of a scene, so that the audience doesn't worry about the fact that someone is addressing it directly from the stage, even though the person sitting next to that someone is still in character. I think David very much wanted to exploit those tools when he wrote *My Zinc Bed*, and was very aware that he could do it.

It's interesting that you mention film, because of course Hare is also a film-maker with a long personal love of cinema, and there's often a filmic quality to his stage writing. But you're not talking about putting film light on a stage, are you? That's a very different thing.

No. I think it's using film 'tricks', using the light to help edit. Light acts like a film editor acts on a real piece of film, choosing which bits to cut together. Light in the theatre can help edit what's there. You look at a certain part of the stage, you look at a certain person, you choose to put two people onstage in different qualities of light – that is like a double exposure in a film – you 'bleed in' from one thing to another, keeping one person in soft focus, putting somebody else in hard focus. Theatrically you can use light to do a lot of that, and there were many times in *My Zinc Bed* when we had people onstage at the same time, but they were inhabiting different, slightly overlapping worlds, and the light was there to follow people around and edit what the audience was seeing of the stage space – so we wouldn't give too much of the stage space away.

The play uses distance a lot as well, doesn't it? Characters are described as being huge distances apart, yet the Royal Court stage is not that big.

No. It's twenty-one feet across, and it's probably barely twenty feet deep, so it is a question of using light to help create that distance on stage just by placement. It's amazing how audiences come *wanting* to have their imagination shaped and worked, and what was great about *My Zinc Bed* was that it did actively engage people's imaginations. You could easily do a television film of *My Zinc Bed*: it would be fine, it would be interesting, and the stories would still come out as well. But the pleasure of having that story told to you would probably not be as great. You would use real locations, and typical television devices of having somebody talking as they are walking into a room, or narrating to camera, or even just doing a voice-over. But in the theatre, you can put someone in a pool of light to talk straight to the audience while the next scene is being set, or slowly conjured, behind you, and it's much more fun that way. It was good to have a piece where we kept teasing that language out and deciding what was good, what worked, what didn't work, you know? 'Do we have all this narration down front? Down front stage right? Just stage right? Did it matter that you set up a convention and then you broke it, because by that point, if you give the audience some tools, they could keep up with you?' Audiences are so much cleverer than we think they are.

You had to decide whether or not to allow the light to connect up various parts of the stage. By allowing some blackness in between the spaces where people are standing you do create a distance, because that little unlit void, even though it's only a metre or two, can seem like a huge distance.

We used a real mixture of techniques on *My Zinc Bed*. One of the tricks that I use is to light actors from the side, which lights their faces and sculpts their bodies very well (like you do in a dance piece), and picks them out of their environment. Then I can choose to light the *environment* in the way that I want to at that moment. So sometimes you can have people lit very well, but, if they're not connected by the light to the floor, that creates a sense of distance and space and the sense that these people are not necessarily sharing that 'grounded' reality. If the light on me as a performer is hitting the floor, I'm connected to the floor. If the light on me is going into the wings, or even on to scenery in the wings, then by the time it gets there it's much less bright, because it's travelled further, and therefore I'm not connected to my environment in the same way. So then you can feed in the environment as you will. There was quite a bit of low-angle lighting in *My Zinc Bed*, just to light the people and to make them sparkle in a way that I wanted them to.

I've seen many of David's plays, and I think that his awareness of the potential of light has grown and grown in the last few years. What lighting itself can do has grown dramatically in the last ten years, and theatres of any size now have sophisticated equipment that means you can do a lot more, even in a smaller space. So I think everybody's appreciation of what light can do has changed, and David certainly has got much more excited about it.

I also think another thing happened when we were doing *Via Dolorosa*. David started to feel what was useful and helpful about light, and how different he felt under different types of light, as a *performer*, and of course, he'd never been a performer before. (You can discount his adolescent rendition of some character from *Measure for Measure* or whatever!)

Ian McNeil (the scenic designer for Via Dolorosa) *talks about the way he designed the thing specifically for Hare – because it was a monologue, because he was an untested performer – to support his performance. So one of the elements that went into the design – the 'bridge' – was a kind of supportiveness of the exposure that Hare was feeling as an actor, that also mirrored the exposure he had felt making the original trip. Were you aware of doing a similar thing with the lighting? Hare himself talks at some point about your lighting and the ways the cues, particularly from side lights, gave him a sort of sense memory of what was going on, and helped energize his performance.*

Rarely have I taken so much notice about what a performer felt about light. In doing *Via Dolorosa*, he was very aware of where he was using light and how it was helping to anchor him; and if it wasn't right you could see, as he was rehearsing, that it was affecting him and throwing him, and catching him out in a way that a more experienced performer probably just takes on the chin. He would say, 'Is it going to be like this?' and try to get a real sense of it so he could use it. We did develop a language where *we* could adapt as he was going through the gear changes of a piece. Sometimes we chose to ignore some of those gear changes from a lighting point of view, to avoid 'over-presenting' the piece and dressing it up to be something that it wasn't. So when we did those few changes they were very, very central for him, and he liked the way that they made him feel. He liked sometimes being dazzled by the light. Interestingly enough in *Via Dolorosa* he initially said that he wanted to see the audience, that he wanted to be able to 'have a conversation with them'. That is something which a lot of inexperienced actors say: 'Oh, it's really important that the light is equal between the stage and the audience, so that *we're* equal, so I'm sure that we're going to want the house lights up'. And I thought, 'Oh, yes, sure!' and we got into the theatre and that was one of the first things to go. We did keep them up a tiny bit longer, but he soon said, 'No, Rick, I love it when the light's in my eyes and I can't see who they are. I need that void, because otherwise I just become too self-conscious.' He liked the fact that it gave him a bit of a 'world' and a bit of 'glue'. It gave him a sense of pace and rest, and I think, having gone through that experience as a performer, it had an effect on his writing, and he could see a more muscular way of using light.

Could you say something about Hare's working relationship with Stephen Daldry, the director? It was very good, wasn't it?
Yes, it was. It had its ups and downs, but that was good. I think Stephen directed it rather brilliantly and brought something out of David, and then worked with him to preserve it. One of the problems was that, as he kept on doing the show, he got better at it, and became a better actor, or a better story-teller; one of the things that he and Stephen worked on was that he didn't become *too* good, in a way. A lot of actors came to see the show and said, 'Oh, I just couldn't bear all that – at the beginning he was flapping his hands around and making gestures, and all that sort of thing'. But that was part of what *made* the show: the truth of what he was saying, and the fact that it was *his* truth, became so overpowering you realized that maybe the fact that he was not as adept as Sir John Gielgud would have been gave it an extra meaning, and for me an extra importance. If he got too good and too clever and too smooth, some of that may have gone, because it would have been just depicted instead of *lived*.

A lot of what Stephen did was to work with David on just this, and David was amazingly methodical about it. He approached it in a way that I've never seen. He was very clear about where his eye-line was, where he looked, where he delivered a line to, and when he wanted to make a change; he was so technically aware it was almost frightening to see him work. I've never seen an actor use a technical rehearsal so intelligently and for his own goals; he knew where he was going, and a lot of times he had to go through various technical things to check lighting cues and sound cues, and he would pace himself very well. It was very impressive.

It was very heartening to see what was in some ways a very exposed piece. I think what is interesting about his book *Acting Up* is that he writes a lot about how exposed he felt as an actor, but it was good to see how he eventually trusted his collaborators, and got angry with them! I think that grew during the piece: I think he felt that we had his interests at heart and were trying things out, and none of us was trying to cast him adrift, even though he sometimes felt like that, as you would. And doing a ninety-minute monologue is no small task.

You've seen Hare direct as well, with both My Zinc Bed *and Wallace Shawn's* The Designated Mourner.
Shawn would not have chosen to use him, I think, unless he felt he had something to give to that play. He was also directing one of the great directors of the age – Mike Nichols – as an actor, and that would put off many another director. Maybe David was too naïve to be put off, and maybe the strength of his own experience as an author helped give him the nerve, the charisma, to pull it off. But he did that piece very well, and it wasn't an easy piece to make work. It was flawlessly done, I think.

He's very detailed at working with the actors, and naturally he's very respectful of the writing; I think the writing is still paramount to him. And it was interesting working on *My Zinc Bed* because the first time I worked with him he was directing somebody else's piece, and the next time he was principally an actor, and one wasn't that aware of him having written the piece. But then to work with him on a new play of his . . . at times you think, 'Is this the director I'm sitting next to, or is it the writer?' There were a lot of times during *My Zinc Bed* when he became a writer, just making sure the beats of his piece were being performed in the way he wanted.

Do you think he's aware of that? Of taking one hat off and putting another one on, or is it one process for him?
I think it became more and more one process as he relaxed about the play, and I was also pleasantly surprised that he was open to discussing the play with anyone who wanted to offer an opinion. He was very open to hearing what either I or Judith [*Greenwood, the lighting designer, who assisted Fisher*] thought about any particular moment in the piece, and he listened to our suggestions about how to stage it or play it; whether or not he chose to act on that doesn't matter. What matters is that he listened, and you would think that someone who wrote and directed a piece would not be interested in listening to anyone else; but, in actual fact, he never stopped being open to other people's impressions of what he was doing, listening to that and using it to refine what he was doing.

At the very end of *My Zinc Bed* there's a little epilogue, and I always said that I never liked it, and I was happy saying that I didn't think the play needed it; he was very sure that it did and so it stayed, and that was fine; but it was great to be able to work with someone where you could say that you didn't like something. That was very empowering.

He had the show in very good shape early on and then it really started to fizz in the theatre. It was very interesting working on it, because we were always tuning and tuning it. It's frustrating, because you don't expect the man to be gifted in so many different areas! I'm disappointed, though, because there was a proposed production by Howard Davies of *Zinc Bed*, and it looked like the show was going to have another life: I was really looking forward to seeing how another person would take it on into another area. But it was not to be, or at least not to be yet. I don't think the play's lost its moment yet, and certainly it should have been seen by more people, and will be, I think, some day.

It's often said that Hare's plays catch the zeitgeist, *the spirit of the moment.*

It's wonderful to have somebody who is writing a play that's about *now*, that's about the things that we're thinking about, and worrying about, and talking about – or not talking about, as the case may be. *Via Dolorosa* only becomes more and more pertinent, unfortunately, as the current situation in the world goes on. In the last month [*September 2001*] it's come home to me how appropriate the play is, and how perceptive, at least in describing the problem. Unless these problems, and how complicated they are, are described to all of us, simplistic solutions like bombing the World Trade Center and/or bombing Afghanistan will continue to be offered as solutions by terrorists and by governments.

Vicki Mortimer

Theatre designer Vicki Mortimer, who has worked extensively with the RSC and the National Theatre, has designed productions of a number of contemporary plays, including pieces by Pinter, Stoppard, Marber and Gilman; she has also collaborated with Random Dance on its multimedia trilogy (Millennarium, Sulphur 16 and Aeon). Her work with Hare includes Shaw's Heartbreak House, which he directed at the Almeida in 1997, a Japanese production of The Blue Room (2001) and the original production of My Zinc Bed ...

What was your initial response as a designer when you saw the script of My Zinc Bed?

In the original typescript (which had emerged from many different re-writes that David had done), there was quite a lot of information about how he saw the space. It was not terribly concrete, but it was quite strongly visualized. It wasn't about an architectural environment: it was more to do with his feeling about how these figures emerged from a sense of a great volume of space. He was very interested in figures travelling across distances to arrive with the audience, which was partly to do with the memory framework of the play. When I read the first version, that was the most striking thing: he wanted this impossible theatrical volume of space, which could expand and contract and stretch in all dimensions. At moments the play could shrink down to the size of a pinspot, but then suddenly go into a great panoramic space. It was very much linked to his passionately felt sense of the play as an epic play, not simply something about this threesome. It needed to have a sense of that in the scenography as well. A lot of how he'd imagined the space was linked with light; he had some really wonderful things, like the scene in the office where the lights go out [*Act One, scene four*]: his idea was that there was a kind of 'plink, plink, plink, plink, plink' down to just one little isolated area. Of course, it was convenient in that there's a naturalistic effect, but actually it's about the exhilaration that those two people feel in being alone together at that moment, and the potential for intimacy.

And then, of course, there was the fact that we were doing the play at the Royal Court Theatre, which is very tiny. It is a fantastically beautiful theatre for playwrights (obviously there is a reason why it has been so successful for new writers), but it's not something that gives you volume, except in height. It meant that at the very beginning I was trying to do things with mirrors, trying to multiply the space, to deliver what David wanted. In a way that kind of theatrical 'sleight of hand' was what personified the script at the time. There is a sense of wizardry in the play, and so old-fashioned theatrical magic was one of the things that we talked about using in the beginning.

So it wasn't at all a process of beginning naturalistically or realistically and then moving away from that?
No, it was quite the reverse, actually: we moved more *towards* naturalism. I think at the beginning Victor's slightly 'Prospero/ King Lear-ish qualities' (which become more clear at the end of the play) dominated proceedings. We made a key visit to the offices of Norman Foster [*the leading architect and proponent*

of 'high tech' modern architecture, whose work includes the new Stansted airport and the controversial 'blade of light' bridge over the Thames]. Because we were talking about Victor's power, and the fact that he is the character who determines the experience of the other two – it all happens within his aura, and his aura is what makes both possible and impossible the exchanges between them – it felt important that somehow we 'hit' his environment properly. Norman Foster seemed like a good model: not on a personal level, but in terms of 'mogulishness'. So the landscape of the scenography came from there. It's an amazing building and – the way that Norman Foster runs it – an amazing bit of social organization and social control; so it was very good for Victor. There is an extraordinary hierarchy of ambition within that environment, and Foster represents something of what Victor's showing in terms of 'charismatic despair'.

Then there was the antithesis, which is where the play starts from: Steven's character [*Paul Peplow*], and how he arrives. David was always immensely keen that he should arrive through the audience, and that the play should begin in a relaxed way, not 'announcing' itself. It was crucial to the way David saw the play that the audience understood Paul's role as a writer, understood the idea that he's colluding with them, and understood that the other two characters, Victor and Elsa, are 'the observed'. Paul is allowed to step in and out of the world of the audience and the world of the play – he has that privilege. So we needed to find how the play started. David wanted it somehow to begin 'magically', so that you didn't quite know *where* it began: he wanted it almost to creep up on the audience. I think Paul's entrance through the audience was one way of looking at that.

Then we needed a kind of environmental support for what Paul's character *is* once he's out of the audience, but not something that was signalling the content of the play too heavy-handedly. I remember thinking that it should be very 'Alcoholics Anonymous', and that maybe there was a frame that could contain all three dimensions of the available space, and that that should be described by a very institutionalized, 'church-hallish' sort of design. In that way we could start Paul off in a quite detailed environment which showed the banal reality which he inhabits, then contrast that with the rather 'blessed' time that he spends within the story of the play. From that initial idea we reduced the design down to the wooden surround that we ended up with, which was supposed to be reminiscent of those institutional places where AA have their meetings. Then we had the big zinc curtain that came in, like a broken-down metallic shutter. That was intended to be a representation of the urban, mundane world, but with a 'metaphysical' slant: we wanted to give a sense of 'shutting off', of separating the two worlds. The metal was actually quite colourful, but it was meant to be – not exactly corroded, but *bruised* metal, whereas everything behind it, in Victor's world, was to be new and exact, with this rather jewel-like precision of glass and colour.

When we were talking about the play as a whole, one of the things that really struck me was that in pretty much every scene there was an *object* that was some kind of turning point, even if it was only a pen on the desk. For example, the margaritas were absolutely the axis of the emotion and the vision at that point of the play [*Act One, scene six*]. That was what was so beautiful about what David had written: he caught the fact that in our memory there is very often something quite odd that we remember from a situation, or *by* which we remember it: some *thing*. It might only be what's in the waste-paper basket. I love that about the play – the partialness, the selectiveness, of memory was very specifically shown in the action.

When you've got that kind of non-naturalistic set, one that's stripped down and where light is doing a lot of the work for you, the nature of the objects that are put on it becomes very important, doesn't it? Did you do a lot of work on that? On getting the cocktail glasses, the plant, the flowers, the glass desk, or whatever, absolutely right?

We did. That was one of the most difficult things, I think, part-ly because one of David's rather likeable qualities is that he quite often talks about things with the absolute assumption that you know what he's talking about. But actually a lot of what he's talking about is extremely personal – it is about memory, and a frame of reference that he assumes you share, but you don't. It takes quite a lot of unpicking: working with David is a process of deduction. His personal memory bank is very close-knit, so getting to the bottom of what's driving his plays is quite a process of investigation. When we were in a design meeting, very often – and sometimes quite a long way into the process – I would ask a question and he would answer in such a way that made it quite clear that he thought he had already answered it. But he never had. He thought he had, and maybe in his own way he had; it's just that you have to have a jolly good pair of ears on to decode what he's saying. I think it is a part of the strength of his writing: as an audience member, too, you really have to pay attention. If he were self-conscious about trying to be clear, you'd end up with something that was heavy and didactic.

Going to Norman Foster's together was very useful, because I took a lot of pictures, and it meant that we had a very con-crete starting point for at least one area of the play. From then on it was easier to piece things together.

David was very interested in archetypes of beauty and luxu-ry in the play, because that's what those characters have built around themselves. The play's about addiction: to people, to love, to power, to beauty, and of course to drink . . . but what David's saying is that the beauty of liquid in a glass is part of addiction to drink, and the characters' addictions hinge on the assumption that what they are doing is *beautiful* as well as sen-suous. I think the whole addictive edge is something that has to be worked into what you have on stage. There has to be some-thing aspirational about what you see – you have to really *want*, on one level, to be in their world with them.

It sounds as if you were intimately involved throughout the whole process . . .

It took us a really long time to design the play: four or five months. We went through a lot of versions, and I think there were still things to be resolved, to be completely honest, even by the time we got into production. The scene David was always unresolved about was the scene at home [*Act Two, scene eight*], which is the most difficult, because it goes right into the belly of home life, and I don't think we ever really got that right. We couldn't quite find the environment. It was odd. In the end, I never fully grasped what privately went on between [Paul and Elsa]. I think David knew, but I could never find enough clues myself to understand what that environment needed to be: how comfortable, how indulgent . . .

In the published text, you can see what he's driving at . . . the intimate domesticity of the situation is part of what pushes Paul and Elsa together, yet all the stage directions ask for is the sense of a doorway. That's quite difficult, isn't it?

It is, absolutely. It's the one thing we didn't deliver, and I think that the problem was that the scene had an uncertain start. That threshold is crucial, I think, for the choice that they both make.

We got extremely distracted by the ficus – the plant that he pours his drink into. We'd created an environment where it was very difficult to include natural life, and suddenly there's this ficus, which is a growing plant. We became quite preoccupied by how to deliver it, probably at the cost of the rest of the scene. At times David said that he was prepared to cut it, but we were determined to solve it, and I'm not sure we did.

There's something important about it, isn't there – something about a living, green, natural thing, in a context that's all cool, blue and straight-edged?

Exactly. Retrospectively, it probably should have been more of a clue to how we designed the scene, and if David hadn't said, 'Oh, it's just a joke,' I think I might have paid more attention.

How did you find Hare as a director? A lot of his collaborators – especially his actors – talk about his eye for detail . . . does that extend into design?

Yes, it does. It's interesting to compare what he was like directing *My Zinc Bed* rather than directing somebody else's play. With the Shaw, he just had a ball – he did it for fun, he had lots of good friends in it, and it was lots of fun watching him do it, because he really enjoyed it. It was different with *My Zinc Bed*, because there's obviously a lot more at stake if you're directing the first production of your own play. He had the same sense of thrill, but obviously there was a more nervous edge to it, and it does matter to David what happens to his plays and what people think. I think sometimes that makes it difficult to enjoy the rehearsal in the same way that he would otherwise. But you were right in what you were saying earlier, about the perception of his writing as cool and controlled, and the experience of working with him, which is exactly the opposite. He's extraordinarily, frighteningly intelligent and perceptive, but in social situations he clothes his perceptiveness with wit. In rehearsal, where 'the clothes have to come off' a little, that passion that you were talking about really is at play. He's very, very knowledgeable about how plays are structured, and about dramaturgy, of course, so he's extremely good technically; in that way he's very detailed. He's got strong opinions about where people should be in scenes, onstage, in relation to somebody else, whether they should move or not, whether they should stay put . . . that's relatively unusual now. People don't block so much, especially in intimate plays like this: actors are allowed to organize themselves more. But that's probably linked to his sense of the epic in his writing: he's got a strong sense that it needs to be bigger in performance than what appears to be required on the page. That's why in *My Zinc Bed* he was very specific about when Tom [*Wilkinson, who played Victor*] for example, needed to stay upstage centre, or sit down, or stand up in the last scene. When there are only three characters, you've got to be on the ball about that anyway, because the physical signals that come off are so strong. A lot of information is given off by those signals, especially in terms of how social dynamics are shifting.

So again, it's like the objects, isn't it? The slightest gesture becomes important.
Especially when all three characters are extremely well-versed in secrecy. Pretty much whatever they are telling each other physically, never mind verbally, is chosen: none of those characters is 'accidental', in physical terms. They want to control. That's why alcoholic addiction is so strong in the play: it's about control and loss of control.

Keeping available as much space as possible is crucial, and in a way one's job is about making sure that the balances are kept moving, scenography-wise, during the show. As the designer, you are very much in a supporting role, rather than – well, it depends which play you're talking about, but certainly with *My Zinc Bed*, it felt very important to be a supporting role rather than something else.

And was Heartbreak House *very different from that?*
Heartbreak House was a bit different, in that the Almeida is a very different theatre anyway, not a proscenium stage like the Court. There are also various '*coup de théâtre*-type things' that need to happen in *Heartbreak House*, whereas in *My Zinc Bed* the *coups de théâtre* come from *within* the characters themselves. Yes, with Victor it is made explicit: there is the thunderstorm, for example [*Act Two, scene ten*]: a 'real' thunderstorm which is reflecting what's going on in the scene emotionally. But on the whole, the audience needs to know that it is effectively a 'psychic' phenomenon, not an actuality, and if you make it concrete at all, then it weakens the point.

Going back to what you were saying about David as a director . . . he's a fantastic orchestrator of the people that he works with. He feels like a conductor, and has the temperament of a conductor as well, especially once you get into the theatre: he's all furious arms and cursing and shouting. He gets thoroughly overexcited, and I think that's one of the charms of working with him: he's an incredible enthusiast as a director. Any caution and anxiety he may feel become overwhelmed by the thrill of it all, and he really understands the power of what theatre can do. Otherwise, he wouldn't be a political playwright. He's convinced of the ability of theatre to change something, and that's not terribly common either. It means that sometimes he gets frustrated and can't get what he needs . . . he's a missionary, basically.

And somebody who consistently throughout a process is soliciting and listening to your ideas?
Yes. He really wants your support, and he really wants you to play a role. He likes what people do, and he likes people who do what they do. Nick [*Bicât, the composer*], crucially, Rick Fisher – he loves the fact that they do what they do well, and that *he* doesn't have to do it because of that. He loves colleagues and he loves collaborators, and, in the best sense, depends on them.

I don't know if it makes him sound too worthy to say that I think *responsibility* and *activeness* are the things that he's interested in: you can't just be a receiver; you have to act, you have to be active.

As collaborator, or audience, or both?
In the world. You can't 'do nothing'. I think one of the things that *My Zinc Bed* is about – or I hope it is – is using what you have. It's a parable of the talents, if you like, and if you choose to waste what you have, then that's your responsibility too. I think he is a moral writer.

Political dramatists are often ultimately seen as moral dramatists.
But the sadness of that is that he is perceived of as this rather 'cool' player. I've just designed a production of *The Blue Room* in Japan. When I saw it here, I had the feeling that other people had: I thought, 'This is well worked out, but I'm not sure

where it's going'. But you could feel that underneath there was something 'hotter' going on. It was very interesting when I came to work on the play, and seeing where its heart lies. The two scenes [6: 'The Politician and the Model' and 7: 'The Model and the Playwright'] with Kelly (the model) and the politician, and then Kelly with Robert, seem to me crucial in terms of the play's argument. There is the incredible, awful blackness and dismay of the Kelly–politician scene, and then in the next scene there is the possibility of tenderness: underneath everything Robert says, there is actually the possibility of something between those two people. It is incredibly moving, because it's so unexpected. They are completely the wrong pair to be together. And then you get the next scene [8: 'The Playwright and the Actress'] with Robert and the actress, who *seem* completely the *right* pair in lots of ways, yet . . . I felt I was sometimes 'outside', sometimes 'inside' the writing. So . . . does it just depend on whether you happen to have had the right kind of personal experience to let you get involved in different parts of the play? I don't think that's true, but it does mean that you have to do productions of his work incredibly carefully to let that passion, and that conviction, out. *Via Dolorosa* was a real treat to see. I thought, 'Thank God he did it,' because in a way, it redressed the balance a little. He showed his own passion. Had somebody else spoken it for him, I think we would have been back in the same territory, but having had that period of selling his own lines to the audience, he's redefined himself. Obviously it was a crucial experience for him, but also for who he is as a writer, so far as the audience is concerned. And it expressed very well that weird combination of perception, toughness and political pragmatism on the one hand, and on the other that part of him which is completely convinced and idealistic and wishful: he has an against-all-odds wish for things to be better, even as he knows, intellectually, that things are terrible.

Jonathan Kent

Following their appointment in 1990, co-artistic directors Jonathan Kent and Ian McDiarmid established the Almeida Theatre Company in London as a theatre with an international reputation for work of high quality and ambition. Hare's association with the company was a signal feature of its work. The Judas Kiss *was premièred at the theatre in 1998 in a production directed by Richard Eyre, whilst Hare himself directed Shaw's* Heartbreak House *there in 1997. The most substantial part of the association, however, took the form of a series of adaptations made by Hare and directed by Kent: Pirandello's* The Rules of the Game *(1992), Brecht's* Galileo *and* Mother Courage *(1994 and 1995, the latter at the National Theatre with Diana Rigg), and Chekhov's* Ivanov *and* Platonov *(1997 and 2001). Kent also revived* Plenty *in 1999, with Cate Blanchett.*

How did your association with Hare first come about?
It came about through *The Rules of the Game*; I knew him only vaguely before. I wanted to do the play: there was something in it that really fascinated me. I knew he'd done a version at the National in 1971 (which I'd seen, but which, to be honest, wasn't the greatest of productions), so I got hold of him and asked if I could meet to talk about it. I hadn't been able to get hold of his version of it, and I hadn't at that point thought of asking him to re-do it. I went to see him at the National (it was the day that [*media tycoon*] Robert Maxwell drowned himself, so we spent a lot of time scurrying around trying to find televisions to see what was happening), and he said, 'Well, if you *are* going to do it, I would really want to work on it'. That was thrilling, because the possibility of a new version hadn't occurred to me. So we worked together on it. David, I think, felt it was a play that didn't work, but, in the end, he was convinced – it *did* work. It's still one of the plays that we've done at the Almeida of which I'm proudest, partly because it re-introduced [*the actor*] Richard Griffiths to the stage. And also

because it began a remarkably fruitful relationship with David. And a friendship.

That's how my relationship with him began. Out of that, and because of Richard, whom I wanted to play the part, I suggested that we do *Galileo*. I think both David's versions of Brecht have been marvellous in that, like all good adapters, he manages to be absolutely true to the spirit of the original, while retaining his own particular voice; they are seen through the prism of his own sensibilities, his own political beliefs. This is even more true of the Chekhov adaptations. There's a sort of meeting between Hare and Chekhov: an empathy between the two of them. As with Chekhov, so with Brecht. *Galileo* was a particularly successful merging of the two writers.

What was the process of adaptation? To what extent was it collaborative?

Our collaboration grew as we learned to trust each other. *Galileo* went back and forth between us three or four times. We both felt that the problem with Brecht is those great slabs of rhetoric; we wanted to 'loosen them', to give them the cut and thrust of passionate argument. The gift of *Galileo* is that within its politics there is a great humanity (it's true of *Mother Courage*, too, though perhaps less so). Brecht has become a prisoner of his devotees: alongside his political beliefs he was a great poet of the theatre, and that has to be honoured as well. He's not done nearly enough, in my opinion. The danger – and this is why audiences have withdrawn from him – is that audiences feel they are going to be button-holed and harangued. He was a far greater writer than that. He created charismatic protagonists, whether it be Shen Te/Shui Ta (from *The Good Person of Szechuan*), Mother Courage or Galileo – these great archetypal figures, who lead you to complex ideas through a simple narrative. He believed in great, high-definition central figures (and performers). He wanted Ethel Merman [*the American singer and actress*] to play Mother Courage, and Charles Laughton [*the British-born stage and screen actor*] to play Galileo; these were both huge, big-hearted personalities as well as great entertainers and performers. He used to sit at the back of the auditorium and shout '*Viel Spass!*' ['*Lots of fun!*']. I think we've traduced him, rather, and I think what David's great contribution is is that he releases the wit and the lightness of the plays – while underlining the politics.

Hare talks about both Mother Courage and Galileo as figures who are 'coping with the effects of bad faith in a fast-changing world'; that could almost be a mantra for his own work, couldn't it?
Absolutely. 'Good faith' is the cornerstone of David's writing. To act in good faith means, I think, to behave properly – honourably, if you like, on a much deeper level than simply being polite. He's a utopian, and words like 'faith', 'decency', and 'honour' have real meaning for him. He's a romantic Englishman (in a sense he is in the line of say [*the English playwright*] Rattigan) and he values an England that he feels is in danger of being smothered – tarmacked over. He has an almost Arthurian sense of England, and that's where his writing is at its best.

What about the affinity with Chekhov you mentioned? Does that reside in their shared ability somehow to catch, even unconsciously, the spirit of their ages?
I think that's absolutely true – they both offer sometimes devastating portraits of their societies, but there is also a great sense of humanity in Chekhov which David has too; with both writers, the most seemingly unpleasant figures acquire a humanity and a dignity. There is also Chekhov's wit, of course, and David is the wittiest of writers. Like Chekhov, he's a great playwright to direct and to act: he's merciless in that you *have* to respect the rhythms of his writing. He's almost metronomic. And at the same time it's like riding a wave, if you can get on to it. His language is precisely calibrated; he's certainly the most rhythmic writer I know. I've just directed Brian Friel's *Faith Healer*, which is a great layered and textured text, but it doesn't have the same pitiless, almost metric, demand that

David's work has. You can do riffs on it, but you have to know what it *is* first; rather as in Shakespeare, where you have to know what iambic pentameter demands before you can begin to play with it. That sense of discipline is endemic to his plays, so you have to listen to his 'voice'. Because I've done quite a lot of his stuff, I recognize that voice – I would recognize a line of David Hare in anybody's play. You have to honour that. Fortunately, it's a rhythm that I instinctively respond to and like, so it's not a huge effort to me, though it sometimes is for actors.

The comparison with Rattigan is interesting, but is it also dangerous? Critics have put Hare's work in that peculiarly bourgeois English tradition before, sometimes to the detriment of its political intentions ...

He's often spoken of as being a Shavian writer, but I don't think he is. *Heartbreak House* is the Shaw I like far and away the best, because it's not the arid, pedantic, slightly arch kind of play which is Shaw at his worst. David is a passionate and a romantic writer: in no sense is he a Shavian writer, except perhaps sometimes in form. Shaw writes long sentences with a lot of subsidiary clauses which are quite hard to pick your way through, and need to be driven through. David does that too, but that's only a question of form.

A play of his which I absolutely love is *Amy's View*. *Plenty* and *Amy's View* seem to share something: they are both laments for a lost England, but the structure of *Amy's View* is so clever in that it is a pastiche of a fifties play – a 'Rattigan-type' play – but then explodes it. I suspect that, because David is such a brilliant craftsman, sometimes he is judged simply *as* a craftsman, and perhaps his craft in a way misleads people into accommodating the work in a particular way. Actually the plays are much more subversive than they appear. I think he's a dangerous and beguiling playwright, and it's an odd combination for some people to accommodate – they can take one or the other, but not both. But then so is Chekhov. And I have no idea what plays critics have been seeing when they describe David's work as 'cold' and 'forensic', because his plays are passionately engaged. Sometimes people say that they don't believe his women; not being a woman, I suppose it's difficult for me to judge. I suppose people feel they are idealized. I don't think they are, but I've given up trying to work out what plays critics have been watching. Fortunately, David is interested in speaking to audiences, not to critics.

Could you tell me about your revival of Plenty?
There are milestones in one's theatre-going and in one's life in the theatre, and *Plenty* for me was one. I saw the original production with Kate Nelligan before I was a director, and (this really isn't an overstatement) it was one of those plays that does change your view of life. I thought it – and she – were just remarkable. It moved me hugely. It fascinates me that David said that the seminal event in his life happened before he was born: the war. The war was the defining moment in the lives of a whole generation. The notion of people rising to that, and then their lives becoming a gradual dwindling away, so that they become diminished as people was, to me, unbearably moving. It's about the loss of life, and not just literally: life bleeds away while you go on living. I feel the same about *Amy's View*: I think they are companion pieces, and *Amy's View* is equally brilliant.

When I came to direct *Plenty* myself, I think I felt slightly inhibited. It had made such an impression on me when I first saw it that I think I was hamstrung by the memory. Normally I don't think it's a good idea for writers to direct their own work (as David did with the first production), but it was a wonderful production. I suppose when I returned to it for my own production, it seemed (this is going to sound pejorative and I don't want it to) a little bit lighter emotionally on the page than I remembered it from the performance, and my reaction to it. It's written as a series of vignettes – postcards sent back from the war front of a life. The scenes are 'moments', and very consciously so. When I went to work on it, that seemed to me to lessen the emotional impact of the play a little. But perhaps that's the way I did it. I think the form *slightly* negates the impact of the play now: the scenes are written to be punctuated by Brechtian blackouts, and I wanted to try and avoid that, because I feel that's now a form we are over-accustomed to. What I wanted to do was to try and create 'a river' on which these little boats of scenes could bob. That proved quite hard to do. I did it with irises closing down the stage picture and then new scenes being revealed. I think perhaps I should have found a form which would have given it a greater fluidity.

One of the things that Hare felt he had got wrong with the original production was that he made the play too much Susan's, too much Kate Nelligan's. Did you find that difficulty with Cate Blanchett?
The difficulty is that her tragedy is so potent that it can hijack the tragedies of other characters in the play, like Brock. That's where I think the strength of the play lies: it deals with people left on the high-water mark of post-war English society, with no place for those qualities we were talking about – no place for honesty and decency and courage and good faith. And it's played out through everybody's story, not just Susan's: we're back to Chekhov again, and writing about small groups of people, not just a hero or heroine, and those groups *are* society. The small tragedies contained within the 'minor' characters are absolutely crucial to the texture of the whole, and that's something that David paints magnificently.

What about Hare as a director?
As I said, I thought *Plenty* was brilliantly directed. When he did *Heartbreak House* for us, much more recently, it was terrific. He loved doing it. He did *Ivanov* on the radio, too, which he also enjoyed. I'm not sure he really enjoyed doing *My Zinc Bed*. I suspect not. He had the pressure once again of it being his own play. I don't think he is primarily a director any more. He has all the skills and he's got such a detailed knowledge of

the craft of theatre, but it's not his presiding passion, and I think whatever you do has to be your presiding passion. David is a great enthusiast and apologist for theatre. He's a 'man of the theatre'. As far as I know, he hasn't designed a play yet, but I'm sure it's only a matter of time. He seems to have done everything else. But to have his kind of energy at the heart of our theatre, when theatre is shifted to the margins of our culture, to have somebody who is a passionate apologist for theatre (in addition to his enormous talent), is a very important and valuable thing. He is both a great spokesman for it, and a dazzling practitioner. He's an enthusiast. He's not a cynic, thank God. The death of most things lies in cynicism.

Sir Richard Eyre

Sir Richard Eyre was Artistic Director of the National Theatre from 1988 to 1997. A signal feature of his regime – generally held to have been the most successful since Olivier's in the sixties and early seventies – was his close association with Hare: he directed the trilogy, Skylight *and* Amy's View *for the theatre. Moreover, both his professional relationship and personal friendship with the playwright extend back into the 1970s, providing him with a unique perspective on Hare's career.*

Am I right in thinking that the first time you worked with Hare was when you directed The Great Exhibition *in 1972?*
Yes. I'd met him about two years before that, through his then wife Margaret [Matheson]. The invitation to direct *Great Exhibition* came more or less out of the blue: David's previous play had been directed by Max Stafford-Clark, so I really don't know why he came to me. I'm not even sure if he'd seen any of my work. I was living in Edinburgh, and I'd been working in Scotland for some time, so my reputation had travelled but was uncorrupted by my work having actually been seen.

What do you recall about that production?
I remember it with some fondness, partly because of the pleasure

of working with [*original cast members*] David Warner and Penelope Wilton, but mainly because I think it was extremely funny. There is nobody writing today who writes as good jokes as David. I think he feels vaguely embarrassed about the play now, in my view unjustifiably. It was a kind of political cartoon, although that does less than justice to that strand of the writing which runs through all of David's work, which is a kind of romanticism. It's a romanticism about the possibility of love to change people's lives, and also about the possibility of politics to change people's lives. In that sense it seemed to me that, although it is not in the top flight of his plays, it is certainly characteristic of his best work.

He has such a profound understanding of what works in the theatre, and a real sympathy and passion for the medium. He doesn't regard it ever as a poor second to any other medium. It's always seemed to him that this is where the action is and this is why, I think, he tends to be rather enviously nostalgic of the position of John Osborne (though in my view he elevates John Osborne's reputation above the point where I think it should naturally rest).

Was that kind of understanding and knowledge of the theatre there even in the early stages of his career?
To some extent he had a sort of preternatural instinct and understanding of theatre. There's a wonderful story: he was doing a production of a play for Portable Theatre, and had an actor say to him, 'I've been in this business for thirty years, and I can tell you that the line won't work if I do it like that'. David replied: 'Well, I've been in this business for six months, and I can tell you that it will'. That seemed to be very characteristic of David's preternatural self-confidence about the medium, and also of his thoughtfulness. There's this wonderful paradox, of the excoriating voice of British political theatre emerging from the petty bourgeois world of Bexhill-on-Sea. He went to the theatre a lot with his mother, so he'd seen a lot more theatre than I had when I first met him, and he knew a lot more. He

was also an usher at the National Theatre during Olivier's time, so he had a rather, I suppose, unfashionable curiosity about the theatre. Where most of his generation would be gravitating towards the movies or television, the allure for him was the theatre. I think that did have a lot to do with a childhood imprint of going to the De La Warr Pavilion in Bexhill and seeing shows on tour, or going with his mother to see shows in London.

That's interesting, because in his own interviews he talks about his early interest in film, but little about the theatre. He stresses his ignorance and naïvety when he began with Portable, saying that he knew nothing about writing, he wanted to direct . . .
David can sometimes seem to have emerged fully formed at the age of nineteen, in Cambridge, as the 'scourge of academia', and I hugely enjoy his critique of 'the gods that failed', in particular Raymond Williams. But I don't think that view of him is quite true. He doesn't talk much about the Bexhill-on-Sea years, but I think that they are actually quite crucial. When he taps into that world, which is the world of petty bourgeois gentility and the quiet desperation of people's lives, it's his very best writing. In a play like *Racing Demon* – which is so uncharacteristic of the banner-waving David Hare, the social critic who at times appears to withdraw compassion from those people he despises – there is nothing but compassion: it's full of love of various sorts.

He talks about finding his politics again in Racing Demon, *and discovering through his research for that play living examples of what he's always talked about: those 'old-fashioned' values, found in the underpaid priests who grind on despite everything. Did you detect that when you directed the play?*
Oh, very much so. I suppose when I first saw David's work, and when I first read *Great Exhibition*, I thought, 'Here is a mannerist; here is someone who is hugely intelligent and witty and confident and iconoclastic'. I thought of him as a sort of dandy, I suppose. There seemed a kind of 'Restoration' feeling to the

work – here was someone who was standing outside society, and having a great time: a satirist. Then I realized that he isn't at heart a satirist at all. He does have a wonderful flair for satire that he can't resist: look at the play that I commissioned from him and Howard Brenton, *Brassneck*, and its sequel, *Pravda*. They are magnificent, bravura satires (and it's interesting that their collaboration draws out of both of them characteristics that strengthen both of their hearts and heads). But David's own, solo voice is much closer to the voice of *Racing Demon*, which, along with *Skylight*, is his clearest, most 'heart on the sleeve' piece of writing. *Skylight*, however, is much more of a dialectic, whereas *Racing Demon* is an exploration of love, of what you believe in, and of human compassion. That was always latent in David; it was just that it was easy to be blinded by his glamour. He was, and is, a glamorous person, and people consistently misunderstand him because of that: they think that it's a lot of swagger, not realizing that the swagger is often concealing a pained and questioning heart.

Could we go back to the Nottingham days? One of the things that strikes me about your time there is that it produced an extraordinary run of some of the biggest and most important plays since the war – The Churchill Play, Comedians, *and so on – and Hare was there, but never produced a solo piece for you . . .*
No he didn't, but then you see David is a very smart impresario. He's got the instincts – though not the patience and the energy, because it would stop him writing – of a producer. He's really, really smart about the particular time to do a particular play, and at what sort of theatre. During my time at the National, I would discuss with David on an almost daily basis what were essentially producing problems. He's a fantastic sounding board and colleague in that respect. He understands the mechanics of producing. At Nottingham, he was smart enough to see that, if he was writing a new play – *Plenty*, which was an expensive play to stage – and he was being courted by Peter Hall to go to the South Bank, it was much better not to

offer it to the Playhouse, but to have it done in London in repertoire with the cast of his choice. That was a very smart piece of producing on his part, and I don't think he was wrong. Obviously I would have loved to do *Plenty*; I thought it was a wonderful play. But I think he made the right decision, and he was pretty (and I think he would admit this now) ruthless in his exploitation of Peter's support of him. So he took the opportunity for all that it was worth, and it was worth a great deal.

Brenton as well was moving into the National at that time with Weapons of Happiness, *which Hare directed. How do you see him as a director?*
Brassneck and *Pravda* were extraordinarily successful pieces of *mise en scène*. He was fearless, really. He would want to put a world onstage. He seemed to me to have learned all the right lessons from Brecht the great director, the great *metteur en scène* (as opposed to Brecht the writer, notwithstanding David's great admiration for *Mother Courage* and *Galileo* at least). They were very accomplished productions. I think, with directing his own plays, that he came to look for conversation; he came to look for a sort of dialectic. But then I think he thought that he could write better if he wasn't doing everything else as well, and I have to say that I think he was right; instinctively, he does find it quite hard to let go. If you're directing a play of David's, you have to be happy with what is the director's role – you are the interpreter, you are not the architect, you are the builder and the decorator. He knows the processes so well that he doesn't tread on your toes, but he is extremely vigilant. The process of receiving notes from David can sometimes be fairly exhausting, as day after day after day you receive five or six pages of faxes of a hundred and fifty notes, which you hope by the time you open them will have reduced to half a dozen. He's very fastidious. I think he now feels that there are things that directors other than himself can bring to his plays that don't necessarily make them *better* but do make them *different*. Different directors add different colours.

So he's not trapped himself in the Edward Bond position of 'Nobody else understands the work, so I'm not going to let them do it'?
Not at all. He takes a delight in what it is that actors do, and particularly what it is the good ones do, what they bring to a part and what instinct and personality provide. He understands that very well, and is very sympathetic to it.

You are suggesting that there is an extraordinary discipline required for Hare's plays. Directors, actors, designers have got to have the work absolutely 'nailed' before they've earned the right to play, to experiment?
Yes, I think you do have to. You can't paraphrase. He's very, very fastidious about his rhythms. To a certain extent all playwrights have their rhythms, that's part of a voice, be it Pinter, Stoppard, or Hare; they all have idiosyncratic rhythms and locutions, and it's important that actors get inside them. If they don't, it's 'nails down the blackboard': it's a very grating sound. So when you see actors trying to paraphrase their way into a speech of David's, it can be quite a disturbing sight and sound, and particularly disturbing for him. You do have to be disciplined, because he's very knowing about what can be done in the theatre. He's supremely professional: there is no playwright who takes his craft more seriously, or who is – almost to a fault – concerned with the construction and the dynamic of a play, and the mechanics of the relationship with the audience.

You could say at times that you wished he weren't *so* knowing, wished that he could in practical terms temporarily abandon his sense of acute self-knowledge and self-examination, and write something that is more outrageously . . . I think he did that more when he was younger – thought: 'I don't know how we do this, but this is what I'm going to write'. I sometimes feel he is trapped or inhibited by his tremendous knowledge of how a piece of work is achieved in the theatre. Maybe *My Zinc Bed* was in some sense the play in which he wanted to abandon the monitoring voice that says, 'Well, David, how are you going to save that, and how is the audience going to understand that?', and, interestingly, it was a return to directing himself. But I think it's difficult, if you're such an experienced practitioner, who is so aware of construction and effect, to let go in that way.

What are the implications of all this for the way you approach his work as a director?
You have to get over the feeling of 'I wonder why I'm directing this rather than David, since David knows perfectly well how to stage this scene'. You have to believe that you're bringing something to it that he couldn't, otherwise you'd just be crushed and diminished. He's good with the occasional aberration, and he's very good at making you feel that you're an equal partner, not just a junior who is in some way merely saving him the trouble of putting something on stage that he could do perfectly well himself.

One of the things that strikes me forcibly about Hare's career over the last thirty years is that he seems to have survived better than many of his generation: he seems to have 'kept going' better than most in terms of consistently getting work on.
Yes. I'd be wary of producing any theory that took him outside of events. You could say of Trevor Griffiths and Howard Brenton that in a sense they were robbed of their subject by the collapse of Socialism. But you could also say that Trevor was, to some extent, destroyed by Hollywood, and you could say that in Howard's writing the will was always stronger than the achievement, whereas David has always been very accomplished as a playmaker. And he's always simply thought the business of a writer is to write, so you keep on writing, and the hardest thing is to keep on writing if you feel that you're not being successful. I think he has, with the craft of writing, a Dickens-like application: you've just got to go on. If you're having problems with writing, the only way you're going to dispel those problems is by continuing to write through them. That might be the distinguishing factor.

Is it also the case that he might have benefited from the critical inclination to lever him into the mainstream tradition of bourgeois English playwrighting? That he's had a kind of 'insurance policy' in that way?

I don't think so. It would certainly be uncharitable to say that he considers his writing in that way, that it's that calculated. He writes from subjects, from stories. Stories attract him that seem to contain the possibilities of dealing with things that interest him at the time. I think more and more the critics are recognizing that it's pointless to ask, 'Is he like X or Y?' He is his own person, and he has this idiosyncratic mix of the man who adores dialectic and is also at least as fascinated with the politics of the heart as with the politics of the state. There is a quirky mixture of the romantic and the hard-nosed, the lyrical and the satiric, that is David. It's not like anybody else.

But if a play such as Skylight *is not to be read in terms of that tradition, not allowed to be seen as a purely private, psychological study about 'the human condition', but as a piece rooted in a profoundly political analysis of contemporary society, do you as director need to force that reading against a tide of received critical response?*

No. It's all there in the writing, and what you need to do is what you need to do with every play: create a coherent world that is fleshed out in a massive accumulation of observed detail. So it's the exhaustive process of making sure that every single aspect of that world is realized. All David's work is autobiographical: he writes about what he's concerned about at the time, and that is the perspective of looking out from a position of security and wealth and status and asking what it actually feels like to live without money. He's very conscientious about not representing the lives of people about whom he has no lived experience. He would feel it to be a lie to write a play about a working-class family, because he would say, 'I can imagine and I can infer, but I can't write that with any real authority'. But he can write the perspective of the schoolteacher who looks at that world and thinks, 'Why are these people's lives so miserable? Why are they so disenfranchised?'

What about Amy's View *in this context? That's a play which deliberately invokes the conventions of the mainstream 'fifties-type' play in order to explode them, isn't it?*
Absolutely. It's a knowing writer's conceit: you set up the world of a country-house play with a vague echo of Noel Coward about it, and you put at the heart of it a character who literally embodies that world of light comedies. It seems to me rather bracingly honest to say, 'Actually, in some sense this is a world occupied by a large number of the people who are seeing this play, who are not from sink estates in Hackney but in reality probably live in detached houses near Pangbourne'. It's an attempt to speak to the much-derided middle-class audience, and to do it by playing with a particular form and then subverting it from within.

By 'launching the missile' of Amy's death, as it were.
That's right.

Finally – and you are better placed, I think, than anybody to answer this question – what is your view of Hare's contribution to British theatre over the last thirty years?
It's beyond argument that he's been one of its leading voices: eloquent, passionate, forceful, romantic, politicized. It's not Shavian, nor is it Rattigan; it's something that is unique, and he has solidly pursued an often difficult furrow of writing about public life and ideas of how people should live, through a variety of different milieux. And, of course, there is his constant proselytization about the medium of theatre, and a demonstrated passion that it's worth caring about this medium. So it seems to me that there is no way of representing David's contribution as anything less than central.

Leabharlanna Fhine Gall

Appendix: Directing Work

Entries in **bold** indicate Hare's direction of his own work.

Christie in Love, by Howard Brenton, Portable Theatre, 1969
How Brophy Made Good, Portable Theatre (at Brighton Combination), March 1969 (co-directed with Tony Bicât)
Purity, by David Mowat, Portable Theatre, 1969
Fruit, by Howard Brenton, Portable Theatre, 1970
Blow Job, by Snoo Wilson, Portable Theatre, 1971
England's Ireland, Portable Theatre, 1972
The Pleasure Principle, by Snoo Wilson, London, 1973
Brassneck, co-written with Howard Brenton, Nottingham Playhouse, 1973
The Provoked Wife, by Sir John Vanbrugh, Watford (Palace Theatre), 1973
The Party, by Trevor Griffiths, National Theatre tour, 1974
Teeth 'n' Smiles, Royal Court Theatre, London, 1975
Weapons of Happiness, by Howard Brenton, National Theatre, London, 1976
Devil's Island, by Tony Bicât, Sherman Theatre, Cardiff, 1977
Licking Hitler, BBC TV, 1978
Plenty, National Theatre, London, 1978
Dreams of Leaving, BBC TV, 1980
Total Eclipse, by Christopher Hampton, Lyric Theatre, Hammersmith, 1981
A Map of the World, Opera Theatre, Adelaide, 1982
Plenty, New York, 1982
A Map of the World, National Theatre, London, 1983
Wetherby (film), 1985

Pravda, co-written with Howard Brenton, National Theatre, London, 1985

A Map of the World, New York, 1985

The Bay at Nice and *Wrecked Eggs*, National Theatre, London, 1986

King Lear, by William Shakespeare, National Theatre, London, 1986

The Knife, New York, 1987

Paris by Night (film), 1989

Strapless (film), 1990

Heading Home, BBC TV, January 1991

The Young Indiana Jones Chronicles: Paris, May 1919 (TV film), 1993

The Designated Mourner, by Wallace Shawn, National Theatre, London, 18 April 1996

The Designated Mourner (film), 1996

Heartbreak House, by George Bernard Shaw, Almeida Theatre, London, 1997

The Judas Kiss (radio), BBC, 1998

Ivanov (radio), BBC, 1998

My Zinc Bed, Royal Court Theatre, London, 2000

Select Bibliography, with annotations

Primary sources

Note: Hare's personal papers are held at the Harry Ransom Humanities Research Center at the University of Texas, at Austin. A catalogue is viewable on-line at:

http://www.hrc.utexas.edu/research/fa/hare.scope.html

Individual plays, teleplays and screenplays
(All published by Faber and Faber, London, unless otherwise stated; arranged alphabetically.)

The Absence of War, 1993.

Amy's View, 1997.

The Bay at Nice and *Wrecked Eggs*, 1986.

The Blue Room. Freely adapted from Arthur Schnitzler's La Ronde, 1998. With a Preface.

The Breath of Life, 2002.

Dreams of Leaving. A film for television, 1980.

Fanshen, 1976. With an Author's Preface.

The Great Exhibition, 1972.

The Hours, 2002 (adapted from the novel by Michael Cunningham).

How Brophy Made Good. Gambit 17, 1971.

Ivanov (adaptation of Chekhov), London: Methuen, 1997. With an Introduction.

The Judas Kiss, 1998.

Knuckle, 1974.

Licking Hitler. A film for television, 1978. With a 'Lecture'.

A Map of the World, 1982.

Mother Courage and her Children (adaptation of Brecht),
  London: Methuen, 1995.
Murmuring Judges, 1991. With an Author's Note.
My Zinc Bed, 2000.
Paris by Night, 1988. With an Introduction.
Platonov, 2001 (adaptation of Chekhov). With an
  Introduction.
Plenty, 1978.
Racing Demon, 1990.
Saigon: Year of the Cat, 1983.
The Secret Rapture, 1988.
Skylight, 1995.
Slag, 1971.
Strapless, 1989.
Teeth 'n' Smiles, 1976. With a 'Note'.
Via Dolorosa and *When Shall We Live?* 1998. (The text of
  Via Dolorosa was also published, with a new introduction
  by Hare, as a four-page supplement to the *Guardian
  Saturday Review*, 28 October 2000. *When Shall We Live?*
  was originally given as the Eleventh Eric Symes Abbott
  Memorial Lecture at Westminster Abbey on 9 May 1996,
  and published by the Dean's Office, King's College London
  that year. An edited version also appeared in the *Daily
  Telegraph Weekend*, 13 July 1996 under the title: 'Why I
  don't believe'.)
Wetherby, 1985. With an Introduction.

Collected plays and films
The Asian Plays, 1986 (*Fanshen, Saigon: Year of the Cat* and
  A Map of the World). With an Introduction.
The Early Plays, 1992 (*Slag, The Great Exhibition* and *Teeth
  'n' Smiles*).
Heading Home, 1991 (with *Wetherby* and *Dreams of
  Leaving*).
The History Plays, 1984 (*Knuckle, Licking Hitler* and *Plenty*).
  With an Introduction.

Plays: One, 1996 (*Slag, Teeth 'n' Smiles, Knuckle, Licking Hitler* and *Plenty*). With an Introduction.

Plays: Two, 1997 (*Fanshen, Saigon: Year of the Cat, A Map of the World, The Bay at Nice* and *The Secret Rapture*).

Collected Screenplays 1, 2002. (*Wetherby, Paris by Night, Strapless, Heading Home, Dreams of Leaving*). With an Introduction.

Collaborations

Brassneck (with Howard Brenton), London: Methuen, 1974. With an Authors' Note.

Deeds (with Howard Brenton, Trevor Griffiths and Ken Campbell). *Plays and Players*, 25, 8 and 25, 9.

Lay By (with Howard Brenton, Brian Clark, Trevor Griffiths, Stephen Poliakoff, Hugh Stoddard and Snoo Wilson), London: Calder and Boyars, 1972.

Pravda: a Fleet Street Comedy (with Howard Brenton), London: Methuen, 1985.

Unpublished plays, teleplays and screenplays

'Inside Out' (with Tony Bicât, adaptation of Kafka's diaries), 1968.

'What Happened to Blake?', 1970.

'The Rules of the Game' (adaptation of Pirandello), 1971.

'Deathsheads', 1971.

'England's Ireland' (with Tony Bicât, Howard Brenton, Brian Clark, David Edgar, Francis Fuchs and Snoo Wilson), 1972.

'Man Above Men' (teleplay), 1973.

'The Madman Theory of Deterrence', 1983.

'The Knife' (libretto, with Tim Rose-Price [lyrics] and Nick Bicât [music]), 1987.

'Damage' (screenplay), 1992.

'The Life of Galileo'(adaptation of Brecht), 1994.

Other work

Books

Writing Left-Handed, 1991. A collection of essays offering commentaries on a number of the writer's plays as well as on aspects of modern theatre and television, and as such a valuable source to students of Hare's work. Together the pieces form 'a concealed professional autobiography'. Eleven of the collected essays had already appeared elsewhere. For example, Hare's 'Introductions' to *The History Plays*, *The Asian Plays* and *Paris By Night* (see above) are all included, as are 'Sailing Downwind' (originally from the *Observer*, 9 November 1996), 'Cycles of Hope' (*Guardian*, 3–4 June 1989) and 'Time of Unease' (Findlater, *At the Royal Court* – see below). The publication histories of some of the other pieces are more convoluted: 'The Play is in the Air: On Political Theatre', for example, originated as a lecture given at King's College, Cambridge, in March 1978, but was also published twice in the same year, as 'David Hare on Theatre', by the Royal Shakespeare Company and, under the title: 'A Lecture', as an appendix to the text of *Licking Hitler* (see above). Similarly, 'Ah! Mischief: On Public Broadcasting' was commissioned for and (under a slightly different title) appeared in *Ah! Mischief: The Writer and Television* (ed. Pike, London: 1982), but first appeared publicly in the *Guardian* 'Weekend' section, 15 August 1981. 'The Awkward Squad: About Joint Stock' is also included (untitled) in Ritchie (ed.), *The Joint Stock Book*, but originated in *Granta* in 1986 as 'Joint Stock: A Memoir' (see below).

Pieces that appear here for the first time are: 'Looking Foolish' (Hare's speech at the 1991 Cheltenham Festival); 'The Dead Heart: A Production Log of *A Map of the World*'; 'An Unacceptable Form: On *The Knife*'; 'Oh! Goodness: On *The Secret Rapture*' and 'Four Actors'. With the exception of the *Granta* piece on Joint Stock, of

which I make use in chapter 2, I have not included in the
list of Hare's journalism below any that appear in *Writing
Left-Handed*: such differences as there are in the published
versions tend to be of a minor editorial nature.

Asking Around, 1993. The documentary background to 'the
Hare trilogy' (*Racing Demon*, *Murmuring Judges* and *The
Absence of War*), edited by Lyn Haill.

Acting Up: a theatrical diary, 1999. Hare's reflections on acting
and performance, prompted by his experience as an actor
of *Via Dolorosa*. An edited extract appeared as 'A month of
bad Hare days' in the *Observer Review*, 14 November
1999.

Journalism and other materials

Arranged by date. Material drawn on substantially in chapter
2 is given in **bold**.

'La Lupa', play review, *Plays and Players*, July 1969, 53–4.

'David Hare on Theatre', Royal Shakespeare Company
Publication, March 1978 ('King's lecture' of 5 March 1978;
also printed in *Licking Hitler* and in *Writing Left-Handed*,
as 'The Play is in the Air: On Political Theatre').

**'Much of what they write is a kind of wail from the far shore
of the English male menopause', *Guardian*, 30 January
1981, 11 (on the critics).**

'Time of Unease', in Richard Findlater (ed.), *At the Royal
Court: 25 Years of the English Stage Company* (Ambergate:
1981), 139–42.

'The New Right has taken over the BBC, distinguished by
their moral self-righteousness and their chilling pleasure in
the exercise of their own power', *Guardian*, 15 August
1981, 7 ('Weekend' section; taken from 'Ah! Mischief: On
Public Broadcasting' in *Writing Left-Handed*; also in *Ah!
Mischief: The Writer and Television*, ed. Pike, Faber, 1982,
where it is subtitled 'The Role of Public Broadcasting').

**'Green Room', *Plays and Players*, October 1981, 49–50 (on
the state of contemporary theatre).**

'I still have the unfashionable belief that critics should try to
see plays as they are, in their fullness, and not concentrate
solely on those parts which flatter their prejudices',
Guardian, 3 February 1983 ('Arts' section, 12; prompted
by the critical response to *A Map of the World*).

'Nicaragua: an Appeal', *Granta* 16, Summer 1985, 232–6.

'Joint Stock: A Memoir', *Granta* **18, Spring 1986, 248–54**
(also appears in Rob Ritchie [ed.], *The Joint Stock Book*;
see below).

'Why I shall vote Labour', *Spectator*, 23 May 1987, 14.

'Just what are we playing at?', *Sunday Times*, 12 December
1993, 10–11 (from a talk to be given 25 January 1994 entitled 'The Unfashionable Theatre', one of *Sunday Times*'s
'Lunchtime Lectures' series).

'A good man let down by third-rate colleagues', *Sunday
Telegraph*, 2 April 1995 (appreciation of Conservative
Prime Minister John Major).

**'Brecht is there for the taking', unsourced photocopy (Faber
archive).**

'John Osborne: a lifelong satirist of prigs and puritans', June
1995 (Hare's speech at Osborne's memorial service).
Available on-line at
http://dspace.dial.pipex.com/town/parade/abj76/PG/pieces/
john_osborne.shtml

'Requiem in blue', *Observer*, 15 October 1995 (*Review* section, 1–2; reporting on Tory Conference under Major at
Blackpool).

'Diary', *Spectator*, 18 May 1996, 9.

'Chekhov the angry young man', *Daily Telegraph*, 19
February 1997 (on adapting *Ivanov*).

**'The RSC won't put them on the main stage, directors seem
frightened of them: what's to become of Britain's living
playwrights?',** *New Statesman*, **14 March 1997, 38–40.**

'David Hare's Campaign', *Daily Telegraph*, April 1997 (daily
general election campaign diary).

'The idea of Amy', programme note to *Amy's View*, **13 June 1997.**

'Give me Broadway's jungle any day', *Guardian*, 25 June 1997, 15 (Broadway v. West End).

Programme Note to *Plenty*, revival by the Almeida Theatre Company at the Albery Theatre, 15 April 1999.

'Don't Panic', *Guardian*, 21 April 1999, 14 (on the revival of *Plenty*).

'Diary', *Spectator*, 15 April 2000.

'Via Dolorosa revisited', *Guardian*, 28 October 2000 (four-page pull-out in *Saturday Review*: text of *Via Dolorosa*, introduced by Hare).

'Why reality is the lifeblood of theatre', *Guardian* (*Saturday Review*, 3) 18 November 2000 (on the social responsibility of theatre; *Via Dolorosa*).

'Hot and Young', programme note to *Platonov*, Almeida Theatre, 30 August 2001.

'Chekhov's wild, wild youth', *Observer Review*, 2 September 2001, 5 (on translating *Platonov* and *Ivanov*).

'Don't give up the Today job', *Observer Review*, 23 September 2001, 15 (book review of James Naughtie, *The Rivals: The Intimate Story of a Political Marriage*, on Tony Blair and Gordon Brown).

'Diana Boddington', *Guardian*, 21 January 2002, 16 (obituary of National Theatre stage manager).

'Why fabulate?', *Guardian*, 2 February 2002 (*Saturday Review*, 3) (on the importance of art responding to the real world).

'Theatre's great malcontent', *Guardian*, 8 June 2002 (*Saturday Review*; extract from Hare's memorial lecture on John Osborne at the June 2002 Hay Festival. Available online at http://www.guardian.co.uk/Archive/Article/0,4273,4428811,00.html).

'An Act of Faith', *Guardian Weekend*, 13 July 2002, 28–32 (on reviving *Via Dolorosa*).

Unpublished letters

To publisher (Faber and Faber, from its archive), July 1973, 1978 (nd).

To the Joint Stock Policy Committee, September 1980 (Modern British Theatre Archive, Brotherton Library, University of Leeds).

Published interviews and interview-profiles

Arranged alphabetically by interviewer. Interviews drawn on substantially in chapter 2 are given in **bold**.

Ansorge, Peter. 'Underground Explorations No 1: Portable Playwrights', *Plays and Players*, February 1972, 14–23 (also Brenton, Wilson and Malcolm Griffiths; covers Hare's work to date).

Billington, Michael, 'Broken Rules', *Radio Times*, 12 January 1980, 17.

—, 'A knight at the theatre', *Guardian Review*, 4 September 1998, 2–3, 11.

Bloom, Michael, 'A kinder, gentler David Hare', *American Theatre*, November 1989, 30–34 (article-interview, with some career context).

Bradby, David, *et al.*, 'After *Fanshen*: A Discussion', in *Performance and Politics in Popular Drama*, ed. Bradby *et al.* (Cambridge: 1980), 297–314.

Brooks, Richard, 'Two lovers and a lino floor', *Observer*, 6 January 1991, 47 (*Heading Home*).

Coveney, Michael, 'Worlds Apart', *Time Out*, 21–7 January 1983, 12, 15–16 (*Map of the World*, with limited career context).

—, 'Impure Meditations', *Observer*, 4 February 1990, 35 (centres on *Racing Demon* and *Strapless*).

Dempsey, Judy, 'Interview', *Literary Review*, 22 August 1980, 35–6.

Dugdale, John, 'Love, Death and Edwina', *Listener*, 15 September 1988, 38–9 (Secret Rapture, Paris by Night, Strapless).

Ford, John, 'Getting the Carp out of the Mud', *Plays and Players*, November 1971, 20, 83 (also includes Howard Brenton and Snoo Wilson; *Lay By*).

Gaston, Georg, 'Interview: David Hare', *Theatre Journal* 45, 1993, 213–25 (career to date).

Goodman, Joan, 'New World', *Observer*, 23 January 1983, 44 (*Map of the World*).

Hassell, Graham, 'Hare Racing', *Plays and Players*, February 1990, 6–8 (*Racing Demon*).

Hewison, Robert, 'View from the top', *Sunday Times*, 11 January 1998, 6–7 (Hare and Richard Eyre).

Isaacs, Jeremy, 'The Director's Cut: David Hare. Jeremy Isaacs talks to David Hare', BBC Television, 16 May 1989 (wide-ranging interview, including biographical material, covering career to date; transcript available on-line at http://www.bbc.co.uk/education/lzone/movie/hare.htm).

Itzin, Catherine, and Simon Trussler, 'From Portable Theatre to Joint Stock . . . via Shaftesbury Avenue', *Theatre Quarterly*, December 1975–February 1976, 108–15 (full career coverage to date). An edited version of this interview appears in *New Theatre Voices of the Seventies*, ed. Simon Trussler, London, Methuen, 1981.

Kellaway, Kate, 'He says people are too backward-looking, but wishes he'd been a black American in the Fifties . . .', *Observer Review*, 3 August 1997, 6–7.

Kuchwara, Michael, 'On Stage: *The Judas Kiss*', *Jacksonville.com* website, 25 April 1998, www.jacksonville.com/tu-online/stories/042598/ent_Sjudaskiss.html

Lawson, Mark, 'Making mischief', *Independent Magazine*, 16 October 1993, 48–54 (wide-ranging article-interview, centred on *Absence of War*).

Lubbock, Tom, 'The Theatre-going Public', BBC Radio 3, 13 April 1986 (on the then current state of political theatre; also includes contributions from Howard Brenton, Trevor Griffiths, John McGrath, Christopher Hampton and Michael Frayn).

McFerran, Ann, 'End of the Acid Era', *Time Out*, 29 August 1975, 12–15.

Oliva, Judy Lee, 'An Interview with David Hare', in Judy Lee Oliva, *David Hare: Theatricalizing Politics*, Ann Arbor and London, 1990, 165–81 (career to date).

Summers, Alison, 'David Hare's Drama, 1970–1981. An Interview', *Centennial Review* 36, 1992, 573–91 (an interview originally conducted in 1981; appears here edited and with an appended commentary by Bert Cardullo).

Tynan, Kathleen, 'Dramatically Speaking', *Interview*, April 1989, 80, 128, 130 (*Secret Rapture*, *Paris by Night*, *Strapless*, and some general career material).

Wroe, Nicholas, 'The *Guardian* Profile: David Hare. Makeover artist', *Guardian*, 13 November 1999.

Wyver, John, 'Brenton and Hare', *City Limits*, 3–9 May 1985, 85 (*Pravda*).

Zeifman, Hersh, 'An Interview with David Hare', in Hersh Zeifman (ed.), *David Hare. A Casebook*, New York and London, 1994, 3–21 (wide-ranging piece, dwelling on Hare's later work).

(Unsigned), '*Via Dolorosa*: David Hare Interview', PBS website, www.pbs.org/viadolorosa/davidhare_interview.html

Previously unpublished interviews
The following are all new interviews recorded by the present writer for this book (listed in chronological order):

'A Conversation with David Hare', London, 8 March 2002.

Rick Fisher, Leeds, 31 October 2001.
Vicki Mortimer, London, 20 December 2001.
Lia Williams, London, 20 December 2001.
Jonathan Kent, London, 21 February 2002.
Bill Nighy, London, 21 February 2002.
Richard Eyre, London, 30 April 2002.

Secondary sources

Critical Studies: Books

Dean, Joan FitzPatrick, *David Hare*, Twayne's English Authors Series 480, Boston/Oxford: 1990 (American perspective).

Donesky, Finlay, *David Hare: Moral and Historical Perspectives*, Contributions in Drama and Theatre Studies 75, Westport, Conn.: 1996 (concentrates on Hare's 'moral vision').

Fraser, Scott, *A Politic Theatre: The drama of David Hare*, Costerus, n.s., 105, Amsterdam: 1996.

Homden, Carol, *The Plays of David Hare*, Cambridge: 1995 (the only British monograph on Hare to date).

Oliva, Judy Lee, *David Hare: Theatricalising Politics*, Theatre and Dramatic Studies 66, Ann Arbor: 1990.

Page, Malcolm (comp.), *File on Hare*, London: 1990 (useful compendium of various materials).

Zeifman, Hersh (ed.), *David Hare. A Casebook*, Garland Reference Library of the Humanities 1240/Casebooks on Modern Dramatists 18, New York: 1994 (useful collection of essays on various aspects of Hare's work, and with a good interview with Hare by the editor).

Parts of books

Bull, John, *New British Political Dramatists*, London and Basingstoke: 1984 (useful on the post-'68 generation generally; chapter 3 offers acute analyses of Hare's work to the early eighties).

Wu, Duncan, *Six Contemporary Dramatists: Bennett, Potter, Gray, Brenton, Hare, Ayckbourn*, London and Basingstoke: 1995 (chapter 6 offers a stimulating discussion of Hare's later work, focusing on its moral dimensions).

General Bibliography

Ansorge, Peter, *Disrupting the Spectacle: Five Years of Experimental and Fringe Theatre in Britain*, London: 1975.

—, 'David Hare: a war on two fronts', *Plays and Players*, April 1978, 12–16.

Barnes, Philip, *A Companion to Post-War British Theatre*, Beckenham: 1986.

Bigsby, Christopher, *Contemporary English Drama*, London: 1981.

Boon, Richard, *Brenton the Playwright*, London: 1991.

Brenton, Howard, *Plays: One*, London: 1986.

—, *Plays: Two*, London: 1989.

Brown, Mick, 'Still angry after all these years', *Elle*, December 1988, 40–45.

Bull, John, *Stage Right*, London: 1994.

Calder, Angus, *The People's War*, London: 1969.

Coveney, Michael, 'Turning over a new leaf: *P&P* investigates the background to *Fanshen*', *Plays and Players*, June 1975, 10–13.

Coxall, Bill and Lynton Robins, *Contemporary British Politics* (third edn), London: 1998.

Craig, Sandy, *Dreams and Deconstructions: Alternative Theatre in Britain*, Ambergate: 1980.

Cunningham, Michael, *The Hours*, New York: 1998.

Debord, Guy, *The Society of the Spectacle*, Detroit: 1970.

Elsom, John, *Post-war British Theatre*, London: 1976.

Ezard, John, 'Look back and marvel at anger of Osborne', *Guardian*, 4 June 2002, 8.

Findlater, Richard (ed.), *At the Royal Court: 25 Years of the English Stage Company*, Ambergate: 1981.

Franzen, Jonathan, *The Corrections*, New York: 2001.

—, 'Perchance to Dream', *Harper's*, April 1996.

Hart, Josephine, *Damage*, London: 1996.

Hiley, Jim, 'The Wetherby Report', *Observer Magazine*, 10 March 1985, 64–5.

Hinton, William, *Fanshen: A Documentary of Revolution in a Chinese Village*, New York: 1966.

Itzin, Catherine and Simon Trussler (interviewers), 'Petrol Bombs through the Proscenium Arch' (interview with Howard Brenton), *Theatre Quarterly* vol. 5, no 17 (1975), 4–20.

—, *Stages in the Revolution. Political Theatre in Britain since 1968*, London: 1980.

Le Carré, John, *The Honourable Schoolboy*, London: 1977.

Lennon, Peter, 'Just leave me alone', *Guardian*, 17 February 1996, 26.

Lister, David, 'Passion is all for idealogue of the theatre', *Independent*, 21 March 1998, 3.

Morrison, Blake, 'He only does it to annoy', *Independent*, 30 April 1995.

Myerson, Jonathan, 'David Hare: Fringe Graduate', *Drama*, 149, Autumn 1983, 26–8.

Peacock, D. Keith, *Thatcher's Theatre: British Theatre and Drama in the Eighties*, London: 1999.

Peter, John, 'Meet the Wild Bunch', *Sunday Times*, 11 July 1976.

Ritchie, Rob (ed.), *The Joint Stock Book: the Making of a Theatre Collective*, London: 1987.

Sierz, Aleks, *In-yer-face Theatre: British Drama Today*, London: 2001.

—, 'To each his Via Dolorosa', *Al-Ahram Weekly*, 5 February 2001; available at http:///www.ahram.org.eg/weekly/1998/1948/396_via.htm).

Taylor, J. R., *The Second Wave: British Drama of the Sixties*, London: 1978.

Taylor, Paul, 'The man who likes John Major', *Independent*, 26 April 1995, 26.

Trussler, Simon (ed.), *New Theatre Voices of the Seventies*, London: 1981.

Whittam Smith, Andreas, '1968', *Independent on Sunday*, 8 February 1998, 7.

Acknowledgements

I thank the many people who have assisted in the preparation of this book: my colleagues at the Workshop Theatre of the School of English, University of Leeds (especially Philip Roberts); Matthew Hopkins; Ruth Arnaud at Casarotto Ramsay; Jean Rose and David Salmo at Methuen; Jane Gater at the Directors' Guild of Great Britain; Anne Hudson at the Almeida Theatre.

My particular thanks go to Sir Richard Eyre, Rick Fisher, Jonathan Kent, Vicki Mortimer, Bill Nighy, and Lia Williams for their generosity in giving me the interviews that appear towards the end of this book, and of course to David Hare himself. I hope my work does his some justice.

For permission to reprint copyright material the publishers gratefully acknowledge the following:

PETER ANSORGE: 'Underground Explorations No.1: Portable Plays and Playwrights', from *Plays and Players*, February 1972, 14–23 © Peter Ansorge; MICHAEL BILLINGTON: 'A Knight at the Theatre' by Michael Billington, © *Guardian*, 4 September 1998; MICHAEL BLOOM: 'A kinder, gentler David Hare . . .' © *American Theatre*, November 1989; MICHAEL COVENEY: 'Worlds Apart' in *Time Out* 21–7 January 1983, 12, 15–16; 'Impure Meditations' from the *Observer*, 4 February 1990, 35; JOHN DUGDALE: 'Love, Death and Edwina' from *Listener* 15 September 1988, 38–9; JOHN FORD; 'Getting the Carp out of the Mud' from *Plays and Players*, November 1971, 20, 83 © John Ford 1971; GEORG GASTON: 'Interview: David Hare', *Theatre Journal* 45:2 (1993), 213–25 © The John

Hopkins University Press, reprinted with the permission of The John Hopkins University Press; DAVID HARE: 'David Hare's Campaign' by David Hare, © *Daily Telegraph*, April 1997, 'Much of what I write . . .' © David Hare, *Guardian*, 30 January 1981; 'I still have the unfashionable belief . . .' © David Hare, *Guardian*, 3 February 1983; 'Diana Boddington' © David Hare, *Guardian* 21 January 2002; 'The RSC won't put them on the main stage, directors seem frightened of them: what's to become of Britain's living playwrights?' taken from an article which first appeared in the *New Statesman*, 14 March 1997; 'Give me Broadway's jungle any day . . .' © David Hare, *Guardian*, 25 June 1997; 'Diary' from *The Spectator*, reproduced with permission from *The Spectator* (1828) Ltd. Extracts from the 'David Hare Papers' reprinted with the permission of The Harry Ransom Humanities Research Center, The University of Texas at Austin; GRAHAM HASSELL: 'Hare Racing' from *Plays and Players*, February 1990 © Graham Hassell; JEREMY ISAACS: 'The Director's Cut: David Hare. Jeremy Isaacs talks to David Hare', BBC TV, 16 May 1989; MICHAEL KUCHWARA 'On Stage: *The Judas Kiss*', from *Jacksonville.com Website*, 25 April 1998, reprinted with permission of The Associated Press; MARK LAWSON: extracts from *Making Mischief* first published in the *Independent* 16 October 1993; TOM LUBBOCK: 'The Theatre-Going Public' from *BBC Radio 3*, 13 April 1986; ANN MCFERRAN: 'End of the Acid Era', *Time Out*, 29 August 1975 12–15; JUDY LEE OLIVER: 'An Interview with David Hare' from *David Hare: Theatricalising Politics* by Judy Lee Oliva, Ann Arbour and London, 1990; ALISON SUMMERS: 'David Hare's Drama, 1970–81. An Interview' originally appeared in *Centennial Review* Vol. 36, No. 2 1992, published by Michigan State University Press; KATHLEEN TYNAN: from 'Dramatically Speaking, interview with David Hare', Interview, October 1997, pp. 80, 128, 130. Reprinted by permission of Brant Publications, Inc.; NICHOLAS WROE; 'The *Guardian* Profile: David Hare. Makeover Artist' *Guardian*, 13 November 1999; JOHN WYVER: 'Brenton and

Hare' from *City Limits*, 3–9 May 1985, 85; UNSIGNED: '*Via Dolorosa*: David Hare Interview' from PBS website; CATHERINE ITZIN and SIMON TRUSSLER: 'From Portable Theatre to Joint Stock . . . via Shaftesbury Avenue', *Theatre Quarterly*, December 1975–February 1976, 108–15; HERSH ZEIFMAN: from '*David Hare: A Casebook*', reproduced by permission of Routledge, Inc. part of The Taylor and Francis Group.

Faber and Faber apologize for any errors or omissions in the above list and would be grateful to be notified of any corrections that should be incorporated in the next edition or reprint of this volume.

Index